$24.75

3 1489 00690 0045

Louise DeSalvo

Chasing Ghosts

A Memoir of a Father, Gone to War

Fordham University Press

New York   2016

World War II: The Global, Human, and Ethical Dimension | G. Kurt Piehler, series editor

Copyright © 2016 Louise DeSalvo

All rights reserved. No part of this publication may be reproduced, stored in a retrieval system, or transmitted in any form or by any means—electronic, mechanical, photocopy, recording, or any other—except for brief quotations in printed reviews, without the prior permission of the publisher.

Fordham University Press has no responsibility for the persistence or accuracy of URLs for external or third-party Internet websites referred to in this publication and does not guarantee that any content on such websites is, or will remain, accurate or appropriate.

Fordham University Press also publishes its books in a variety of electronic formats. Some content that appears in print may not be available in electronic books.

Visit us online at www.fordhampress.com.

Library of Congress Cataloging-in-Publication Data available online at catalog.loc.gov.

Printed in the United States of America

18 17 16   5 4 3 2 1

First edition

For my parents,
as they were,
and,
as they might have been
and for

      Ernest DeSalvo, Edvige Giunta,
    Audrey Goldrich, Christina Baker Kline,
      and Pamela Redmond Satran,
        who helped immeasurably

CONTENTS

Four

Five

Epilogue

War stories. Let your guard down for a moment, and
they come rushing in on you, one by one by one. . . .
Paul Auster
Man in the Dark

Where do words come from? They come from the dead. We inherit them.
Borrow them. Use them for a time to bring the dead to life.
Ruth Ozeki
A Tale for the Time Being

The flame of that wild battlefield
Rushes in fire through our rooms.
Muriel Rukeyser
"Letter to the Front"

PROLOGUE

Flushing out the Enemy

2004

The last time my father came to supper at our house, he could barely climb the stairs. I stood at the top of the landing, wanting to help, knowing that if I tried he wouldn't let me, knowing that if I tried to touch him, he'd wave me off, and maybe yell, or worse.

"Goddamn stairs," he said, glaring at me, as if I'd put the stairs there just to bedevil him. "Goddamn it to hell."

I stood there holding my breath, watching him, hoping he wouldn't fall as he staggered, then gripped the railing with both hands to pause and rest for a few moments before hauling his once wiry and strong, but now enfeebled, body up the next step, and the next, and the next. I stood there, hoping he could make it to the top of the stairs unaided so that, after all his effort and hard work, he might enjoy the merest of victories.

This is the way it so often was with us. Me, standing and watching. Me, wanting a different kind of father, a phantom father who'd be happy to see me, a father who wouldn't fly off the handle. A father I wouldn't have to lock into the crosshairs of my sightline to see what he would do next, and so what I would do next: exchange a few words; leave him alone; or duck and run for cover. A father I could, again, love.

And what did he want from me? That I would become a different kind of daughter? A daughter who wanted to please him? A daughter who adored him? But who that daughter might be, I couldn't yet figure out.

I had been that daughter once. But I'd stopped being that daughter a long time ago, on the day my father shipped out to war. And he'd stopped being the father I'd loved in that way on that day, too. And it wasn't his fault and he couldn't have done anything to change it, and it wasn't my fault, either, and this was the greatest sorrow of my life.

Still, I wanted that father back before he died, if only for a little while. And I wanted to be that daughter again, the one who loved him utterly: I wanted to roll back the brutal engine of time. But how to get from here to there was the great mystery of my life. And on the day my father came to supper, it wasn't a puzzle I'd yet tried to figure out, for I didn't then realize how little time we had left.

A few days before, my father asked me why I never invited his wife and him to supper anymore. I couldn't say, "You're a dangerous driver, that's why I always come to see you," for then we would have fought.

So I invited him and his wife against my better judgment, and the rest of the family—his two grandsons (my sons), their wives, his two great-grandchildren—all of them pretending he was still the man he'd been. The man who'd fought fires into his sixties until he was too old to scramble into his gear and climb onto the hook and ladder. The man who'd played Frisbee with his great-grandchildren well into his eighties. The man who'd labored as a machinist into his early nineties because he couldn't imagine a life without work.

He'd wanted to come to supper, was happy he'd been invited. And I'd wanted him to come, too. This was something new for me, my wanting him to come. For years, I'd done my daughterly duty—visiting him, having him over to our house, making him supper, taking him on holidays, caring for his household, and done it far better than he deserved, my husband said. But I never knew which father would greet me: the father who wanted me to join him in the sunroom for tea and conversation, or the father who lashed out at me for not having come to see him sooner, or more often, or at a different time of day.

When I'd invited my father to supper, I'd wondered if it was a good idea. If it was a good idea for him to leave his house, given that he could barely make it up and down his stairs, couldn't make it to the toilet without wetting himself. If it was a good idea for him to drive given that I suspected his driving was a danger to himself and others, having seen the dents and scratches on the car with too much horsepower for anyone, let alone a man in his nineties, losing his hearing, losing his eyesight, losing his reflexes. Wondered whether he'd still remember where I lived, whether he'd get lost on the way, whether he'd get into an accident and die. Wondered whether he and his wife could get themselves organized to get out of their house and over to our house by a certain time.

I thought he could because he wore the same shirt, same pants, same socks, same shoes every day, changing them only when I went to his house and forced him into clean clothes while I did the wash. But I doubted whether his wife could because she never knew where anything was, couldn't find anything she needed, and my father spent most of his energy returning her belongings to their proper places so she could get them again and put them where they weren't supposed to be.

I'd heard through one of her daughters that a few days before, a neighbor had discovered my father in the supermarket parking lot, asleep at the wheel of his car with the engine running, and she had found his wife wandering the parking lot, trying to find their car.

"It's dangerous," the neighbor said. "They shouldn't be doing this kind of thing anymore. You should stop them."

"Stop them?" I said. "Stop him?" She had no idea.

Later the same day, their cat climbed a tree in the back yard and refused to come down, and my father had gotten a ladder out of the garage, carried it around to the back, wedged it against the tree, and tried to climb it to rescue the cat who climbed into and out of trees all the time. This was a routine occurrence, the cat climbing the tree, my father believing it needed rescuing or deciding that it had spent more than enough time in the tree and that it was time for the cat to come back into the house where it belonged. But this time my father lost his balance and fell.

The neighbor saw him fall. Rushed over to help. She wanted to call an ambulance. But he refused.

"It's a wonder," she said, "he wasn't killed." Then she added, "And he wasn't very nice."

I'd had a conversation with my father about this tree-climbing cat of theirs. Told him to let it be, told him the cat would come down when it wanted to. But there was no arguing with him.

"Cats don't belong in trees," my father said. "That's why I go and get him."

I told the neighbor we were doing the best we could, that my father wouldn't let us hire anyone to help in the house, that he wouldn't let us shop for them, that he refused to stop driving his car and his doctor said there was no legal way for us to stop him. He was still clearing leaves out of gutters, still cleaning the filter in his heating system, still shoveling snow, still lugging the garbage out to the curb.

"There's nothing a man half my age can do that I can't," my father said.

Still, now most days my father moved from his bedroom to the bathroom, down the stairs to the kitchen, into the sunroom, and back upstairs again, one slow step at a time, trying to find whatever his wife had lost. Other times, he'd stare at the television, stare at a book, stare at the bird feeder out back, stare at his wife when he wasn't yelling at her to do what good wives were supposed to do—fix his supper, clean the house, make the bed—even though all she could do now was sleep, lose things, and wander the house. This was driving him crazy; she was driving him crazy. If things didn't change soon, he told us, he was going to find his own apartment, he was going to move out, even though we knew he never would.

"Leave me alone," my father would say whenever I went to their house and tried to wash a small load of laundry or cook something simple. "Let me be. I can take care of myself. I'm fine." But he wasn't fine; she wasn't fine; they couldn't take care of themselves, and so our family did the best we could to help them even though every time we tried, they yelled at us, told us to go away, told us it was their house, not ours.

The night they came to supper, my father wore his usual: khaki trousers, plaid shirt, brown belt, and sneakers with Velcro closures, the only footwear he could pull onto his swollen feet. I was relieved to see that his wife wore jeans, a sweater, and her more-or-less clean sneakers, because she'd tried to leave the house in her bathrobe a few times before.

"Why should I get dressed?" she'd say. "I'm not going anywhere important. I'm not going to have tea with the queen."

But here they are now, atop the stairs, my father and his wife, looking more or less normal, if you overlooked the stains on the fly of my father's pants, the black-and-blue marks from his recent fall on his face and hands, her disheveled hair, the terror-stricken look in her eyes: did she even remember who we were? And here they are now, after even more effort, sitting at the dining room table, awaiting their meal.

So far, I think, *so good.*

To pass the time until supper, my daughter-in-law proposes a game of charades. The kids know how to play and my father and his wife have played with them many times, but not recently.

The children go first. Julia is a purring cat, Steven a baying dog. My father and his wife say nothing. Julia and Steven's mother guesses both.

And then it is my father's turn.

"Think of something you want us to guess and act it out," my daughter-in-law reminds him. "A book, a movie, a play, a TV show, an animal, anything."

My father pauses. Thinks. Picks up a knife from the dining room table. Hoists himself out of the chair. Hobbles into the living room. Hides himself behind the doorframe.

This is a very bad idea, I think, remembering other mealtimes, other knives.

But my grandkids are smiling; my daughter-in-law is smiling. They love playing games with my father. They've never seen him become someone else.

We see the knife in the doorway. Then my father's hand holding the knife. Then his face, eyes wide, peering into the room, focused now, not on us, but on another time, another place. He is on a mission to survive and to destroy.

He sidles into the room, slices the air, disappears, lunges back into view. I move toward him slowly, at the ready.

"Zorro?" my grandson shouts. He's sure he's right.

My father shakes his head.

"*Star Wars?*" my granddaughter asks.

My father shakes his head again. He's getting pissed off.

"World War II?" I ask, thinking, *That goddamned war.* But my father shakes his head. I want this to stop, I want to stop this right now before he scares the kids.

"Come on, you win," I say, moving slowly, prising the knife from his hand. "That was a good one. We can't figure it out. Tell us what it is."

My father relaxes. Sinks down into his chair. This time I've been lucky, averted catastrophe.

"Couldn't you tell I was flushing out the enemy?" he asks. He's disgusted. How could we not know?

I'd heard my father's war stories about how, when the Americans landed on that island in the Pacific where he was stationed during the war, even after the island was captured, there were still Japanese soldiers hiding in caves, secreted in the interior. You never knew when one would emerge from the jungle at night and lob a hand grenade into your tent, killing you and all your buddies. When one who'd tied himself to the top of a tree would fire at you when you were out on patrol. When one would emerge from the bush late at night and slit your throat as you slept.

He'd heard stories about how Japanese soldiers tied missionaries to trees and used them for target practice, how they disemboweled their captives, how they hacked off the top of their enemies' skulls and scooped out their brains. There were stories, too, about how, elsewhere, Japanese soldiers, taught that surrender was dishonorable, would dig themselves into caves, subsisting on rice, roots, grubs, and whatever else they could scavenge, for they knew how to survive in the jungle, these fighters, who, my father said, were unlike any others, and they would wait and wait for weeks, for months, for years, even, and then come out of hiding in a suicide mission to kill as many men as they could.

"But where is the enemy?" my grandson asks.

"The enemy," my father says, "could be anywhere."

One

War Stories

It's two weeks later. I'm at my father's house. We're sitting in the sunroom. I've made us tea.

"I'm so sorry you had to go to war," I say, remembering my father playing charades, remembering the look in his eyes.

The war is a subject we've never discussed. I wonder whether he's been unwilling to talk about it because he wants to forget the past, or because the past is too difficult for him to discuss, or both. And I wonder whether I've been reluctant to ask him about it because I'd rather not learn why the man who'd come home was so different from the father who'd gone away.

"You're not sorry for me," he replies. "You're sorry for yourself."

At first, I'm angry. Why can't my father accept my expression of concern? I turn away to look out the window at the bird feeder he's rigged up in the yard. It's late autumn now, the leaves are off the trees, the birds desperate for the food my father brings them.

But then I have to admit to myself that my father *is* right: I can't possibly feel sorry for what he's lived through because I don't know and because I can never know.

"Look," my father says. "It's only the two of us now. We'd better learn to get along."

2004–2014

I started writing this book when my father was still alive. I'd heard him mention the war ever since I could remember. But his stories were brief, sporadic, disjointed, attenuated, and they said little about what had happened to him. I listened to them—it was impossible not to—but I did not hear them.

But during the last two years of his life, my father talked about the war more than ever before. The United States was at war again, and the footage my father watched on the evening news brought back memories of his war. I would stop by his house to visit on my way home from work. It would be late afternoon. His second wife would be upstairs sleeping, her days and nights reversed. For the first time since I was a little girl, my father and I would be alone.

At first, during those long afternoons we spent together, I nodded through his stories while I looked outside at the birds feeding, the sturdy oak in the back yard, the apartments beyond the fence, occupying myself with my own thoughts, catching snippets of what my father would say while I urged him on, thinking it would be good for him to unburden himself. But then my father's stories began to claim me. I thought that maybe in telling me these stories, my father was telling me what he believed I needed to know—why he was the way he was, why my mother had been the way she was, why he and I had never gotten along. This was his opportunity—and mine—to make peace with the past, our chance to right something that had gone terribly wrong between us. It wasn't as simple as his wanting to make amends, though. It was as if he knew that if he helped me try to understand him, we could move to higher, safer ground. Maybe, too, he hoped his stories would claim me after he was gone, his way of continuing to make his presence felt. And in time, as he told me the story of his life, that I felt sorry only for myself and not for him became less true, and then not true at all.

There was something about the silence in the house, something about the light in late day, something about his—and my—knowing it was now or never, I suspect, that prompted him to speak. He wanted to tell me about his life, wanted to explain himself, wanted me to understand him, although he never had before, either because he'd been locked into silence or because he couldn't scale the wall I'd built to protect myself from him. It was as if he wanted to give me something in return for what the war had taken away.

His narrative was not chronological; he never started a story at its beginning; he never picked up where he'd left off; he didn't make it easy for me to figure out what had happened to him. His answer to my question "And then what happened?" might come later the same day, or the next day, or the next month, or year, or not at all. He left it to me to fit the pieces of the puzzle together, to make order out of the chaos of his memories, to fill in the blanks of his stories with information I'd later learn from other sources, from the books about the military and World War II and naval strategy that I'd read. Often, he'd circle back to what he'd told me a long time before, adding a new detail or another observation.

During that time, he told me about his childhood, too; about his parents; his first tour of duty in the Navy during the 1930s and what he'd learned about the build-up to the war in the Pacific during that time; how he'd met my mother and courted her; how they'd fixed up the apartment where they would start their life together; my birth and my mother's depression afterward; when he'd returned to the Navy during World War II and the time he'd spent on that island in the Pacific, and how he'd come home. It was as if he were trying to understand his place in history, trying to see how living during that time had affected him, had affected us all.

Still, it took me until near the end of my father's life to understand that World War II had taken the man I had loved away from me. I knew he'd been utterly changed by his wartime service. But it took me a long time to understand that the reason I hated him, and had, for as long as I could remember—although, of course, I loved him, too, and with a fierceness I chose to deny—was that his rages were directed mostly at me, but also because I'd had another father before the war, a good father, a father who'd cared for me, the father I'd yearned for through all these long years.

Near the end of his life, I got a glimpse of that father as he told me stories about his past and his service in the Navy before and during World War II. And in some sense, during that time, I *did* get that father back, although temporarily. His stories answered the great overarching riddles of my life: why he was such a violent, angry man; why we never got along; why he courted danger throughout his life; why he felt worthless.

And what did telling me these stories do for him? Thinking back upon those long afternoons we spent together, I would have to say that my father was trying to listen to his voice for the first time, trying to make some tally, some assessment of the man he'd been and, so, trying to understand himself. But whether this was really his purpose, and whether he achieved it, I can't say, for, as I write this, he's been dead for almost a decade now and so he can no longer speak for himself. I have tried to render what he told me as well as I can, to do him some small honor, for, from this vantage point in time, I believe he deserves it. But in assembling his stories and retelling them, I think I have begun to understand something of the man and something of men like him—working-class men who'd joined the military because of the limited opportunities they had to better themselves in civilian life, and men who'd had to go to war because a great evil had overtaken the world and they were enlisted to eradicate it—men whose lives were irrevocably changed thereby.

My father's stories weren't self-aggrandizing. If anything, he downplayed what he'd done. But in telling me the behind-the-scenes story about ordinary men like him called upon to perform workaday tasks in extraordinary times that made extraordinary feats possible, he shifted my understanding of that war.

"Are you going to write a book about this?" my father asks as I take notes when he tells me about the war.

"I don't know," I answer. "I might."

"Don't waste your time on me," my father says. "You have better things to do." But I knew that writing this book was not only important to me; it was essential. I am the only one of my family still alive. The only one left. And so the only one who can do this work of remembering and reconstructing the past. To many, this man I am writing about will be regarded as unimportant, insignificant, and so not worthy of being remembered, of having his story told. For this man was no hero, and this is no hero's story. This man did not storm an enemy encampment singlehandedly; did not shoot down enemy aircraft; did not survive a sinking ship. So this is only (only?) the story of a man who started out poor, tried to better himself, fell in love and married, did his duty, but a man who was, and whose family was, nevertheless, undone by war.

The work of understanding the past is, as Paul Auster says, condemned to futility. Still, I must try to understand this man who's vanished and this time that will never return. So in this sense, I am a ghost writer, a writer who is chasing ghosts.

During those afternoons we spent together, it was as if my father knew that if he didn't share his secrets with me then, they'd be lost forever. And I knew that if I didn't listen, I'd miss an opportunity for us to reach a détente, no matter how temporary, in our relationship, and the only chance to understand why he'd been such a volatile man. I learned more about him, his military service, his hopes, his dreams, his thwarted ambition, and his sorrows than I'd ever known. What I learned allowed me to love him in a way I couldn't before, and to make a fragile though temporary peace with him.

As I listened, I began to understand that his story represented that of many men like him whose lives had changed because of military service both before and during wartime (and whose families' lives, too, were besieged by the continuing presence of war), but whose work and sacrifice weren't necessarily honored because it wasn't conventionally heroic, men who couldn't understand, and whose families didn't realize, that they, too, had been harmed by what they'd experienced and witnessed. For, as my father said, there were two kinds of dying in that war: the death of the body, and the death of the soul, and although not everyone in that war experienced the former, everyone who survived experienced the latter.

It wasn't until after my father died that I understood I'd been trying to find out what I could about him and men like him for a long time. In high school, I was that girl who read books about war—Pierre Boulle, *The Bridge Over the River Kwai*; Ernest Hemingway, *A Farewell to Arms* and *For Whom the Bell Tolls*; James Jones, *From Here to Eternity*; Boris Pasternak, *Doctor Zhivago*; Erich Maria Remarque, *All Quiet on the Western Front*; Leo Tolstoy, *War and Peace*; Sloan Wilson, *The Man in the Grey Flannel Suit*—and read them obsessively in my Physics class, where my compassionate teacher told me I could do whatever I wanted in the back of the class as long as I did my homework and did well on his tests, for he must have understood the urgency of my need. In college, I was that anti–Vietnam War pacifist who studied Revolutionary War battles and military strategy. In graduate school, after reading about the character

Septimus Smith in Virginia Woolf's *Mrs. Dalloway* (a veteran of the Great War who manifested symptoms of post-traumatic stress before the condition was understood), I was that student who became temporarily sidetracked from writing a dissertation by reading everything I could about attitudes to "shell shock" and "battle fatigue" during Woolf's time. As a literary scholar, as I was researching D. H. Lawrence's life and his and Frieda Lawrence's expulsion from their coastal home in Cornwall on the charge that she was a German spy, I read first-hand accounts of submarine movements along the Cornish coast. On preparing for a holiday to Tuscany, I'd read Iris Origo's *War in Val D'Orcia: An Italian War Diary, 1943–1944* and, while there, searched out the location of the places Origo mentioned. On a trip to Piedmont, I'd asked the Piedmontese I met if they remembered the war and I listened to their stories (one woman telling me that since the war ended, there hadn't been a day her family didn't talk about it), and I was taken deep into the countryside to visit a hillside monument to the soldiers from that region who'd walked home from the Russian front.

For me, it always came back to that war, although, until my father started telling me his stories, I couldn't have said why. I didn't realize that in learning as much as I could about war, I was trying to find my father but that I was also trying to understand the fathers of my friends, for we were a generation of children whose fathers had fought that war. And that my need to understand him—and them—would continue even after his death, as I tried to piece together his narrative.

If I am anything, I am the child of a man gone to war and a woman left behind to raise me. Or, as Doris Lessing has said, "We are all of us made by war, twisted and warped by war, but we seem to forget it."

But this is not a story of transformation. It's not a narrative about how one day my father changed, and how I changed, and how our relationship changed because he opened up to me and I finally understood him. It's not a narrative about how, because my father decided to break the silence about his life and his wartime service—a silence so many veterans of war maintain—everything between us was transformed, although I wish I could write that narrative, and indeed tried to write it for the many years I attempted to force the messy story of what happened to him and to our family into a narrative of redemption and forgiveness. But transformation doesn't happen all at once, or even after a while. It comes after a long period of sustained effort and it can be fleeting; it can vanish and has to be hard-earned all over again.

The truth is that the father I'd yearned for did come back, but only for a little while. Then he left again, as absolutely as he had before, and what we had, then, was something like the complicated relationship we'd always had before. Only now I felt I'd lost him for the second time, and there was pain in that, and yearning. But what remained, both throughout the last months of his life and after he died, and what remains still, is the memory of that time we'd spent together, him telling me about his life and me listening, a beacon I sought after he once again became that irascible bastard he'd been before. For during that brief time, he was the father I had desired for so long. And, of course, what I have left are his stories, his final and, I sometimes thought when I was angry at him, his only gift to me.

"Join the Navy, See the World"

1935/2004

"That day, I almost kill him," my father says.

My father comes home from work earlier than usual. His father is beating his mother.

"I had my hands around his throat," my father says. "I could have killed him. But then I would have gone to jail for murder. And what good would that have done her? My mother stops me. My father kicks me out. I hated to leave her with that bastard but I had no choice. I figured I'd join the Navy, go away, learn a trade, earn some money, come back, and see if she'd leave him. I told myself that it was time for my sisters to look out for her. If I didn't believe they would, I never could have left her with him."

It's seventy years later, and my father is telling me why he joins the Navy in December 1935, years before the United States declares war on Japan. During these afternoons we've spent together during the last year and a half, I've learned much about his life, much about his wartime service. But he's never told me about how he was in the Navy before the war, never once mentioned why he'd joined the Navy in the first place. And now that I'm hearing this story, I'm wondering if he hasn't wanted to tell me that he'd joined because he tried to kill his father because then we might get around to talking about how, once, he came at me with a knife. We might have to talk about how what my mother always said, that he came back from the war an angry man, wasn't altogether true, or maybe not true at all. Maybe the military and the war didn't make him a violent man. Maybe he was a violent man and that's why he'd joined.

1956

We're sitting at the supper table, my father, my mother, my sister, and me. And before I know what's happening, my father picks up a carving knife and comes after me.

I don't remember what I did, if I did anything. I don't remember how this all started. I might have disagreed with him. I might have come home too late the night before. I might have refused to do something he told me to do.

But what I do remember is the look in his eyes, the redness of his face, his upraised arm, the knife, the knife, the knife.

And the next thing I remember is running down the street, away from my father, away from our house, the back of my blouse in shreds, my eyes hot with tears.

1996

Many years later, I have to tell my father that I've written a memoir about our family and an account of that time, and I suggest that he doesn't read it.

I'm sitting in the living room with him. Neither of us is speaking. My husband is in the kitchen with my father's second wife, making supper. My husband and I have invited them to our house so I can tell them about this book. I have to tell him, though I thought I could publish it without his finding out. After all, he doesn't go to bookstores. But a few of their friends have come to a reading I've given at a local bookstore.

"Does your father know about this book?" his friend asks me after the reading.

"No, he doesn't," I answer.

"Well, you better tell him," she says. "Because I'm seeing him for supper next week and I won't keep it a secret."

So we invite my father and his wife to supper and I tell him and I tell his wife. At first, neither my father nor his wife says a word. Then, after a long, uneasy silence, his wife speaks.

"So, what did you write about?" she asks.

She's known my family a very long time. She's lived across the street and down the block from us. I babysat her kids; my sister and her daughter were best friends; my parents and she and her husband socialized; she was a widow for many years; my father and she got together just days after my mother's death; and since he's married her, he's been nicer than he ever was during his marriage to my mother.

"I wrote about everything," I say.

"Everything?" she asks.

"Yes, everything," I say.

"Well, Lou," she tells him, "she was only a little girl and you were a very scary man."

"I never meant to hurt you," my father says, and nothing more. And that's the closest he ever comes to apologizing and it's the first time I realize that our neighbors knew what was going on in our house.

1935/2004

And I can see them now.

My father slams his father against the wall, starts choking him, watches him turn blue, almost kills him.

"No, my child, no," his mother cries.

Her words stop him.

My father recovers, lets his father go. Tells him that if he ever touches his mother again, no matter what she says, he won't stop, he'll kill him for sure. But my father knows it's an empty threat, knows his days of living with his family are over.

"Get out, and don't come back," his father says. "This is my house. What I do here is my business."

"Go," his mother says, "go." By now one or another of his four sisters is home from work. They steer clear of the old man, steer clear of my father. His mother helps him gather his few possessions, ties them into a small bundle.

"Where will you go?" she asks.

"Don't worry, Ma," he says. "I can take care of myself. And you have to take care of yourself now."

His father is still in the kitchen. He's sitting down at the table. My father knows that once he leaves, his mother will make his father a cup of coffee, give him a biscotti out of the tin she keeps on top of the icebox. She'll say nothing about what he's done to her, say nothing about her son leaving. She won't cry, though she'll mop her tearing eyes with the handkerchief she keeps tucked into her sleeve. It will be a few weeks before she sees her son again. By then, he will have joined the Navy, and she'll weep, for she'll know it will be a long time before she sees him again.

Coming home from work, walking into one of his parents' arguments, was a staple of my father's life. Their fights had been going on ever since he could remember. His father accuses his mother of not tending to her duties, of not doing things the way he wants. Or his mother needs more money to feed the family and his father kept most of his income for himself. Or his father wants to go off by himself, once again, to Italy.

Although he's witnessed their arguments, never before has my father caught his father beating his mother. He's seen the black-and-blue marks on her arms and legs, witnessed her silent tears. But whenever he's asked what's happened, she tells him she's bumped into something.

"I'm clumsy," she's always replied.

After my father is kicked out, he spends the next few nights with a friend's family. There's a picture of his buddy in our family photograph album that my father shows me when he tells me why he enlisted in the Navy. Shorter than my father, slimmer, far less handsome, less well groomed, but cockier and feistier, he sports a well-worn sailor's hat, though he wears civilian clothes. He's always wanted to join the Navy, sees it as a way out of poverty, and tries to persuade my father to join up with him. But until now, my father has refused, his loyalty to his mother trumping his desire to leave the family.

"Join the Navy, see the world," his friend says. My father got so sick of hearing him, he'd cuff him on the back of his head so he'd stop.

"I can't," my father says. "I have to take care of my mother."

Like my father, his friend lives with his family in a crowded tenement in North Bergen, home to many Italian immigrants. There are six people jammed into three small rooms, so my father knows he can't stay there long, though his friend's mother likes him.

During the time he stays with his friend, my father realizes he has no alternative but to join the service because he can't go back home and he can't afford to rent an apartment on his own on his pittance of a salary working in a pen factory. The Navy is his obvious choice. Being in the Navy will keep him away from his father, will keep him out of trouble. So what drives my father into the service is his father's behavior, that lethal combination of machismo, the belief that his wife is his chattel, that his children were made to serve him and must obey his every command, no matter how irrational, his verbal and physical abuse. And I wonder how many men like my father were driven out of their homes for similar reasons, and I see, too, how much of my family's history has repeated itself.

In the service, my father won't have to worry about making ends meet: he'll be fed, clothed, housed—in the mid-1930s, the security of service in peacetime is a tremendous allure for a working-class man like him. The excitement of a new world opening for him—the opportunity to spend time on the open sea, to visit countries he can't afford to visit—replaces the trepidation he feels when he knows he can't go back home.

"Join the Navy. See the world."

My father and his buddy hope to join up together, hope they can stay together during their twelve weeks of basic training, perhaps even wind up in the same company and serve aboard the same ship. My father will learn as much as he can in the service so that when he leaves, he can get a better job. His service in the Navy will serve as the apprenticeship he's always wanted.

Joining the U.S. military is unusual for a southern Italian American man at this time, and if his mother knew he was going to enlist, she would have tried to stop him. His people are suspicious of government. To them, military service doesn't mean bettering yourself; in Italy, moving from one class to another is almost impossible. In Italy, joining the service means fighting—and perhaps dying—for someone else's interests. His people are loyal, not to their country—what is Italy, after all, but someone's invention?—but to their families.

After a war, the rich stay rich or get richer, and the poor stay miserable if they're lucky enough to survive. My father's parents know that peasants were sent to fight in the Great War without boots on their feet and with nothing more than sticks to serve as weapons. They know how any uprising of the poor is met with violent reprisal. And my father's parents have read about the Italian invasion of Ethiopia in *Il Progresso*, the Italian American newspaper.

"The 'haves' want Ethiopia so they can send all the 'have nots' like us out of the country," he's heard his father say.

Years later, I read that by December 12, 1935, when my father enlists, the Nazi Party has complete power over Germany's political process, making it a one-party state. Germany has quit the League of Nations. Hitler has ordered the assassination of those who threaten his sovereign leadership. He's abolished due process and filled concentration camps with his enemies. He's declared himself Führer of Germany and has placed the Army under his control. His regime has instituted the Nuremberg Race Laws, stripping Jews of their rights.

Hitler's regime makes an open show of its tanks, airplanes, and naval vessels. Hitler violates the Treaty of Versailles and introduces military conscription—a half-million men are conscripted in March—without any interference from other signatories to the agreement.

I ask my father whether he was concerned about joining the Navy during Hitler's rise to power in Germany and whether he thought that, in time, perhaps even during his tour of duty, there would be a war in Europe and that the United States would ultimately have to become involved. He replies that he didn't think about it in that way back then, and neither did anyone he knew. By the end of 1934, Germany was better off than it had been since the end of the Great War. The country was in a state of economic resurgence—roads and public works projects too numerous to count were being built. There were more jobs available in Germany than in the United States.

Yes, Hitler was an absolute dictator, and, yes, he was rearming despite the restrictions placed on Germany by Versailles, and yes, he was persecuting Jews. Still, my father thought Germany had no reason to wage war because its people were better off than they had been before. Most of the people he knew thought that what was happening in Germany had nothing to do with them.

At this time in U.S. history, the working and unemployed poor couldn't afford to be concerned with Europe. My father believed that the United States had to take care of its own people first, that keeping the United States out of war was essential, and that the Atlantic Ocean provided all the protection the United States needed. Finding a way to earn enough money to put food on the table and a roof over your head was about all the people he knew had the energy to worry about.

1922

When my father moved to Italy with his family in 1922, when he was eight years old—his father had dreams of making himself rich in Scafati, the village he'd left years before—he'd witnessed the early stages of Fascism. The country his family moved to was in the midst of great turmoil—workers' parties and Socialists were facing off against Fascists.

My father remembers learning the words to the *Bandiera Rossa*, the rallying cry of the labor movement—"Forward people, to the revolt"—remembers seeing a group of Blackshirts marching through town, remembers seeing a group of Socialists jeering; remembers a pushing, shoving crowd singing the *Bandiera Rossa*; remembers singing the song along with the crowd; remembers being chased by Blackshirts and outrunning them; remembers thinking that it was a thrilling game of tag; remembers learning that it wasn't.

To a young boy, he says, this was more exciting than terrifying, though when he hears about how the Blackshirts have beaten people senseless, he understands there's a battle raging in Italy. But he's just a kid and can't understand its significance.

He hears grown-ups arguing about strikes, revolution, freedom, oppression, Mussolini's secret political police, Fascism, Communism, Socialism. On every street corner in Scafati, men stand in groups, raising their fists and shouting at one another about the best way to save Italy, to make it into a viable republic that can feed its poor and help the ever-beleaguered South. Standing on the edge of such a crowd, my father has a taste of the tumult that will ravage Europe. But he's far too young to understand what's at stake if the Fascists take control.

1935

My father and his buddy go down to the local Naval recruitment office together. They read the brochure promising excitement, adventure, training. They see the poster announcing the service's motto of Honor, Commitment, and Courage. They ask a few questions and begin the enlistment process.

My father is twenty-one and doesn't need permission from his family to join up, not like the young, wet-behind-the-ears kids who are trying to enlist, lined up with their mothers in tow to sign papers. Most of them are unemployed and a drain on their family's meager incomes. They have no choice but to try to join the service, but it's not likely they'll be taken.

My father knows the Navy isn't taking many men—just one or two a month from this center, he's heard. So many men want to join during these tough times that the Navy can afford to be picky about its recruits. He hopes he and his buddy stand a chance.

My father believes he has something to offer. He knows how to fix engines and machines, knows how to repair automobiles. And, because of these abilities, my father gets accepted into the Navy but his buddy doesn't. What my father doesn't know then, what he doesn't realize, is that what happens to him in the Navy, what happens to him during World War II, will be governed by the fact that he knows how to repair automobile engines. With modern warfare increasingly dependent upon aircraft, the Navy will need scores of mechanics to repair airplane engines. My father will become one of those men.

"I was one lucky son of a bitch," he says. "I spent most of my time out of the line of fire just because I knew how to fix engines."

After my father enlists in the Navy, he goes back home to visit his mother during the day when his father's at work to make sure he doesn't run into him. He tells her he's joined up for four years, tells her he'll soon be leaving—he'll do some basic training at the Brooklyn Navy Yard before he's transferred to the Naval Station in Newport, Rhode Island. After Newport, he has no idea where he'll be, but he suspects he'll be assigned to shipboard duty.

His mother doesn't want him to go away; she doesn't want to lose her only son. She worries that something will happen to him. Still, she knows she has no choice but to let him go.

She pleads with him to make peace with his father before he leaves. In southern Italian households, where family rifts can last for years and sometimes for generations for far less reason than what has occurred within my father's family, an uneasy truce between father and son would be something of a miracle.

His mother asks him to stay until his father comes home from work. My father says he'll go out to shop for food for supper and come back to help her cook. While he's gone, she can tell his father he's joining the Navy. She can tell him she hopes they'll make peace.

My father helps his mother cook while his father changes. He stays for supper, sits at the same table with his father. His mother doesn't sit, she never sits, she hovers between stove and table, table and stove, serving the two men. This is what she's always done, this is what she'll always do.

As she serves, she dabs her eyes. Her tears come easily. But they come with good reason.

The reconciliation between the two men—if you can call it that—happens wordlessly. There is no apology on my father's part, no forgiveness on his father's, no promise from his father that he won't harm his wife.

The Sea, the Sea

2004

So who was this young man who joined the Navy in 1935? And what forces in his life had propelled him to that defining moment when he tried to kill his father, that moment which set in motion the events of the next several years and perhaps those of rest of his life?

About his childhood, my father never held back. These were the stories my father loved to tell me, the ones he repeated, and repeated, again. They were the stories he returned to whenever he approached the telling of something more difficult, like his first encounter with the reality that even in peacetime, in the military, good men die, which he'd begin, and then interrupt, by saying, "But before I tell you this, did I ever tell you when I . . . ?"

And then we'd move back in time to 1922 with my father's family moving back to his father's village in Italy, to my father on the deck of a ship somewhere in the middle of the Atlantic Ocean, to my father being chased by the Blackshirts in Scafati, the same year Benito Mussolini declared his intention to rule Italy when 30,000 Fascists marched in Rome (about this, my father didn't know). And then we'd move forward in time to 1926—or was it 1928?—when he got caught by the cops in North Bergen, New Jersey, for breaking and entering. Then back in time to how his father met his mother. And it's when I reassemble these pieces of the puzzle of his life that I begin to realize something about the hopes and dreams my father had when he was young.

1922

It's 1922 and his father decides to move the family back to Italy to his hometown, Scafati, near Pompeii, to try to make his fortune by buying property and becoming a landlord. His dreams of earning enough money to indulge his expensive tastes haven't materialized in the United States. Members of his family write him that everyone back home is expecting a postwar boom. With the steep rise in taxes in the States, his father isn't taking home the kind of money he needs even though his barbershop is a cash business and he can hide some profits. So he'll try his luck back in Italy.

On the long ocean journey from New York to Naples, my father escapes the family's cramped quarters whenever he can to stand in the bow of the boat where he can see the horizon. The sea mesmerizes him. He watches the sunrise, when the sea turns orange, magenta, purple, and the sunset, when the water blazes. In a fog, you can't see the ocean and the ship seems to float in a vast, empty space. In a storm, the ship dips into the trench of a swell, then rises, and takes a lashing spray over its bow.

Until this sea voyage, the only places my father has known are the crowded neighborhoods and cramped tenements where his family lived, and the Brooklyn neighborhood of his father's relatives.

"On the ocean," he tells me, years later, "I felt as if I could breathe."

It is on this journey that my father develops a passionate love for ships and for the ocean. For the rest of his life, he will imagine himself traveling to faraway places, standing at the bow on the deck of a ship in the middle of the ocean. And by the time he dies, aside from his time in the Navy, he takes but one such journey—a cruise to Alaska with my mother a few years before her death.

My father is the only member of his family, the only passenger, who doesn't get seasick. He is so at home on the water that he rollerskates all over the deck. Crewmembers adopt him as their mascot and tell him he has sea legs. They show him the engine room, the kitchen, the storerooms. A ship, he learns, is like a great floating city, entirely self-sufficient—dependent, however, upon the skill and knowledge of its captain to bring the vessel safely to port.

1918

Before my father's family moved to Italy, young as he was, he helped his mother wash clothes, shop, and cook. And although she had five children to care for, she worked in the garment industry, either at a factory on Bergenline Avenue in North Bergen, or at home doing piecework. Before they attended school, she left her younger children alone in the care of the eldest, still a child herself, locking them into the apartment, leaving their food on the kitchen table, asking a neighbor to look in on them.

My father hated being left with his sisters. They bullied him, teased him, held him down, dressed him as a girl, just as his mother had when he was small. (She had no clothes for boys, couldn't afford them, he says, so he was dressed in his sisters' hand-me-downs.)

When he was young, he had hair so blond it was almost white. His mother kept his hair long, in ringlets, until he was four years old. When he turned four, his father yanked him out of his carriage.

"You're making a sissy out of him," he shouted at his wife.

His father sat him down in the kitchen, took his scissors, and cut off his curls. His mother was outraged. Until now, her husband had paid no attention to their only boy. She picked up her son's curls, put them in a box lined with blue velvet, and gave them to him as a keepsake.

My father's family of seven lived in four tiny rooms. His parents shared a bedroom; his four sisters, another; my father slept on the sofa or on two chairs pulled together in the living room. The kitchen table wasn't big enough to seat the entire family, so they took turns eating. His mother ate, standing, at the stove.

Caring for a family of seven aged her. She washed laundry in the sink on a washboard, dried it outside during fine weather, inside in foul. The family ate simply: meat, once a week, or less, reserved for the family's workers; otherwise, soups and pastas. As soon as they could, the children had to find work. There were, as yet, no laws against children working. Without their children's help, poor families would have starved. My father started working with his mother when he was four years old, buttoning the shirts she sewed at home. She was paid by the piece, and although he didn't earn any money doing this, his work saved his mother time; she could sew a few more shirts and so earn a bit more because of his help.

His father never provides enough money for the family and disappears to Italy for months without support. Somewhere in Italy, perhaps in Naples, his father has another family with another woman, his *comare*. This is common among Italian men, my father says, but his father isn't well off, despite his pretensions. He's a barber and he's good at his trade and could have provided his family with a comfortable life. But he takes much of the money he earns for himself, buys hand-tailored three-piece suits, linen handkerchiefs, silk shirts, silk ties, handmade leather shoes. *La bella figura.* And all those steamship tickets to Italy and what he gave that other woman cost *un occhio.*

When his father left for Italy—and they never knew when that would be—the family dressed in their best clothes and trooped into New York to see the reprobate off, his mother keeping up appearances, making it seem as if she didn't mind his desertions. They'd stand on the dock, waving their handkerchiefs until he vanished. His mother wept, but whether it was because he was leaving or because she didn't know how she'd support the family while he was gone, my father couldn't say.

My father didn't miss his father. The family scrambled for money, but a holy calm settled upon the household: There were no decrees about proper behavior; no lamentations about the family's drain on his father's resources; no lectures about the respect his father deserved as head of the household; no shouting matches between his parents. Still, my father never learned by example how to be an attentive father. Instead, he was either the butt of his father's endless criticism or the object of his neglect. And in their household, his father did whatever he pleased and no one held him accountable for his bad behavior.

Even though she worried about money when her husband was gone, his mother was more cheerful. And she didn't have to care for his finery. He'd wear a shirt once; take a fresh linen handkerchief each day; demand that his suits be aired and brushed, his trousers pressed, his shoes polished.

"My father acted the swell," my father said. "And then there were the rest of us."

There are very few photographs of my father's father with his family. There's one of the family in the kitchen after a meal. My father's father stands behind the family, distracted; he's wearing a pressed shirt, a vest, a tie. My father's mother wears a housedress covered by an apron; you can sense her exhaustion, her grim forbearance. The frame slices her body in half—she's almost not there.

Although my father claimed the family was better off when his father was away, and that he didn't miss him, he kept a photograph in his wallet of his father in a horse-drawn carriage taken on one of his father's visits to Italy. Was this mute testament to an unacknowledged yearning he felt for a father whose absence was the most powerful presence in his life? And I see how my own yearning for a father who wasn't there replicates my father's desire for his father who was, so often, far away.

1923

His father's scheme to make his fortune in Italy doesn't turn out: He goes bankrupt. His mother is forced to work in the local canning factory to earn enough money for the family's passage back to the United States. After a year of living in squalid circumstances, the family moves back to North Bergen, but they are poorer than before, and his parents' marriage is worse than ever.

My father is nine years old and he's told it's time for him to pull his weight in the family. He'll have to find a way to earn money after school. So after school, he begins working odd jobs. During the growing season, he runs fruits and vegetables up tenement stairs and collects money for the itinerant vendor who hawks his goods from a horse-drawn cart. He sweeps the horse dung off the streets and loads it into a burlap bag; the vendor will sell it for fertilizer. During winter, my father shovels snow from stoops, steps, and sidewalks in his neighborhood and scavenges coal alongside railroad tracks.

When I'm young, my father often accuses me of being spoiled. I have no idea what he means. We don't have much; I never ask for anything; I work at odd jobs every chance I get beginning when I'm eleven years old. And until I learn about my father's childhood, I can't understand what he means.

1888

Why his parents marry or, rather, why his mother marries his father, my father could never understand. For his father has been uncaring and cruel toward his mother for as long as he can remember.

Like most late-nineteenth-century Italian marriages, theirs was arranged through a marriage broker. She was living in Positano on the Amalfi coast; he was living inland in Scafati, near Pompeii. When my father asks his mother if she ever loved her husband, she shrugs, as if to say, "Love, what's that?"

My father's mother was born in Bella in Lucania, the poorest part of Italy, but her family moved to Positano after an earthquake ravaged the village in 1857. During the most severe shock, a monstrous crevasse appeared, swallowing people, animals, and houses. The quake forced many inhabitants whose homes had been destroyed to move; others moved to settle in less dangerous locations. And that's how his mother wound up living high on a hill in a poor fishing village that was then nothing like the luxurious resort on the Amalfi coast that it has become today—the inhabitants subsisting mostly on fish and whatever vegetables they could grow in the soil that had to be transported into the village by donkey.

Still, his mother told my father of how much she loved the sea, and how the sight of it at the foot of the terraced hillside cheered her after her long days of working indoors as a seamstress bent over a garment. She told her son that one night when she stopped work and stepped outside, the moon was a giant orange ball, glowing in the southern sky.

"And the sea, the sea," she continued, "it blazed and shimmered with color and I thought at that moment that I would never leave this place."

A young, beautiful, marriageable woman with money-earning skills could become her family's passport to a better life, but only if she married a prosperous man. My father's father wasn't well off, but he was a barber, not a peasant, not a farm worker, and so, a good enough catch for a poor girl.

Pasted into the family photograph album are pictures of my father's parents before they married, the ones exchanged by the marriage broker.

And here she is, sitting tall and proud, and she's beautiful. Straight back; set shoulders; well-defined, sensuous lips; aquiline nose; smart eyes; lush mane of dark, wavy hair pulled away from her face. Who wouldn't want her to be his bride? She wears a simple, elegant suit, a high-necked lace blouse, a tiny gold necklace. You couldn't predict from this photo that she will become a drudge and that she will look like a charwoman in middle and older age. My father never remembers her dressed this elegantly (around the apartment, she wears shapeless housedresses; and even at his wedding, she wears something simple and severe), and he doesn't remember her ever looking this self-assured, proud, and self-possessed.

And here he is, the scoundrel, and he's magnificent. He wears a striped suit, a stylish high-collared shirt, a light-colored pinstriped tie. His hair is slick with Brilliantine and combed back from his high forehead, and he sports a groomed handlebar mustache. You can see why a country girl would want to marry him, if indeed she even had a choice. Perhaps he was her only suitor, or her most promising suitor, or perhaps the family insisted she marry, or she was desperate to marry.

Look closely at this photo, look into his eyes. He looks like that silent-film villain who twirls the tip of his mustache before grabbing the innocent, unsuspecting girl from behind to do her harm.

And so they met, courted, and married, and she moved with him to Scafati, his hometown. He wanted a woman to bear his children, a workhorse to keep his house, cook his food, wash and press his and the family's clothes. And he expected his wife to let him do whatever he wanted without complaint. This was the way southern Italian men behaved, my father said.

1889–1923

After their first child, a girl, was born, they moved to the United States, where he expected to make his fortune. Soon after they emigrated, a second daughter was born. My father was the next child—there would be two more daughters. After my father's birth, any affection or grudging respect his parents might have felt for each other vanished, and his father started leaving the family to their own resources to travel back to Italy alone. And each time the family troops into New York to wave his father off on one steamship or another, my father tells himself that one day he'll follow in his father's footsteps and leave the family and sail across the sea.

On the Road to Nowhere, Moving Fast

2004

"It's a miracle," my father says, "I didn't wind up in jail. I have to thank my mother for that. I could have turned out to be a punk kid. I could have wound up in the mob. She kicked my ass when I got in trouble, insisted I make something of myself."

And then my father tells me about why he thinks he began his "life of crime," as he called it.

1920—1930

My father doesn't go to high school, doesn't make it past eighth grade. His father moves the family constantly—to cheaper digs, to better digs, to cheaper digs again, to one city, then another, to Italy and back—so he attends a score of schools, can't keep up with the other pupils, and gets left back several times. Because he's always working after school at one odd job or another, he has no time for homework, and when he's in school, he's tired and falls asleep during lessons.

He's ashamed of himself, believes he's dumb, is told he's stupid, and becomes a Peck's bad boy in school. Teachers often make him sit under the desk for misbehaving.

In grammar school, he doesn't learn to write well, can't spell, and can just about add and subtract. But he's learned how to read, though haltingly, and he loves it. He runs his finger across the page under a line of print, like a child learning to read, so he won't get lost in a sea of words.

As a poor boy, he reads anything that comes his way, and not much does—magazines, car repair manuals. All his reading is serious, all of it instructional. He doesn't read pulp fiction or girlie magazines like his friends. He decides to teach himself arithmetic because he hasn't learned it well enough in school, and he solves problems from a textbook he steals when he leaves school for good. He finds it's easier to learn on his own than from a teacher.

When he's sixteen and still in elementary school, he decides to quit and find a job. But he's young and can't find steady work. He knows he has to bring money home, so he joins a gang of teenagers who loot construction sites, mostly make-work government projects.

My father's specialty is copper pipe. He's small and can crawl through fissures in chain link fences and through tiny openings. He's wiry and strong and can carry heavy loads. Sometimes he's the first one who breaks in through a window or a rent in a fence to reconnoiter what's there.

When night falls, the gang meets up and the leader tells them the site they're hitting. They break in, swarm all over the place, find what they can, and run away carrying as much loot as they can haul. They're in and out within fifteen minutes.

After the goods are fenced, my father gets his cut depending on how much he's stolen, and how much it's sold for. But it's never much—there are men up the line who have to get their cut.

One night, the cops catch my father. The rest of the gang flees. He's handcuffed, hauled into the police station, and thrown into a cell. His mother comes to post bail. He hasn't been caught with anything and the cops don't link him to the gang they've been chasing. He knows he could've been charged with breaking and entering, but it's chalked up to a case of juvenile mischief. He's given a stern warning and let go.

When they return home, his mother beats him with a broom handle.

"She saved my life," my father says. "I was a stupid punk. I might have gone on to bigger and better things with that gang, by which I mean, bigger and far worse things. I needed work, I couldn't get work, and we needed the money. I didn't think I had a choice."

His mother doesn't tell his father. But she tells her son if he gets caught again, she'll let him rot in jail. She knows the consequences of a life of crime. Her husband has relatives who are connected; some have done time, and she doesn't want this life for her son, her pride and joy.

"My life of crime," my father says, "didn't last long."

After my father quits the gang, his mother works longer hours. She enrolls him in Jersey Prep, a trade school. She hopes that if he learns a trade, he'll straighten out and that when he graduates he'll be able to support himself. There, he learns the rudiments of operating and repairing machinery, and because of this training he'll eventually become a skilled laborer.

His mother forces him to join the Boy Scouts to teach him discipline. At first my father resists. He thinks his friends will mock him or beat him up. But his mother insists.

"Join the Scouts or get out of the house," she says.

This marks a turning point in my father's life. It's the first time he feels like he belongs to something important. It's his first move out of the insular world of his poor Italian neighborhood into a place where boys from diverse backgrounds mingle without acrimony and for common goals. His Scout troop—its orderly, disciplined environment—is a welcome change from his chaotic family life.

Poor boys don't often join the Scouts. There are dues, and the uniform is expensive, but the Scout leader gives my father one that's a hand-me-down. His mother takes in laundry to wash at night after her day's work and makes enough money to pay his dues.

And here is my father in a photograph, wearing his well-worn uniform, standing at attention outside the tenement where his family lives. The sleeves are too big; the trousers are too baggy. But the stiff, broad-brimmed Baden-Powell hat seems brand-new. My father wears the uniform with pride, as he will wear each of his uniforms throughout his life—his sailor uniforms, his fireman's uniforms. And it seems he's looking forward to the life that is ahead.

"There's nothing like a uniform," he says, "to make you feel proud, to make you feel like you matter." My father starts paying attention to his appearance; he starts spit-shining his shoes.

He becomes a good Scout. He learns the Boy Scout oath—doing your best; doing your duty to God and country; obeying the Scout law; helping others; keeping yourself strong, alert, and morally upright—and he takes it seriously. He promises himself that whatever he does, he will do it right.

He learns the Boy Scout law. The part about being obedient and cheerful will cause him trouble: He doesn't like to play by the rules and he sometimes has bursts of temper that frighten his sisters. Still, he'll try. The Scout motto, "Be prepared," he takes seriously. When there's the threat of a hurricane, he gathers flashlights, a crank-operated portable radio, water, canned goods, and dry goods sufficient to last for more than a week, and he puts them in a safe place. This, his mother doesn't understand: His preparedness differs from how her people deal with potential calamity by resigning themselves to fate.

He learns knot tying, orienteering (using a map and compass to navigate from one place to another), and survival skills that he uses throughout his life. Being a Scout prepares him for being in the Navy. And when my father joins the Navy, he's already learned how to be a member of a group in which discipline, regimentation, and fellowship are valued.

He's required to learn about the life of Lord Robert Baden-Powell, the founder of the Scouts, his service in India, Africa, and the British secret service. He learns Baden-Powell's creed, that in any life-threatening military situation you must think independently, be self-reliant, and use initiative. This contradicts the rule about always following orders issued by superiors, Baden-Powell explains, because men on the front lines understand the terrain and the enemy better than officers far removed from the fighting. Though my father knows he'll never become a leader, he emulates the man's ideals.

1930

When my father is seventeen, he gets a job in an automobile repair shop because of the skills he's learned at Jersey Prep. Few people own automobiles, so there isn't much work, which my father doesn't like, so he makes work for himself—straightening up the shop, cleaning the tools. When he's at work, he wants to work, not waste time. He doesn't think repairing cars will ever turn into a big enough business; he can't foresee a time when so very many people in the United States will own a car; he can't imagine a country crisscrossed with highways.

During his stint at the shop, my father becomes an expert Ford Model A and Model B repairman—they're the most common automobiles brought in for service. But once, a Rolls-Royce Phantom is brought in for repair.

"A honey of a car," my father says. "Probably belonged to a gangster. Who else could afford one?"

My father can't afford a car, won't be able to own one until years after the war, but he wouldn't want a fancy car even if he could have one.

"A car's a car. It takes you from one place to another. When you're inside, you can't see the outside. Expensive cars are a waste of money," he says. Still, my father will treat every car he owns as if it were a Rolls-Royce Phantom.

During winters, work in the garage is brutal—it's unheated—so after a year he looks for other work. His cousin who works at a pen factory puts in a good word for him, and he gets a job working on an assembly line. He welcomes the job because it pays more and the work is steady. His salary is enough to contribute to the support of his family, but not enough for him to live on his own.

With the country still feeling the effects of the Great Depression, with recovery still a political promise, with so many workers unemployed, my father knows he's lucky to have work, and he works hard to make sure he keeps his job. Workers are expendable, and a slip-up can get you fired. Like every other laborer, my father knows he's replaceable.

My father works harder and faster than everyone else. "Work like hell or lose your job" is his motto. It's the way he works for the rest of his life. It's the way he teaches me I must work when I get my first "real" job as a file clerk the summer after ninth grade, and it's the way I work at every other job I get: another filing job the summer after tenth grade; a key punch job the summer after eleventh grade; an office job in New York City the summer after twelfth grade and throughout college; my first high school teaching job; my college teaching jobs. Throughout all these years, when I tell my father that I landed a new job he reminds me that I have to work harder and faster than everyone else, and even though I scoff at his advice, even though I pretend we're different and that it's a different time in history, many of my diary entries speak about how tired I am because of how hard I'm working.

Because my father works so hard, he says the men he works with resent him.

"Slow down," they tell him. "You make us look bad." The boss loves him, my father says, but the workers don't.

My father's job is to operate a machine press that shapes the casings for pens. It's a dead-end job, but it's a job, and the money he brings home makes it possible for his mother to work fewer hours. He tries to persuade his boss that because he knows how to fix machines, he should be made responsible for preventive maintenance that will keep the factory running smoothly. But his boss doesn't want to stop production long enough to check the machinery to prevent breakdowns, so the press breaks down often, and it takes a long time to repair. The wages of the men working piecework like my father suffer.

Grateful as he is for work of any kind, my father hopes for a better job than work on the line in a factory. But it's one of the worst times in U.S. history for a young working-class man from an immigrant family to fulfill his aspirations. He continues to work at the pen factory until he's twenty-one years old, when he joins the Navy.

When he was younger, when he left Jersey Prep, he'd hoped to find an apprenticeship to learn a trade—any trade, but preferably one that had to do with machines. But during the Depression and the years after, such opportunities have vanished.

When, after my father leaves home and realizes he has no choice but to join the service, although he regrets having fought with his father, he knows he would never have left that dead end job voluntarily.

"I wasn't the kind of man to risk losing work at that time," he tells me. "If I didn't fight with my father, if I didn't have to join the Navy, I might have stayed at that job for years, until I got drafted into World War II. And I would have entered that war without the skills I learned during my first tour of duty, and who knows what would have happened to me. I probably would have been on the front line somewhere and died." And this is when my father tells me that he's read somewhere that, during wartime, the greatest number of men who die are from the working class.

Fly Boy

1935, 2004

The day my father enlists in the Navy, he tells the Specialist recruiting him that he wants to learn how to fly.

"Sure," the Specialist says. "We'll see how you make out in training."

"Thanks," my father replies, imagining himself in a flight jacket, scarf, goggles, and gloves, climbing into the cockpit of an airplane, knowing he's turned out to be that rarest of men, a natural flyer.

"But what he meant," my father says, "is 'No way.'"

My father tells me this story seventy years later, and he's still furious about it.

If you were an enlisted man, becoming a pilot was almost impossible. While my father was in the Navy, he would meet just one. You had to have a high school education and rise through the ranks to become a warrant officer, a chief warrant officer, a petty officer, or a chief petty officer. And you had to re-enlist after your first four-year tour of duty. Then maybe you'd be considered for flight training.

When my father enlisted, the Specialist who recruited him didn't tell him that flight training for enlisted men had been suspended indefinitely. Besides, he never could have qualified.

"I should have known," my father said, "but I was stupid. They wanted someone who could fix engines, and that's what they got. A grease monkey. Someone who'd learn to take an engine apart and put it together blindfolded. But that's not what *I* wanted."

For the first time during our conversations, I've learned that my father's innermost desire in joining the Navy, perhaps the *real* reason he joined in the first place, was to become a pilot. And how holding out the hope that you could become something you could never attain in civilian life was a powerful means of luring poor men into the military. Joining the Navy *did* help my father better his life. Still, what he wanted most—to become a pilot—he learned he could never achieve, and this left a residue of bitterness that lasted his entire life.

When I was in college, a friend of mine used to call desires like my father's a "dashed hope": an impossible-to-achieve desire because of the odds stacked against you. As she saw it—and this was long before I had the conversation with my father about his "dashed hope"—the United States encouraged working-class people to think that bettering themselves and fulfilling their dreams were possible. But for most people during our parents' day, the odds were against them. Yes, it did become possible after the war to move out of the gritty cities into the suburbs. And it did become possible for people like my parents and my friend's parents to educate their children. But it remained impossible for most working-class people back then—and even now—to fulfill their dreams of substantially changing their lives. Or as the Marlon

Brando character, Terry Malloy, puts it in *On the Waterfront*: "I coulda been a contender."

My father's desire to become a pilot was the first "dashed hope" of his that I learned about. There would be, there had been, others. And as I listened to my father talk about his love of airplanes and his hope of becoming a pilot, I had to wonder how wishing that he could have become something that he wasn't permitted to be affected him. Could this have been one source of his rage and disappointment? And then I remembered all those times I wished he'd told me he was proud of something I'd achieved—graduated from college or gotten a teaching job or earned my Ph.D. or published my first book—and how angry and empty I felt when his praise wasn't forthcoming. And I do know that he must have been proud. But I also now know that it must have been hard for him to see me fulfill my own desires because of his hard work when it had been impossible for him to fulfill his.

1932–1934

Before he enlisted in the Navy, my father was in love with flying. Improbable and astounding, he thought, that human beings could fly.

He'd read about the Wright Brothers. They could have died pursuing their dream, but still they risked their lives. He wanted to visit Kitty Hawk. But he was young and couldn't afford to travel there.

(My father finally travels to Kitty Hawk in his seventies, when our family takes a holiday on the Outer Banks of North Carolina. Crouched on the sand, holding my sons close, he tells them how brave the Wright Brothers were. How they chose Kitty Hawk for their first flight because there was always a wind. He asks my sons to imagine what it must have been like for those men to leave the Earth and fly like a bird for the very first time in history.)

My father has read about the legendary Great War airplanes. The Sopwith Camel. The Zeppelin. The Fokker. The Nieport. He studies diagrams of their engines. He learns that, during the Great War, the United States didn't have enough aircraft; they borrowed their allies' obsolete planes. He wonders why the United States had been so unprepared to fight an air war. If the enemy has an air force, you have to have one that's bigger and better than theirs, he thought. If you don't, you're leaving your people unprotected and exposing them to great danger. Warfare now depends upon technology. The country with the most sophisticated weapons, with the greatest number of them, will have a strategic advantage.

But there are peacetime uses for airplanes too, and my father hopes he'll one day board an airplane to visit a foreign land. In May 1932, he reads about Amelia Earhart's transatlantic flight. And when she attempts to break the women's nonstop transcontinental flying record in August 1932, he wants to camp out near the airstrip in Newark, New Jersey, to watch her land at that dredged stretch of marshland.

Amelia Earhart is scheduled to arrive from Los Angeles on a Wednesday. My father asks his boss for the day off so he can be there.

"Sure," his boss says. "You can have the day off. Just don't bother coming back." So my father has to settle for reading a newspaper account about her perfect landing at 10:31 A.M.

She climbs out of her plane looking exhausted, wearing her signature brown jodhpurs and leather flight jacket. She's mobbed by the press and an excited group of spectators, mostly young women. Reading about Earhart thrills my father. He hopes that one day he can become an adventurer, too.

After his father buys a Ford Model B in 1934, the year before my father enlists in the Navy, his father lets him borrow it and drive to Newark via the Pulaski Skyway, that historic series of steel bridges spanning the Meadowlands that connects North Bergen to Newark. (His mother is furious about the car; it's a waste of money they could use on more important things. A few months later his father sells it; he can't afford its upkeep, although he'll buy another in a few more years.)

For the few months his father owns the Ford, my father drives to Newark on weekends and stands watching planes take off and land. He imagines where the plane is heading, imagines himself taking off and flying to some distant landing field, imagines himself bringing the plane safely back to Earth. He wonders how it feels when the flow of air lifts the wings and the plane leaves the ground. He imagines the sight of the Earth from the sky—the vast distance beyond, the strangeness of the Earth seen from above, that great dome of sky.

His desire to travel and explore foreign lands becomes a deep, searing urgency. He remembers how acute his senses became when his family moved to Italy. He remembers how, when the ship docks in Naples and his family debarks, the look of everything—people, houses, ancient monuments, trees, the light, the ships in the harbor—excited him. It's as if he's awakened from a long sleep.

When his family returns to the United States, he misses how he felt when he was in Italy. He buys a small notebook and pastes in photographs of San Francisco, the Bay of Fundy, Diamond Head, Glacier Bay. He'll visit these places, he tells himself. And he does, but not as a young man seeking adventure but as a hardworking Navy man, when he's in the service.

For their first three weeks in the Navy, my father and the other new recruits are confined to their receiving unit. The spread of infectious diseases is a huge threat. Doctors examine them every day, vaccinate them against smallpox and typhoid, and teach them hygiene.

These first few weeks are dangerous—communicable diseases can spread rapidly through confined quarters, as the influenza virus did during the 1918 epidemic that killed so many servicemen. The recruits are told to err on the side of caution and to report to sickbay if they don't feel well. They're instructed to report any man who seems ill but refuses to go.

When they have free time (of which there isn't much), they can rest, write home, visit the canteen in the receiving unit. And they can watch movies.

"The Navy got terrific movies," my father remembers. Going to the movies isn't something he's done in civilian life. But in the Navy, he sees *Captain Blood*, *The Lives of a Bengal Lancer*, *Mutiny on the Bounty*.

"If there was a movie about any navy, we saw it," my father says. "If there was a movie with a sea battle, we saw it. And the more bombardments, the better we liked it." And hearing this, I know that these movies are also initiating these men into the military ethos of comradeship, bravery, and self-sacrifice.

For most inductees, leaving home and entering the service was wrenching. They'd left their family, friends, maybe even a sweetheart, and lost their familiar way of life. For many, this was their first time away from home, the first time they lived a communal life—sleeping in a bunkhouse, washing in common showers, doing your business in a toilet without a door, standing in line for food, eating at a long table in a mess. You quickly learned you weren't any better than the next man.

Most of the enlisted men my father met had never been more than a few miles away from home. Many came from poverty-stricken small farms scattered across the Midwest. The Depression had made their families poor, and sending a son into the military who would send his pay home was the only way they could keep their farms.

These farm boys had lived in wide-open spaces, so living in a crowded naval base unnerved them. A few couldn't make it and were sent home. Most came from homes without electricity, and their citified buddies loved to scare them by switching on the lights after "lights out" even though they got into trouble for doing so.

These green recruits were warned against houses of prostitution (venereal disease, assault, robbery), tattoo parlors (you'd regret it when you were older), boozing (you'd pass out and get robbed). They were told they'd be sorely tempted, because there were whorehouses, tattoo parlors, and saloons in every port of call and they'd have to learn to resist temptation. A sailor was always on duty, even when he was on shore leave; he was a representative of the Navy and the U.S. government, no matter where he was, so his good behavior was imperative.

My father has less of an adjustment to Navy life than most of the new recruits. He's always lived in crowded quarters, never had any privacy, never had a bed of his own or a place to store his few possessions other than the small suitcase he tucks behind a parlor chair. He doesn't mind sleeping in a barracks. He's never had a moment's peace living with four sisters, so getting away from them and their incessant chatter is a relief.

He now has more clothing, and of better quality, than ever before. Having a cot and locker of his own is more private space than he's ever had, and he relishes it. In the Navy, a man's bunk, his footlocker, his duffel, and his possessions are sacrosanct. There are strict penalties for taking or borrowing anything that doesn't belong to you without permission.

Like all the recruits, my father isn't crazy about the food—meat, potatoes, vegetables—and he misses his mother's cooking, those simple pastas and soups she serves for supper. All the recruits say they miss their mother's cooking; it's a way of admitting they miss their mothers without getting mocked. But Navy food is hot, plentiful, and nourishing, and my father doesn't have to worry about whether there will be enough for everyone.

Although my father has friends back home, he has a streak of the loner in him, and he likes disappearing into a crowd. He can turn on the charm if he has to—he's a good storyteller and he can sing, too—so he has no problem making friends in the service. He's dated women but has never been serious about anyone, so he isn't leaving a sweetheart behind. He misses his mother most, but he's relieved to be away from his parents' arguments.

Because he's lived in a crowded neighborhood near New York City and in Italy, my father is worldlier than most of his peers, more able to roll with the punches and capable of handling anything the Navy throws at him. But he doesn't brag and he isn't smug. Behaving like you're better than the next man can get you in big trouble.

Still, he finds Navy discipline difficult. He dislikes that there's only one correct way to do everything (mark your clothing, fold your uniform, launder your clothing, stow your gear, lash your hammock), the Navy way. The Navy prides itself on having the cleanest sailors in the world; there are rigorous unannounced inspections, and because many officers feel contempt for enlisted men, anyone with dirty fingernails or rumpled uniforms is punished even though enlisted men do all the grunt work.

My father despises the officers' sense of superiority, hates the inviolate chasm between officers and enlisted men. But he knows that any infraction, violation of protocol, or sign of disrespect will be punished. Extra duty for minor offenses. Solitary with a diet of bread and water for major offenses. Courts-martial for crimes. Assignment to more dangerous duty aboard ship that can get you killed.

He doesn't like to leap out of his chair whenever a superior enters the room. Doesn't like backing up against the wall when one passes by ("bracing the bulkhead"). Doesn't like being reminded that he's a nobody—is constantly told that he's a nobody. Doesn't like to march everywhere—to mess, to class, to barracks, to drill. Hates drilling—everyone does—but tolerates it. But he can endure what he hates. He comes from a people who've learned not to hope for too much and to wait for hard times to pass (though hard times sometimes don't pass for decades, if they pass at all).

Throughout the long, hard days of training, my father tells himself that if he endures and works hard, he'll learn how to fly. He repeats to himself that conversation he had when he enlisted.

"Do you think I can learn how to fly?" my father asks.

"Sure," the Specialist who recruits him says. "We'll see how you make out in training."

Man o' War's Man

2005

After my father dies, I clean out his house. His wife still lives there. She can't understand what's happening. She doesn't always realize my father is dead.

I don't want much of what he leaves behind. But, as I go through his drawers and his bookshelves, I find treasures, artifacts he's referred to in the stories he's told me. And now, his stories come back to me and they come alive as I find them.

A large photograph of my father in his dress blues.

A photograph of my father and his father, standing before their tenement in North Bergen.

A dog-eared, annotated copy of *The Bluejacket's Manual*, the "bible" he told me he studied diligently when he was in basic training.

His Aviation Machinist Mate, Third Class insignia—a two-bladed propeller, given to him at his graduation ceremony after his training.

Photographs that he took on his ports of call and that his buddies took of him.

And I can see that young man now. I can imagine him having his photograph taken to bring home to his mother. I can see him bent over *The Bluejacket's Manual*, running his finger beneath the words so he won't lose his place. I can see him taking his insignia back to his quarters, fetching his sewing kit, sitting on his bunk, and sewing it onto the uniform that he wears with great pride. And there he is, on the deck of a ferry, posing with a few of his buddies, all of whom are clowning around, and he's so young, so handsome, and so hopeful, before he discovers what being in the service during the late 1930s is *really* all about, before he loses the first of his friends during peacetime, a time when military men weren't supposed to die.

1935–1939

When my father gets a day of liberty, he has a formal portrait taken in his Navy uniform at the Electric Studio in downtown Newport that he'll give to his mother. He doesn't tell the other recruits; he's afraid they'll make fun of him. He's received his orders and he'll soon be heading to San Diego, to the naval air base on North Island. And after that, who knows? Sea duty on an aircraft carrier, maybe? His absence is hard on his mother, he knows, and he hopes this photograph will help her remember his love and devotion, despite the distance between them.

For his portrait, my father wears his dress blues. He poses before a painted backdrop of a sylvan scene viewed though a painted window framed by lush drapery. This imaginary environment is far different from his family's tenement, his Navy digs, and maybe that's why he chooses it. He's seated on a leather bench, his upper body leaning into the camera. He's smiling: he wants his mother to think he's content, and, the truth is, he's happy. Life in the Navy seems to agree with him.

Against regulations, he wears a pinky ring and a watch, not permitted by the strict Navy dress code. He'll remove them after the photograph is taken. His hands are clasped; they rest on one knee. They're the strong, scarred, muscled hands of a man whose hard work requires strength in his hands and fingers.

During the next four years, from December 1935 to December 1939, my father will see his mother only twice when he's on shore leave, but he doesn't know this yet. Once, before he travels to San Diego, when he brings home the photograph. And again, near the end of his tour of duty, just before his discharge. Each time, he'll stay home the whole time; he won't see any of his friends unless they visit him. His free time is precious and he doesn't want to waste it.

Mother and son sit together in the kitchen, drinking espresso. He won't talk much, nor will she. He tells her a little about what he's learned, though not so much to frighten her—he doesn't want to worry her with tales of how he's learned to break down a rifle and put it together. She talks about her hopes that her daughters—and he—will find good spouses. He sleeps on the sofa in the parlor, as always. He realizes he has more space and privacy in his barracks than he's ever had at home.

The first time he comes home, his mother makes him a steak for supper. He and his father speak, but not much. My father brings home money, nearly every dollar he's earned, except for the small sum he's held back for cigarettes and soft drinks. He wants his mother to buy something nice for herself. But instead, she saves it, as she'll save all the money he sends home.

She'll wrap the bills in a linen handkerchief and squirrel them away in the back of the pantry behind the grease can where her husband never looks. She'll do without so she can surprise her son and return the money to him when he comes home. He'll not want to take it, but she'll force him to. She'll tell him to save it for when he gets married. And he will. He'll be happy and proud he has a little nest egg if, or when, he meets the woman of his dreams.

When his mother opens the package containing the photograph, she weeps. Her boy, now such a handsome man, who'll travel so far away from her. Families should stay together; families shouldn't drift apart. When will she see him again? *Will* she see him again? She fears—no, she knows—that something terrible will happen to him.

"Your life is in God's hands," she says.

She doesn't frame the photograph of her only son, doesn't place it on her chifforobe. She doesn't want to provoke her husband, doesn't want him to ask why she displays her son's photo and not his and not their wedding portrait. She stores the photograph in her top drawer beneath her undergarments. It will make a nice gift for the woman his son will marry. (And she *does* give the photo to my mother as a wedding present, and after my father dies, I'll find it, and I'll know it's the photograph he's told me about because he's told me that he joked with the proprietor about the name of his studio—the Electric Studio—as the man was setting up his equipment. "So," my father asks, "Are you going to take a picture of me or are you going to electrocute me?")

During my father's first leave, before he travels to San Diego, one of his sisters takes a photograph of him and his father in front of their North Bergen tenement. My father is wearing his dress whites, his father a three-piece suit. They're clasping hands. It's the only photograph I've found of father and son.

It was his father who grasped his hand, my father tells me, when he shows me this photograph, and this gesture makes it easier for my father to stay away from home for so long. He hopes it means his father loves him, and that all will be well between his parents while he's away. He knows he might be kidding himself. But if he were to think otherwise, he'd be forced to go AWOL and stay home. And that wouldn't help anyone.

After my father arrives on the West Coast, his sister sends him the photograph. My father keeps it with him through all his years of service. Whenever he feels downhearted, I imagine, he takes it out and looks at it. He looks more like his father than he's realized and this might frighten him. He wants to be a better man than his father. Less prone to fly off the handle. Less self-centered. More of a family man. If he meets the right girl.

When my father went through basic training, *The Bluejacket's Manual* was his textbook.

"There is much work to be done," the manual states, "and success in battle, the primary aim in every military organization, necessitates implicit obedience to orders. It necessitates that men be trained to do instinctively everything that must be done in battle when under the fire of the enemy . . . . Discipline is necessary for success in battle."

My father tells me he should have known that he'd be preparing for battle, that he was stupid not to realize it. But a combat-ready Navy wasn't the one my father thought he'd joined. He'd enlisted in peacetime, thought he'd get training for a better job, leave the service, and make something of himself. But everything he's taught, everything he learns, is how to make him a man o' war's man, a cog in the wheel of an efficient, deadly fighting machine.

He learns how to carry, break down, clean, assemble, and fire weapons. Learns to recognize naval vessels from afar. Learns shipboard routines and safety precautions. Learns how to use a compass, to steer and sound. Learns how to evacuate a sinking ship, and how to swim. Learns how to survive in the water. He is taught he should never discuss naval operations with a civilian, not while he is in the service, not after, not ever, because doing so will endanger lives and his country's security.

My father takes this command seriously. He doesn't break the silence of what he knows, witnesses, participates in, and learns, until he's an old man, although he'll reveal snippets of his life in the military every so often, and then he'll clam up and refuse to finish the rest of the story.

But the military *does* change him, because in the Navy, my father learns that he can learn. And this is something, this is everything. He studies so hard he qualifies for, and attends, Aviation Machinist Mate School. The Navy is buying airplanes and training pilots. And it needs men to service these planes.

My father learns how to assemble, repair, and maintain aircraft engines and their exhaust and propeller systems. He learns how to do preflight checks, how to inspect a plane after it lands. He learns how to repair and make airplane parts.

The Navy believes that a machinist's mate should understand the principles of flight, that he should be a jack-of-all-trades, not just a Specialist trained to repair only one part of an engine or airplane. So my father learns the principles of flight, how the flow of air lifts the wings, how the airplane is carried into the sky by air. My father is trained to do everything from routine daily engine run-ups (checks before takeoff of the carburetor, the magnetos, the oil pressure, oil temperature, cylinder head temperature) to an engine tear down and rebuild.

After his training, my father becomes an Aviation Machinist Mate, Third Class. (Before he leaves the service, he progresses to Aviation Machinist Mate, First Class.)

2009

When I'm writing about my father's first tour of duty, I'm reviewing notes describing the disagreement among naval strategists at that time which profoundly affect the everyday lives of men in the Navy, and I realize that I don't know enough about the Navy he entered, so I decide to learn.

What my father said was, "The higher-ups couldn't agree among themselves whether they should build more battleships, or whether they should build more aircraft carriers."

In 1935, when my father enters the Navy, some naval strategists believe the Navy should build more battleships, not more aircraft carriers. They believe sea battles will be fought as they always have been: battleships seeking out and engaging enemy battleships. But other strategists believe the Navy should build more aircraft carriers because carriers provide a significant strategic advantage: They can launch aircraft to attack distant targets on sea or land; a few airplanes taking off from a distant aircraft carrier can sink a battleship. Aircraft carriers, not battleships, these strategists argue, will win future wars. (And it is Japanese aircraft deployed from their distant aircraft carriers that attack Pearl Harbor.)

During the Great War of 1914–18, aircraft were used for reconnaissance, anti-submarine patrols, shipping-lane protection, penetrating and bombing enemy lines, defending against airborne attacks, bombing strategic targets (factories, mines, railroad and supply routes), and fighting other aircraft. If the United States were to enter another war, airplanes and aircraft carriers would be essential for the defense of the country, one group of naval strategists argue. Without them in significant numbers, the United States would be at an enormous strategic disadvantage.

There are now three great dictatorships: Japan, Germany, and Italy. Japan has occupied Manchuria. Germany will be moving into the Rhineland. Italy has invaded Ethiopia. Military strategists believe that, in time, European powers will have to intervene to stop Germany's and Italy's expansion, and that the United States will have to stop Japan's.

Unless the United States can build more airplanes and aircraft carriers, in addition to battleships and submarines, the Navy will be powerless to defend the mainland and its possessions in the Pacific against Japanese aggression. The Italian invasion of Ethiopia in 1935 proves how quickly an army with modern weapons can overrun a country with antiquated and inadequate ones, even if the aggressor is fighting far from home. And the United States isn't yet well armed.

Still, the carnage of the Great War has made politicians and civilians in the United States and other countries (England and France, especially) decide that no war is worth fighting. Politicians in the United States argue that the Atlantic and Pacific oceans will protect the United States. And with a series of Neutrality Acts, this sentiment is written into law.

But despite President Roosevelt's public stance of isolationism, he's visited Pearl Harbor in 1934 and proclaimed that military force is necessary to ensure peace. In 1935, he orders the building of runways on Wake Island, Midway, and Guam (ostensibly for commercial purposes). The Japanese protest and claim that these bases will be used to launch an offensive attack against them. In April 1935, the U.S. Navy engages in the largest maneuvers in its history near Midway. A Japanese admiral says it was like "drawing a sword before a neighbor's house." The chief of U.S. naval operations replies that it's too damn bad.

And during my father's first tour of duty, the Navy continues to test its ability to fight a sea war in the Pacific with a series of military maneuvers and war games, many of which my father will participate in aboard the *USS Ranger*, the aircraft carrier on which he's stationed. But before that, he'll finish his training at the Naval Air Station in North Island, San Diego.

Dead as a Doornail

1975

When my father is still an energetic, late-middle-aged man, years before he gets sick, years before he goes into the hospital, years before he lives in the nursing home, years before he dies, my two young sons are playing model airplanes with him in the driveway of our house in Teaneck. The three of them have spent an hour at our patio table putting together three balsa wood pre–World War II model airplanes. At the time, I don't know that they're models of the kinds of planes my father worked on when he served on the *USS Ranger* in the late 1930s.

A diagram explaining how to build it comes with each plane, and there's a little booklet that tells you the plane's history. First, you punch out the pieces.

For this, my father's little blue pocketknife, the one he's carried with him ever since he joined the service, comes in handy. Then you assemble them—you don't need glue; these kids are too young to use glue. Last, you affix the decals onto the fuselage just so.

My father bought these kits as presents for my sons. But he's bought them for himself, too. He had a rough childhood, didn't have much time to play, never had enough money for toys like these, inexpensive though they are. My father is getting as much of a kick out of this project as his grandkids.

I'm in the kitchen cooking. But I'm listening, too, and watching through the screen door.

When my father works at something—building a model, fixing his car, putting up screens—if things don't go perfectly (and they often don't), he swears.

"No good cocksucker."

"That no good fucking carburetor."

"Piece of shit screwdriver."

"Goddamn it to hell."

This makes me want to run for cover. But it always makes my sons laugh. When my father's not with us, and they're building something, they imitate him.

"No good frigging thing."

"Son of a bitch bastard."

"Jesus fucking Christ."

They think my father's funny. But they've never seen him at his worst. Never been there when the shouting turns to throwing. When the throwing turns to breaking. So far, with this project, he's had only one outburst, when one of the planes splintered.

"Son of a bitch. Cheap shit thing."

Now they're down to two planes, one for each kid, none for my father.

These planes are powered by rubber bands, a step up from the simpler balsa wood models the three of them played with when my sons were smaller. To fly those simpler model planes—"baby planes," the boys now call them— you just pitched them into the air. They went up; they glided a while; they came down. The boys spent more time running to fetch the planes than they spent flying them.

But now my father wants the boys to build model planes that fly by themselves. To make these planes fly, you have to twist a rubber band tight by turning the propeller round and round and round. When the rubber band is fully wound, you aim the plane skyward, let go of the propeller, and the plane takes off and flies until the rubber band unwinds, and then the plane plummets back to Earth.

So far, there haven't been that many successful flights. But my father and my sons greet the few that worked with shrieks of joy as they race down the driveway to see who can get to the downed planes first.

Soon, though, the kids are tired of this game. Tired of how long it takes to wind the rubber band. Tired of how many times the rubber band unwinds before they get the plane to fly. Tired of chasing the plane. And my father seems annoyed. But as I've tried, and failed, to explain to him, kids always want to do something either longer than you want to, or for far less time— that's just the way kids are.

My father takes the kids into the back yard, sits them down on the lawn, and reads aloud the little booklets explaining the planes' histories. My sons are mesmerized as they always are when my father reads them what they call "really cool stuff." My younger son asks my father how real planes take off and land. The kids know my father knows a lot about airplanes, that he fixed them during World War II.

My father takes a model and demonstrates how a plane takes off from an airfield, explains how the air lifts its wings, shows how it banks for a landing, and shows how it lands. He tells them about taxiing to the start of the runway, about revving the engine, about headwinds and crosswinds and wind shear.

Then he shows them how a plane takes off from an aircraft carrier, and how it lands on a carrier deck. He tells them that an airfield doesn't move, but the deck of a carrier rocks and dips and rises and falls with the movement of the swells in the ocean.

"A thing of beauty," my father says, "to see an ace pilot landing a plane on the deck of a carrier."

My father makes a plane take off from an imaginary carrier for a gunnery run. Makes the plane fly to the target, a convoy of enemy ships, a line of pebbles he's positioned at a distance. Shows my sons the long, descending bank of the plane as it approaches the target, mimics its sudden burst of gunfire and then the plane's steep ascent back up into the sky so "those sons of bitches on the guns don't shoot the plane full of holes," the run back to the ship.

"But now it's getting late," my father says. "Late and dark. Landing a plane on a carrier in broad daylight is hard. Landing it at night is almost impossible."

"What happens," my younger son asks, "if the pilot can't find the ship?"

"He runs out of fuel," my father says, "goes down into the sea, and the plane takes on water, and sinks like a stone."

"What happens to the pilot?" my older son asks.

I'm outside now. I've run outside as fast as I can. But not fast enough.

"Dead," my father says. "Dead as a fucking doornail."

I tell the boys that's it for now. Tell them they need to wash up for supper. I take the airplanes, kick the pebbles aside, don't say a word to my father; it wouldn't do any good anyway, it would just start another of one our rows about how he thinks it's important to toughen up boys and let them know what's what.

"School of hard knocks. That's how I grew up," he's told me more times than I can remember.

"You're no fun," my younger son says to me.

"Killjoy," my elder son shouts, as he grabs a plane out of my hand and runs away.

A Very Smart Ship

1936

My father is happy he'll be finishing his training at the Naval Air Station at North Island, San Diego, the most famous air station in the United States. Lindbergh's plane, *The Spirit of St. Louis*, was built in San Diego, and Lindbergh took off from North Island on the first leg of his historic transatlantic flight. North Island is home port to all four U.S. aircraft carriers: the *Langley*, the *Lexington*, the *Saratoga*, and the *Ranger*. My father hopes he'll be stationed aboard one of these carriers.

After he arrives at North Island, my father's life is centered on airplanes. The base is filled with the sound of engines revving during testing, warm-up, and takeoffs. There are planes everywhere, parked at the edge of the runway, inside hangars, flying overhead, in the near-distance, on the horizon.

The air is filled with the smell of exhaust fumes, the sweet, sick smell of burned rubber from the tires of landing planes. These smells mingle with the humid, briny San Diego air. My father loves the romance of the air base, and he never leaves it to go into the city. If he doesn't have a work order, he'll stand by another machinist and ask if he can help.

Though he knows the rudiments of his trade, my father hones his skills on North Island, becoming that all-around machinist's mate the Navy requires. He loves climbing onto the wing of a plane and settling into a cockpit to do his work. He knows there is an unbridgeable distance between a pilot and an aviation machinist's mate. Yet he tries to draw out the pilots he works with to get to know them, so he can better service their planes.

Although he isn't learning how to fly, at least he's near airplanes. A pilot's safety depends upon my father's work—his care and attention to detail. It's an awesome responsibility. Every time he picks up a tool, he realizes that he holds a pilot's life in his hands.

Each pilot has his own plane. When a machinist's mate is checking out an airplane, a pilot often stands watching the servicing of the plane that will take him tens of thousands of feet into the air.

By the end of the day, a machinist mate's hands are black with grease. Sailors are supposed to have clean hands, so mechanics rub their hands raw with a harsh, strong soap and dig the grease from under their fingernails with the blades of their little penknives. Cleaning your hands takes a long time, and they're never as clean as they should be.

My father hears an officer call machinist mates "grease monkeys." He wants to confront the officer but a buddy holds him back, calms him down.

" 'Grease monkeys'?" my father says. "Where would the Navy be without us?"

When the machinist's mates walk around the base, they put their hands in their pockets. When they appear in photographs in aeronautical magazines, they hold their hands behind their backs. Except when they're working, machinist's mates are always hiding their hands.

* * *

My father completes his training on North Island and is assigned to shipboard duty on the *USS Ranger*, the first Navy aircraft carrier built from the
keel up. Only the most qualified mechanics are assigned to aircraft carriers.

It's April 1936, and the *Ranger* will soon be leaving North Island with other
vessels of the naval fleet. Where they'll be going, they don't yet know.

Aboard the *Ranger*, my father learns how important and how dangerous it
is to deploy aircraft from a carrier. He is sworn to secrecy about what he
knows and what he witnesses on board. He keeps that promise for decades.

After my father tells me about his tour aboard the *Ranger*, I try to fill in the
gaps in his story by learning everything I can about the vessel, and then I begin
to understand why my father was so proud to serve aboard this carrier.

The *Ranger* was special, not just because it was the first aircraft carrier the
United States built (the others at North Island were converted battleships). It
was named after the first *Ranger*, Captain John Paul Jones's ship, the first U.S.
naval vessel to hoist the new national flag, and it was the ship that defeated the
Drake in the English Channel.

The *Ranger* was a "smart ship," one that manifested that grand old Navy
spirit. In the ship's newspaper, called *The Ranger*, her Captain, Arthur LeRoy
Bristol, wrote that a "smart ship" was clean and neat and that its sailors were
clean and neat. Daily life and special maneuvers were conducted quietly and
in an orderly manner on a "smart ship." Its personnel were cheerful, self-
reliant, and respectful. Every sailor aboard was "ready to perform any duty,
at any time, any where." All hands worked "hard and faithfully, accomplish-
ing tasks in a timely manner."

The *Ranger* was built to deploy and land the greatest number of aircraft in
the shortest period of time. Takeoffs and landings are timed, my father
learns. The squadrons compete with one another for the best time. But this
isn't just a game. Getting planes into the air quickly and landing them safely
is essential in combat.

The *Ranger* is small, but she's fast and maneuverable. Her job is to protect
battle lines, search for submarines and enemy ships, and attack enemy shore
installations. Her deck is a little longer than twice the length of a football
field, her width about the same as one. She's armed with five anti-aircraft guns
plus machine guns.

"We wish we had more guns," his superior, a Machinist's Mate First Class, tells him. If there's a war, the *Ranger* will most likely be attacked by enemy aircraft or torpedoes. No one on board thinks five anti-aircraft guns are enough to protect her. "But we can't think about that," he's told.

"Sitting ducks, that's what men aboard the *Ranger* would be in battle," my father tells me, "and the designers knew it. But they didn't have the money to arm her as heavily as they should have."

The *Ranger* cruises at 30 knots, but she's top-heavy and has what are called "lively tendencies" and lacks sea-keeping ability in bad weather—she rolls and pitches—so then it's impossible to deploy or land aircraft.

"The enemy better attack when it's calm," the men aboard the *Ranger* joke, "otherwise we're goners."

Before coming aboard, my father's been told that the *Ranger* is a small ship, so he thinks the *Ranger* will be small. Nothing prepares him for the reality of the ship's size—the warren of corridors below deck, the vastness of the aircraft hangars, the number of aircraft on board, the size of the dormitories. When he's shown how to set up his hammock, my father is warned that the hull of the *Ranger* groans in heavy seas. This drives some sailors crazy, lulls others to sleep.

He's shown the cafeteria-style mess hall, "First in the Navy," and the machine shop and the below-deck airplane hangar where he'll be working. He learns where the pilots' ready rooms are located. Each squadron has one. The members of each squadron keep to themselves, and they're fiercely competitive.

The vessel is a self-contained, self-sufficient sea-bound city. There are more than 1,500 sailors aboard. Pilots. Commissioned officers. Crews to care for and help deploy and land planes. Crews to chart courses, steer, and care for the carrier. Gunnery and ordnance crews to deal with the weaponry on board. And there are chaplains, carpenters, storekeepers, printers, photographers, pharmacists, medics, firemen, butchers, bakers, cooks, shopkeepers, painters, and even two mascot dogs, one called "Popeye." And there are the aircraft—squadrons of bombers, fighters, and a few amphibians—and tools and supplies to repair them. And enough provisions to last for months.

Standing on deck, my father imagines what it will feel like to work here when the ship is far out in the Pacific. He imagines the deck dipping and rising, the wind shear that makes takeoff and landing difficult. He's eager to watch maneuvers, to see the crew readying planes for takeoff, to watch plane pushers position a plane, to see the signalman communicate with a pilot. Learning a procedure is one thing; seeing it, another; participating, still another. But it will be a while before he works on deck.

My father learns that airplane handlers scramble to the ledge that runs alongside the ship a few feet below deck to get out of harm's way and that arresting gear crews wait there for airplanes to land. It's hard to keep your balance and it's against regulations to lean on the rope lifeline. A plane can go over the side; a man can fall off the ledge into the drink.

My father is surprised the deck is made of wood and he asks about the gouges he sees. "Hard landings," he learns. One deep groove down the length of the deck is from the wing of a plane that tipped over during landing.

The glare on the deck is so bright, my father shields his eyes when he first experiences it. He can't imagine what it's like working there. "They tell us to wear sunglasses but they don't do a damned thing," he's told. You can't work wearing sunglasses; they impair your vision. A lot of men become snow-blind.

Crews work on planes at the end of the deck in the deck park, where planes are stored—fighters, scouting planes, bombers—with the pilots' names painted on the fuselage. When my father serves aboard the *Ranger*, there are seven different kinds of planes, a mind-boggling number of different planes to work on, although many of them use the same engine.

The crews, when they work, are often shirtless and hatless, and they don't wear sunglasses. They're sunburned and the backs of their necks are bright red. My father's been told to be careful on deck, to take cover from the sun whenever he can, under the wing of an airplane, in the shade of a smokestack. He's told to paint his nose with zinc oxide, to cover his neck, and the top of his head. Still, if you're working, standing on the wing of a plane, he knows there's no way to take cover.

"And whatever you do," he's warned, "don't back up when you're on deck because you might back up into a propeller." A machinist's mate did just that; he got lucky and survived.

First, my father works below in the machine shop. He repairs and services engine parts. Then he graduates to engines. Later he works in the utility unit and hangar where planes are lowered from the deck by elevator for service, repair, and storage. Much later, he works on deck. The machinists' work carries an enormous responsibility. Any slip-up can mean an entire maneuver might get bungled, a pilot might die.

"Good luck in the machine shop," my father is told. "I hope you don't puke easily." The shop is too far aft. He has a hard time calibrating anything when the *Ranger* is underway.

When the more experienced machinist mates trust him, my father learns of a secret cache of landing-gear struts stored in the materiel section. Struts are always breaking, but he's told not to take any from the secret cache unless it's absolutely necessary.

1933–1935

Before my father came aboard, the *Ranger* had cruised to Argentina, Brazil, and Uruguay as part of the "Good Neighbor Policy." When the vessel crossed the equator, first-timers participated in the traditional ceremony. Sailors dressed up to impersonate Davy Jones and Neptunus Rex cleansing the ship of pollywogs. On the cruise south, there were boxing matches, tumbling exhibitions, and comedy shows put on by the "Old Home Town Boys." The sailors had shore leave and participated in parades and air shows; there were parties for officers in each port. After, the *Ranger* transited the Panama Canal and stopped in Guantánamo Bay.

The *Ranger* had also participated in fleet maneuvers in the Pacific near Hawaii and Midway. During these war games, the *Ranger*'s first, they discovered that every sailor in the fleet needed to learn how to recognize friendly aircraft at great distances; otherwise, they might be shooting down their own planes. But the Navy is flying so many different kinds of aircraft that recognizing each of them is difficult, especially from a distance, or at dusk, or when one is flying toward you.

"We learned a lot," my father hears. "But we lost a lot of planes and too many good men."

Lost too many good men?

This is the first time my father understands that it's almost inevitable that pilots and crewmembers will die during training maneuvers.

The *Ranger* lost three F2Fs—single-engine biplane fighters—because they were brought in to land too high and too slow; luckily, no men were killed. But a pilot and five crewmembers died in an accident off Midway in May 1935. Patrol planes found no survivors, only some debris, but not enough for the Trouble Board, the group onboard responsible for investigating accidents, to determine what went wrong. Despite this fatal accident, the *Ranger* passed her first war games with flying colors and she was declared a valuable member of the fleet.

"But what if you were the machinist's mate who'd worked on that plane?" my father wonders. "How could you live with yourself, worrying if something you did—or didn't do—made that plane go down?"

In time, my father learns that he must focus on the job he has to do; all he can think about is the task at hand. If he worries about making a mistake, he'll be more likely to make one. But sometimes you have to work so quickly, you're more likely to make an error. Like the crewmember blamed for a plane leaking gasoline into the cockpit during a flight because he didn't fasten the gas cap correctly while he quickly refueled the plane in total darkness. Under those conditions, he said, there was no way he could tell if the cap was secured.

He told the Trouble Board the cap needed redesigning to ensure that a crewmember wouldn't make a mistake in darkness. The Trouble Board split the blame for the accident: half human error, half mechanical problem. The crewmember wasn't punished.

After these fleet maneuvers, the *Ranger* participated in a cold weather test up north. The constant work in freezing cold with gale-force winds, williwaws, and a blizzard, was exhausting. But the men had good cold weather gear and hot food, and they were shown movies every night to keep up their spirits.

"Wouldn't want to do it again, but it was beautiful up there," my father hears.

"Why go north?" my father asks. He's told that the Navy has to learn to operate in cold weather in case they have to protect shipping lanes in the North Atlantic, or in case there's fighting off the coast of Alaska.

1936

Until my father settles into shipboard life aboard the *Ranger*, until he learns about the *Ranger*'s previous maneuvers, until he hears about the likelihood of war, my father hasn't realized—although he says he should have—how dangerous his work on this aircraft carrier will be, and how responsible he'll be for men's lives.

"Until then I thought it was all about the engines, all about the planes. I know it's stupid, but I didn't realize it was all about the safety of the pilots and their crews."

It's peacetime. My father knows that flying's dangerous. Even civilian pilots die. But he didn't realize how many men would die testing planes, how many crewmembers would be injured, how many lives would be lost before the enemy fired a single shot.

My father wants every plane he works on to take off and land perfectly. And if not perfectly, then safely.

"And do they?" I ask.

This question, my father doesn't answer.

A Flower, a Sunburst, a Star

1936/2004

My father is standing in the utility unit of the *Ranger*. He's being shown an engine they've pulled from a Boeing F4B fighter.

Everything about this aircraft is astonishing. Its top speed is 188 mph. It climbs at a rate of 1,666 feet a minute. It can cruise at an altitude of almost 27,000 feet. Its range is 370 miles. My father's shipmate loves this plane, even though its controls are too sensitive.

The engine, a Pratt & Whitney R-1340 Wasp, an air-cooled radial piston engine, weighing less than 650 pounds, powers the F4B. This is the legendary engine that has made aviation history. The one that powered Charles Lindbergh's Lockheed Sirius when he broke the transcontinental speed record in 1930. The one that powers Amelia Earhart's Lockheed Electra 10A. Any motor head knows about this engine. My father does, too, although he's never before seen one that's been taken out of a plane, overhauled, and refurbished. He's read that it looks like the wheel of a giant bicycle without the rim and without the rubber tire.

My father reaches out his hand to touch the shiny metal, runs his fingers down one of its spokes. Right now it's a gleaming work of art.

"It's a honey," my father says.

"You won't be saying it's a honey," he's told, "when you're up to your armpits in grease, when you can't figure out what the fuck's gone wrong with the goddamned thing."

And, yes, my father would swear at the R-1340 Wasp many times when he was repairing one. When he was replacing the piston or the piston rings, reboring or honing the cylinder walls, replacing the main and connecting rod bearings, regrinding the crankshaft, restoring the valves. He'd fly through a string of curses, then fly through them again. But he would still think it was the most beautiful thing he'd ever seen.

Years later, I learn about this defining moment in his life. When he saw the Wasp engine, he said, he knew he had found work that was important, that made him feel he was making a contribution to a communal effort.

"That engine," my father tells me, "looked like a flower, a sunburst, a star." This is the most soulful comment I've heard my father make. His love of this engine is palpable. I'd always known that my father was good at what he did, always known that he was exacting about his work. But I now realized that, by his example, he'd taught me to be passionate about my work; he'd taught me that getting to do the work you love is a privilege; that working with a deep and profound attention to the task at hand is its own reward; that being internally motivated is far better than looking outside oneself for motivation and praise.

"You're your father's daughter." I've heard this all my life. My mother said it. My husband said it. People who knew us both said it. I thought it meant that I looked like him, and I did. But as my father told me about his work, and his life, I learned that it meant much, much more. That I was as determined as he was. That I was as active as he was—we both had "ants in our pants," as my mother phrased it. That my form of relaxation was making things, just like him. That I could focus on a task for hours at a time, like him. That I hated interruptions, just as he did. That I could fly off the handle like him, and often with little provocation. That I was as quick to take offense and as slow to forgive as he was. That I was moody and not that easy to get along with. That I was, indeed, my father's daughter. And as much as he'd harmed me, he'd helped me immeasurably. But it took long for me to admit this. Hating him was easy; loving him was harder.

1936

Before my father leaves for sea duty, he watches Movietone News film clips of Hitler addressing a crowd of more than a million people; of Hitler's troops goose-stepping in review; of Hitler's forces marching into the Rhineland through Cologne and Coblenz; of German soldiers building the Siegfried Line, that insurmountable armored fortification of concrete and steel Hitler promises will protect the western boundary of his empire.

Who can stop him? my father thinks. *There are more soldiers in that parade than we have in our entire military.* And for the first time he realizes how powerful Hitler is and how vulnerable are those nations that will try to stand in his way.

Hitler has ordered the reoccupation of the Rhineland. France does nothing. Great Britain agrees that the German Navy is partially liberated from the terms of the Versailles Treaty.

"Just what we need," one of my father's shipmates says. "They already have 2,000 combat planes. Now they'll start building more ships, more U-boats. How can anyone stop him?"

"Sacrifice," the Führer says. "Struggle." "Hard work." "Achievement." Sacrifice. Sacrifice. Sacrifice.

"Sacrifice means a lot of people are going to die," my father suspects.

One of my father's buddies asks an officer if he thinks there'll be a war. The officer laughs.

"Of course there's going to be a war. What do you think we're doing here? Training for a Fourth of July celebration?"

I know that my father wasn't a kneejerk patriot, and that he hadn't joined the military to serve his country. During the early months of his first tour, his primary loyalty was to his mother and, to a lesser extent, his family, except for his father. But in listening to my father's response to watching news clips of Hitler, I realize that he becomes a patriot in the service of his country when he learns how hard-earned and fragile peace is, and how rare. And it is because of his family's adopted country's vulnerability, not its might—for it is, compared with Germany, far from powerful—that he grows to love this land and to want to do his part to protect it.

"If there was one thing I learned from looking at those film clips," he told me, knowing that I believed myself to be a pacifist, that I was against the Vietnam War, the Gulf War, the invasion of Iraq, "it was never to let a maniac have the upper hand." And as I learn more about those times, I can better understand those men of my father's generation who were, paradoxically, both against war—"There never has been a good war," my father says—and in favor of a strong military, capable of entering combat at a moment's notice.

I imagine my father back then, wondering what the future will hold for him, wondering whether, or when, he'll see action. Did he worry about it all the time? Or did he put it out of his mind and just hunker down and do his job as well as he could?

So many years of his early manhood will be spent in the military; so many years of his early manhood will be spent living with the likelihood of impending catastrophe. These years, I realize, will form him. These years will create the man who will become my father. During all those years I've had a difficult relationship with him, I haven't considered the impact of historical events upon my father's life. Yes, I've busied myself learning about war, about his war, I always have. But not to discover how it shaped him. But to figure out how it harmed me.

Knowing this, I begin to understand something about the mystery of the man. As I begin to fill in the blanks of my father's early life in the Navy, as I try to understand what it was like for him to be a sailor who would witness, first-hand, his country's preparation for participation in a war that many civilians felt sure wouldn't happen, I begin to sense how those years must have affected him. But I don't begin to understand this until long after he's gone. And this, I believe, is the human condition: that we learn what we need to know about our parents after they've vanished from our lives.

APRIL 27, 1936

The *Ranger* is ready to stand out of North Island together with the *Langley*, the *Lexington*, the *Saratoga*, and other vessels in the naval fleet. She's about to set her course for somewhere in the Pacific, but exactly where, my father and his shipmates—except for Vice Admiral Frederick Joseph Horne, Commander Aircraft Battle Force and the rest of the high command—don't know. Whether she'll cruise north, south, or west or transit the Panama Canal, the ship's company hasn't been told. And whether she'll be doing reconnaissance work or participating in another series of war games hasn't yet been announced.

I can see my father standing at attention on the deck of the *Ranger* with the rest of the ship's company. They've been under review just prior to the *Ranger* setting out to sea. He hears the shrill sound of the boatswain's pipe over the loudspeakers. Hears the words "Set the watch!"

The U.S. flag is hauled up the halyards. It unfurls high above the deck. The ship's company salutes smartly as the *Ranger*'s band plays the national anthem.

What my father and all the machinist's mates on board know is that there will be plenty of hard work. They have some new planes aboard—F2F-1s for the bomber squadron VB-5B. But the squadron is short of pilots—mumps, emergency dental work, and transfers have cut into its ranks. The experienced machinist's mates suspect that the remaining pilots will be given extra duty, and this will mean pilot fatigue.

Tired pilots mean misjudgments, close calls, or accidents. New planes pose challenges too—until they're tested at sea, there's no predicting how they'll perform taking off and landing on the relatively short deck of the *Ranger*.

"Each of the pilots testing a plane or an engine for the first time at sea," my father says, "was an unsung hero."

"Hope for the best. Prepare for the worst." This motto is tacked up in the machine shop. It becomes my father's shipboard motto.

The officers' "cruise widows" and their children stand on the dock. They wave white handkerchiefs at the *Ranger*. They hope to catch one last glimpse of their husbands or their fathers.

The children are outfitted in their Sunday best—dresses and bonnets for the girls; suits, shirts, and ties for the boys. Their mothers hold the littlest among them up high so they can see what's going on. The older children clutch their mothers' skirts and wave little flags. They're excited by the ceremony and they've been given special treats to blunt the fact that they won't be seeing their fathers for a very long time. And some of the more seasoned wives know that a few of the ship's company might die at sea, might not come home. It's happened before; it'll happen again, even though it's peace-time. Still, their job is to pretend that nothing tragic can happen, that being a sailor participating in military maneuvers is as innocuous a job as selling auto-mobiles.

The children have been through this ceremonial leave-taking before and they know that, soon, they'll hear the blast of the ship's horn announcing its departure. When it comes, the littlest children put their hands over their ears to shut out the sound, and they'll cry. The oldest children will be caught up in the excitement and the ceremony.

If my father meets a woman and marries, if he re-enlists in the Navy, he too might one day have a wife standing on the dock waving her handkerchief at his ship as it departs, he thinks. He too might have a son or daughter waving a little flag. He too might be trying to catch one last glimpse of his family as his ship stands out to sea.

But, no.

He doesn't want that life. He's a sailor. But he's not that special breed of man who's made for a lifetime of departures. Although he's looking forward to this, his first military voyage, and although he knows he loves being far away from land, and loves the excitement of shipboard life, and loves the sea, when he meets the girl of his dreams, he won't want to leave her like these sailors leave their wives.

He'll give up his love of the sea to make a stable life on land with the right girl. He won't want to leave her behind. He'll want to stand by her side for the rest of their lives.

The First Death

MAY 1936

Less than a month after the *Ranger* is at sea, the ship participates in maneu-vers near Panama to train patrol plane squadrons and test anti-submarine operations.

My father's job is to repair engines, not ready planes for takeoff, the responsibility of more experienced machinist's mates. He works steadily and carefully, double-checking everything, making sure he makes no mistakes and hasn't overlooked anything. One mistake can spell disaster. A machinist forgets a rag when a firewall is repaired; it stops up the oil outlet; fortunately, the pilot glides in to a safe landing.

My father spends most of his time below deck working in one of the ship's utility units or in the machine shop. He's not on deck to witness the excitement of takeoffs and landings, although he can hear the elevator raising planes from the hangar onto the deck and the sound of revving engines.

As he's helping with a thirty-hour overhaul of an engine, my father learns of a fatal plane crash. A *Ranger* crewmember is dead. It is the first time someone aboard the *Ranger* dies during his first tour of duty. But it won't be the last.

A *Ranger* pilot is flying an amphibian transporting a $20,000 payroll to an outpost in the Panama Canal Zone. The pilot takes off from Coco Solo Naval Air Station with two *Ranger* crewmembers as passengers—the assistant paymaster in the compartment behind the pilot and the storekeeper in the lower compartment.

At first, it's an uneventful routine flight, although it's raining. The pilot follows the Panama Canal over Darién Province on his way to the Gamboa Panama Canal Dredging Station where the weather is unpredictable—there's a rainforest nearby. He's flying low, at 500 feet under a 600-foot cloud cover. But when the plane reaches Gamboa, there's an immense flash of light near the nose of the plane. The plane's been struck by lightning!

The plane loses power. The pilot tries to stabilize the plane, but the controls don't respond. The plane plummets toward the water, ricochets across it, overturns, and starts sinking.

The pilot and crew are upside down underwater. But the pilot frees himself from his safety harness and parachute, kicks himself free of the plane, and surfaces. It's not easy. His flight suit is sodden with water—a pilot's nightmare is being dragged down by the weight of his gear.

Before he surfaces, he grabs the fuselage and looks for his passengers—a pilot is responsible for trying to save his crew. But he can't see them, so they must still be trapped in the plane.

Although it's dangerous, the pilot dives to try to free the assistant paymaster. But the impact of the crash has jammed the sliding hood over the upper compartment and the pilot can't open it.

He dives down to the lower compartment to try to free the storekeeper. He struggles to release him. But the storekeeper's parachute tethers him to the plane. The pilot struggles to hold his and the storekeeper's heads above water. But he soon has to let go or he'll drown.

A launch from the Dredging Station is nearby, sees the crash, and races to help. The launch's crew recovers the pilot. A crewmember dives into the water to free the trapped storekeeper. The plane is sinking fast but the crewmember releases him, and drags him to safety.

Other launch crewmembers try to free the paymaster. But no one can open the hood to his compartment. The paymaster can't be freed before the plane sinks. The launch rushes the two survivors to the hospital ship sailing with the fleet.

When the crash site is dredged and the plane is recovered, the body of the paymaster is found.

After each accident, a Trouble Board is convened. Witnesses are called; the aircraft is inspected; machinists are queried. The board issues a Trouble Report assigning blame, in percentages, to equipment failure, pilot failure, and crew failure. The pilot's performance, the machinists' logs, the signalmen's instructions are always carefully scrutinized. If the Trouble Board determines a pilot or crewmember was negligent, if anyone violated pilots' or crewmembers' protocols, they are disciplined.

"You had to keep careful records," my father says. "You had to prove you'd done things by the book. Even so, mistakes happened."

After the pilot of the amphibian recovers, the Trouble Board meets to reconstruct the accident. They decide it's impossible to determine why the plane crashed. It's likely it was struck by lightning, or an electrical disturbance affected the plane's carburetor, causing the engine to lose power. They decide the pilot bore no responsibility for the crash.

"Still it must have been hell," my father says, "to lose a passenger even if they said it wasn't your fault." He imagines the pilot will ask himself if there was anything he did wrong, if there was anything else he could have done to save the man's life. After a pilot recovers from an accident, when he starts fly-ing again, he's watched. Is he flying as well as before? Or has he lost his nerve? A pilot who's lost his nerve is dangerous.

I want to ask my father whether he knew the pilot or the crewmembers. Was there a ceremony for the paymaster? Did the crew mourn him? Sometimes my father continues his story; sometimes he doesn't. When he doesn't, he gets an-gry. Does this question force him to think about what he'd rather forget?

"You never get used to it in case you're wondering," my father says. He's been sitting, brooding, staring out the window. The only way I know he's feeling some-thing is when he goes quiet. And then, when he starts talking, there's no telling what he'll say next.

"We hoped the paymaster was unconscious when the plane went down," my father says.

"Were you ever a crewmember on a plane?" I ask. I'd imagined my father's job was as safe as any job on an aircraft carrier could be, and that he hadn't been exposed to enormous risk.

"Of course," my father says. "We all took our turns."

Being trapped in a sinking airplane was everyone's nightmare. Pilots and crewmembers practiced releasing their safety harnesses, wriggling free of their parachutes, kicking themselves free of the plane, surfacing. But they practiced on land or on board ship, so there was no way to know if you could wriggle free of your gear while you were upside down, in the dark, under water.

"Every death is like that first death," my father says. "You're supposed to get over it. You pretend you're over it. You go about your business, do what you have to do. There's always something to do, and work takes your mind off it. But you never get used to it, no matter what anyone says."

Into the Drink

2011

When I'm writing about the dangers of landing planes aboard the *Ranger* and reading relevant material in Robert J. Cressman's *USS Ranger, The Navy's First Flattop from Keel to Mast* (2003), the definitive work about that ship, I ask my sons whether my father ever told them anything about witnessing serious accidents during the time he served on board. When we'd discussed this, he'd often evaded my questions or spoken in vague generalities, as if someone else had witnessed the events he was reporting.

Once my sons were grown, my father was far more open with them than he had ever been with me about the challenges he'd faced, even during those years when he'd told me so much about his life in the military. Maybe it was because he didn't believe death was a fit subject to broach with me because he still retained vestiges of the idea that women were the weaker sex and should be protected from difficult narratives, although he'd told me plenty of gruesome tales by the time we were finished talking about his military service and the war. Maybe it was because my father liked to tell my sons his stories because they adored him and thought he was a hero and he needed their adulation. Or maybe it was simply that I'd never had the courage to repeat those hard questions if he failed to answer them the first time, telling myself that I was trying to protect him from talking about upsetting material when I was really trying to protect myself from hearing it.

My son Justin replies that my father told him that a pilot who'd befriended him overshot his landing and missed the grappling hook that catches the plane and slows it down. The plane, as my son recalled my father's narrative, had slowed as it made its approach, but the engine lacked the power to resume vertical lift, and so it plunged into the water at landing speed and broke apart and sank.

The crew gathered at the edge of the carrier's deck, hoping the pilot would escape. But they believed he died on impact.

My son told me that my father continued to be very upset about his friend's death, and that he told and he retold the same story to him many times. But my son couldn't say whether my father had worked on this plane because he'd never asked and my father didn't say.

Trouble Board

1936

My father tells me that whenever he and his buddies are relaxing when they are operating from North Island Naval Station near San Diego, California, or on the *Ranger* out at sea, the conversation always turns to talk about accidents.

"We talked about how accidents *could* happen."

High winds could blow an aircraft off the deck. A pilot could experience vertigo during a dive-bombing exercise and spiral down to his death. He could forget to crank down his landing gear. A plane could fail to engage an arresting wire. A bad wave-off by a signalman could cause a plane at full throttle to go over the side and into the sea. A plane, coming in, could be caught in a slipstream and tossed upside down. A pilot could misjudge a landing and crash onto the carrier's island or roll onto the stacks. A pilot's neck could snap while the plane catapulted off the deck.

"And we talked about accidents that *had* happened."

The crew of the *Ranger* avidly read accident reports published in the *Bureau of Aeronautics Newsletter.* And they discuss—and argue about—the findings of the Trouble Boards that are convened after each accident and that assign blame, in percentages, to equipment failure, pilots, crew, machinists, and/or extenuating circumstances.

By reviewing each accident, pilots and crew hope they can avoid accidents and better prepare themselves for what might happen if one occurs. After there is an accident, the Trouble Board might determine how to fix what has gone wrong with an aircraft or might determine whether onboard procedures to launch and land aircraft need to be changed. Then the same thing might not go wrong again, the same accident might not happen again.

August 4, 1936

A pilot is flying an F2F in an approach pattern to the landing field on North Island when his engine fails at 300 feet. Without a place for an emergency landing, he heads for deep water. When the plane hits the water, it turns over. The pilot frees himself and surfaces, unharmed.

The Trouble Board decides that "a low fuel supply had caused a lack of suction in the main fuel tank," causing the engine to fail. The pilot is disciplined.

August 31, 1936

A pilot, flying an F2F-1, stalls, skids, and turns over upon landing at Long Beach. The crash throws the pilot forward in the cockpit, smashing his head into the end of a gun sight, lacerating his right eyelid.

The Trouble Board determines that the accident, which requires a major overhaul of the plane, was caused by the pilot neglecting to crank his wheels down. The pilot recommends a change in the design of safety belts, so that the pilot's upper body can be strapped against the seat—they are currently strapped only over the pilot's thighs. This would have prevented the injury.

Accidents Concerning the *Ranger*, October through December 1936

October 1936

An SBU-1 skids upon landing, and the tail wheel assembly collapses, forcing the landing signal officer "to scramble out of the way to avoid decapitation." The pilot doesn't realize the "amount of throttle needed to regain level flight" once the plane starts to settle. The Trouble Board blames the pilot's "poor technique" for the accident.

A VF-3B's left wheel collapses during a nighttime landing. The Trouble Board assigns 25 percent of the blame to the pilot for "poor technique"; 25 percent to the landing gear; 50 percent to the hazards of night flying.

A BM-1 crashes upon landing into a barrier on the flight deck.

An O3U-3's tail hook breaks upon landing, hitting the barrier, bending the propeller and damaging the wings and landing gear beyond repair.

An F4B-4 crashes into a barrier during a night landing because the pilot has failed to lower his tail hook.

November 1936

Maneuvers en route to San Francisco. A pilot flying an F3F-1 inadvertently reduces his altitude to below 100 feet on his landing approach to the deck of the *Ranger*. As he descends, he loses sight of his plane guard and collides with it, ripping off the foretopmast of the vessel. The plane sinks within 30 seconds after impact. There is no sign of the pilot. The Trouble Board faults the pilot for losing sight of his plane guard.

During the remainder of November, four more, nonfatal accidents occur. During one, a pilot, not feeling the hook pick up the wire, fully applies his brakes, causing his plane to hit the barrier and pitch forward onto its nose, "with the propeller blade sticking into the deck."

December 7, 1936
A pilot flying a BM-1 with an aviation machinist's mate aboard dives at 10,000 feet to carry out a mock dive-bombing attack on the *USS Utah*.

At 1,000 feet, the pilot makes a "low release" and pulls up the nose of the aircraft. The plane, however, turns nose down and plunges into the sea. Neither crew nor plane is recovered. The crash remains a mystery.

Later the same day, two nonfatal crashes occurred, both the result of "poor technique," carelessness, and equipment failure. One pilot can't close the throttle at 500 feet; a piece of sponge rubber has fallen and lodged behind the arm on the end of the throttle control. Mechanics working on similar planes rectify the problem by securing the sponge rubber with bolts and washers.

"Those pilots and their crew were human guinea pigs," my father says.

They test new engines. They test engines after they've been re-jiggered. They test planes no one has flown before under difficult conditions, like the *Bouncing Girl*, a BG-1 that flies ten feet up into the air after it lands. There are planes whose struts tend to give way when they land hard. And the crew aboard the *Ranger* learns by trial and error that the deck is too short for landings made from the bow approach to the carrier.

Navy pilots during the 1930s tested new planes and new engines. No pilot wanted to be the first to detect a defect. But that's what was exciting about their work. Each test flight was a journey into the unknown. For every aircraft, every engine, every landing on an aircraft carrier, there was a first flight. And in many ways, every flight was a first flight, for no two flights were undertaken under the same conditions.

Pilots were superstitious. They kept lucky charms hidden in their uniforms—a piece of cloth, a stone, a letter from a girl. A pilot who lost his lucky charm feared his flight would be jinxed; a fellow pilot had to talk him down. Pilots had rituals and routines before they entered the cockpit, before they took off. They sequestered themselves in the "ready room" to prepare themselves for flight.

If you were a machinist like my father, you knew to stay out of a pilot's way when he was getting into his plane. Everything he did—the way he hoisted himself into the cockpit, adjusted his gear, touched his charm, was vital to his safety. If he screwed up his ritual, if you interrupted him and made him screw it up, there was a chance he might lose his nerve and go down. That's why each squadron had its own "ready room" below deck. No one but the pilots in a given squadron could enter that room. It was a familiar space where flights were planned and evaluated. But it was a sacred space, too, where a pilot could prepare to take his life in his hands with comrades who understood how risky each flight, no matter how routine, might be.

There was a tradition of gallows humor aboard the *Ranger* about accidents. My father thought joking was a way of coping with risk, a way of relieving tension. If you weren't a sailor, you'd be outraged at the way crewmembers talked.

"Did you hear about that poor bastard on board the *Langley*?" someone asks. "Stupid fuck backed into a revolving propeller when he was working on deck. Damn near got his head torn off. Taught him a lesson, I'll bet."

My father wonders how this accident could have happened. When on deck, the safest way to move about is to "crab crawl" from one place to another, to look behind you, in front of you, and to both sides to see if it's safe to stand. You never move backward unless you know exactly where you are because you can be backing into a propeller or stepping off the deck. And you have to wear protective headgear that covers your head and snaps under your chin so your hair won't be caught in a whirling propeller. You're supposed to wear that gear, but many sailors don't—it's hot and uncomfortable.

Still, working on deck you can easily make a mistake. The glare from the deck can blind you temporarily. An unexpected noise can trigger a flight response that might put you in harm's way.

The listeners laugh when they hear the story. They shake their heads in disbelief. No one could be that stupid. (Every one of them could be that stupid.) Things happen so fast on a flight deck when planes are being deployed that you don't know whether you're coming or going, and orders are shouted at you and you have to respond quickly. The men laughing about that poor bastard on the *Langley* who backed into a propeller know the same thing could happen to them on the *Ranger*. But it was as if by laughing about it, you could pretend getting your head sliced open wouldn't happen to you.

My father doesn't like discussing accidents or joking about them. He just wants to focus on the job he has to do. If the talk goes on too long, he'll try to stop it.

"I'd tell them to shut the fuck up, that enough was enough," he says. "I didn't think making fun of someone who got hurt was funny."

Aside from the pilots, my father thought the signalman, the crewmember responsible for using signal flags to wave planes off the deck of the carrier and wave them in to land, had the hardest job. He had to judge, in a split-second, whether a plane was coming in too high or too low, too fast or too slow, and signal his observations to the pilot. He had to assess the pitch and roll of the ship, take into account the wind speed and direction. He had to signal the pilot when to cut the engine. Whenever there was an on-deck crash, it was possible that the signalman had wrongly judged what the pilot should be doing to bring the plane home safely.

One signalman was so obsessed with accidents that he kept a log of every on-deck accident he witnessed or heard about. (Keeping a private journal was against regulations; if he'd been caught, he'd have been severely punished.)

This signalman, by reading his log, figured out that F2Fs were being brought in too high and too slow on the *Ranger* and that's why there were so many accidents. The practice aboard the *Ranger* was to bring F2Fs in high, just above full stall, with the "gun on." When the throttle was closed, the plane dropped quickly, the elevators controlling the lateral attitude of the plane had little effect, and unless the stick was brought back "smartly," the plane would land hard. So the signalmen started bringing in the F2Fs low and fast, the way they were landed on the *Langley*, and there were fewer accidents.

I tell my father that I've found online the log kept by the signalman aboard the *Ranger* and I ask him if he knew the man, if he knew anything about that log.

"Of course I would have known him," my father says. "But I never heard anything about anyone keeping such a record. Even though it sounds like his log helped save lives, if it had been discovered, he'd have been courts-martialed. The only records were supposed to be the official ones."

When my father tells me about the signalmen having such a responsible job, I tell him I think that machinist's mates had a responsible job, too.

"I guess you're right," my father says. "But, really, I was one of many, just a cog in a wheel."

War Games

2005

My father has told me about how he met and courted and married my mother, about how they set up their apartment while the war was raging in Europe, about my birth and my mother's depression after I was born. But it isn't until near the end of his life, and well after he tells me these other stories, that my father tells me about one of his deepest regrets. And because he's waited so long to tell me, I think he must have wanted to keep this information hidden, and that it must have troubled him greatly throughout the years.

"After I met her, I never told her," my father says.

"I was 99 percent sure there'd be a war in the Pacific because of what I'd learned when we were on maneuvers there. I was almost certain that I'd have to go back into the service. But your mother married me thinking she'd be one of the few lucky girls who'd have a man at home if the United States went to war," he says. "I told her that because I'd been in the service before the war, I wouldn't have to go back in. And I still can't forgive myself for it. But I was afraid that if I didn't lie to her, she'd never fall in love with me."

My father looks away. That's the extent of our conversation on this day. His eyes tear. I know he's lost in thought about my mother, his one, his only true love, as he always calls her.

Still, my father has told me that he wasn't permitted to say anything about his military service—he was even reluctant to talk to me about it all these many years later. And so I remind him that he *couldn't* tell my mother what he suspected because what he'd learned when he was aboard the *Ranger* during the war games in the Hawaiian Islands was classified information.

* * *

It's a few days later, and I gather the courage to continue our conversation.

"So what *did* you tell her about your time in the service?" I ask.

"Not much," my father says. "Only that I was in the Navy. That I did my basic training in Newport. That I spent some time in California. And some more time at sea."

"And she didn't want to know more?" I ask.

"No," my father says. "You know how your mother was. She didn't like to talk about anything that might upset her. And besides, I couldn't have told her the truth, anyway."

"Loose lips might sink ships?" I ask.

"Yes," he replies. "Defense of the sea begins on shore."

"Well," I say, "since you know you couldn't have told her, maybe you can forgive yourself."

"I *could* have said I'd probably have to go back in," my father replies.

"How could you have known that when you got married?" I ask. "You got married before the United States declared war."

My father doesn't reply. And then he tells me about the war games in Hawaii for the first, and last, time. And so I learn that, yes, he did know that the United States was going to war. And that, no, he couldn't have told her anything.

APRIL 16, 1937–APRIL 28, 1937

The *Ranger* is sailing toward the Hawaiian Islands. There, together with the rest of the naval fleet, crewmembers will participate in a series of large-scale war games. One phase of the games is designed to simulate an attack on Oahu by one part of the fleet, and a defense of its shoreline by another. Does this mean that military strategists are anticipating a Japanese attack on Pearl Harbor?

My father's role, before each simulation, is to prepare aircraft for flight, to determine whether an aircraft is ready, to stand by and repair (as quickly as possible) anything that's wrong.

My father is servicing Grumman F2Fs. Pilots belonging to the "Red Rippers," the legendary fighter squadron, are flying them. The Grumman F2F is the standard fighter in the U.S. Navy from 1936 to late 1939. It's a single-seat bi-plane armed with two .30-inch machine guns. It has a watertight compartment to improve the possibility that the plane—and the pilot and crew—will survive water landings. It's powered by a Pratt & Whitney Twin Wasp Jr. 700 horsepower radial engine, can reach a speed of 231 miles an hour, with a range of 985 miles, a flying ceiling of 27,100 feet, and a climbing rate of 2,050 feet per minute. Its short, stubby frame has been designed so that many planes can be packed onto a flight deck. It's a plane my father loves.

Building aircraft during that time was still a cottage industry. Many parts are tooled by hand. This means that, on board, replacement parts often have to be tooled on the spot in the machine shop under less-than-perfect conditions while the ship pitches and rolls. My father has sea legs, and so unlike some of his buddies he never gets seasick. It's why he gets a lot of bum jobs in the machine shop, he says—he can tolerate working under the worst conditions.

Preparing a plane to fly isn't a by-the-book matter. There are never enough spare parts. Sometimes, my father says, they fixed things with bailing wire and masking tape. Sometimes, my father says, machinists squirreled away spare parts like struts that malfunctioned often in places where other machinists couldn't find them.

I imagine my father on the flight deck of the *Ranger*, crawling crabwise toward a plane, climbing into the cockpit for a final check before the pilot takes over. I imagine him starting up the engine, checking the gauges, listening to the sound of the engine—if you know how to listen, the sound of the engine tells you everything you need to know.

I see him signaling "All's well" to the deck crew, watch him climbing down from the plane and scrambling to the side of the flight deck.

I imagine the mad rush of pilots in their gear scrambling across the deck toward their planes, climbing into the cockpits, attaching and adjusting their restraining gear and parachutes, and fixing their goggles. They do their final check, pull the cover over the cockpit, get ready to watch the signalman cue their takeoff.

My father is one of the sailors squatting down on the ledge below the flight deck. He's at the ready, listening to the sound of engines revving. If you hear anything you don't like, you signal to the crew on the flight deck that something is wrong.

You can't let yourself get carried away by all the excitement. The only protection from falling off the carrier into the sea is a rope you're forbidden to lean against. During takeoffs, a man can easily fall into the sea and not be noticed.

There's the whip of the signalman's flag, the roar of aircraft engines, the smell of fuel, the snap of the catapult that flings the craft off the deck and into the sky. There are planes circling overhead, waiting for other planes from their squadron; there are planes flying in formation to their targets. You see them, you see them, and then you don't.

Now it's time to go below to the shop, time to make parts, repair disabled planes, maintain and overhaul engines. And then, when you get the signal that the planes have appeared as small specks in the sky, you come above and wait, and hope that every plane launched has a safe return.

Taking off is risky, landing even riskier. You peer into the sky. You hear someone shout, "They're coming in." You wait and pray for a series of safe landings. But you know accidents happen. You've already witnessed too many of them.

Afterward, you check out your assigned plane, talk to the pilot, hear what he says needs to be done to get that plane back up into the air. But sometimes, my father says, a pilot has had enough flying and is flight-weary; sometimes he's worn out because he's had a close call and doesn't want to fly and he might pretend something's wrong with his plane.

You try to find out what's wrong with the plane and you can't. You decide that the plane's airworthy. You're the one who decides, and it's a hell of a responsibility, my father says, to tell a pilot you can't find anything wrong with his plane and to send him back up into the sky when the pilot might want to stay grounded.

During war games, everyone is exhausted. The rate of takeoffs and landings necessary to carry out maneuvers pushes even the best machinist, the best pilot, the best signalman, and the best deck crew to the limits. During an eight-day period, from April 21 through April 28, the *Ranger* logged 333 landings, with no barrier crashes.

The crew's job on an aircraft carrier, according to one of their commanders, is to train for the "quick and almost continuous handling of planes" required during wartime. And the *Ranger*'s flight deck crew has become so skilled that they can deploy planes more quickly than the larger carriers in the fleet. Admiral William D. Leahy, the Chief of Naval Operations, says that the men are proving themselves to be "well trained and highly contented."

APRIL 25, 1937

The *Ranger* launches its planes during a moonlit night. She is part of the task force simulating an attack on the Pearl Harbor Navy Yard (the very place the Japanese will attack) and destroying it. Her planes are "attacked" by "enemy" bombers and engage in mock dogfights with the "enemy." It's evident to those who participate just how vulnerable the Navy Yard is, and just how vulnerable the *Ranger* will be in any sea battle.

MAY 4, 1937

The *Ranger* engages in war games simulating an offensive campaign against the Hawaiian chain of islands. During this phase of the war games, the *Ranger* defends the islands.

The weather, at first, is rainy and foggy. The crew hears of a disagreement between two officers about whether to launch planes. One wants to send the planes into the air. The other thinks it will be deadly for pilots to fly. Luckily, the weather breaks. But it's clear that some officers put carrying out the war games first and the safety of the pilots and crew second. It's a sobering—and infuriating—lesson. Still, if this were wartime, they'd have to fly no matter what.

During this series of fleet problems, a pilot flies his Vought into the water at full speed, killing himself and his passenger, a grim reminder of how dangerous maneuvers can be, even in peacetime.

Umpires whose job it is to score opposing sides, analyze the mock battle, and decide upon a winner and a loser declare the *Ranger* gravely crippled by attacks. They decide almost half of its flight deck is damaged and the ship's planes are inoperable because they have no place to land. Still, even though umpires declare that the smallness of the ship means that procedures for getting the planes into the air must be carefully planned and carried out, her planes have been launched more quickly than those of the other, larger carriers in the simulation.

MAY 26, 1937

While the *Ranger* is en route to San Francisco from the Hawaiian Islands, a crewman sights a Japanese ship cruising at a distance, its movements in tandem with that of the *Ranger*. Until the ship slips beyond the horizon, the crew is jittery.

The crew has good reason to be jittery. Eleven days later, Japanese and Chinese forces will fire at each other near the Lugon Bridge on the route to Beijing; shortly thereafter, Beijing and Tianjin will fall to Japanese forces, and Japan's full-scale invasion of China will begin.

In six months, on December 12, 1937, in the early afternoon, Japanese aircraft will strafe the deck of the *USS Panay* and bomb the vessel lying at anchor in the Yangtze River, several miles away from Nanking, which is being viciously attacked by the Japanese. On board are the *Panay*'s crew, newsmen covering the Sino-Japanese conflict, and officials from the U.S. Embassy in Nanking, fleeing the carnage. The United States and Japan aren't yet at war; the *Panay* has the right, under international law, to patrol the Yangtze River to defend U.S. commercial interests from river pirates.

Because of the attack, seventy-four men are wounded, and three die—the first Japanese attack against the United States during World War II, my father says, when he tells me to go read about the attack on the *Panay*.

President Roosevelt, through Secretary of State Cordell Hull, conveys shock and concern to the Japanese ambassador. The Japanese government apologizes, claiming the attack is a case of mistaken identity. Impossible, say eyewitnesses. After an investigation, the Japanese offer a second apology, the Japanese admiral responsible for the attack resigns, and $2 million in reparations is paid.

Roosevelt accepts the apology; he holds Japan to its promise to respect the United States' interests in China. The attack on the *Panay* hardens the leadership of those committed to neutrality.

An investigation reveals that the attack on the *Panay* is no accident. Some believe the Japanese are warning off the United States from aiding the Chinese—the United States has been sending bombers and pilots to China. Some believe the attack was instigated by a group of Japanese military fanatics wanting to provoke a war with the United States before it is prepared for combat.

"So," my father says, "just why was that Japanese ship shadowing us a few days before the Japanese began to attack China? And why did they attack the *Panay*? To provoke a war with us before we were ready? That's what I thought. That's what I still think. And I knew—we all knew—we weren't anywhere near ready."

MAY 28, 1937

After the *Ranger* arrives stateside, the results of the most recent war games are analyzed and policy decisions are reported to the crew.

There has been a controversy over whether aircraft carriers like the *Ranger* are more effective if they stay with the fleet to defend it or if they operate offensively against the enemy independently of the fleet.

For now, the decision has been made that aircraft carriers will stay with the fleet to protect it.

"But carriers sailing with a fleet are sitting ducks," my father explains. "A carrier is the enemy's first target. Cripple a carrier, wipe out its ability to launch aircraft, and you wipe out a significant part of a fleet's offensive capability."

But one of the "top brass"—Admiral Claude C. Bloch—reasoned that aircraft carriers should stay with the main body of the fleet to defend destroyers and battleships.

"It's better for the carriers to be sunk incident to winning a fleet victory than to escape from a defeat or an indecisive engagement," Bloch said.

But Captain John S. McCain Sr., the captain of the *Ranger* during these games, and the pilots on board the *Ranger* who've participated in the war games in Hawaii, argue that aircraft carriers should operate independently, away from the fleet, to seek out and destroy enemy carriers. They know that carriers will be prime targets because they are the most valuable, but the most vulnerable, component of a naval fleet—carriers aren't heavily armed nor do they have protective armor.

(This is the heyday of the internal battle between the "battleship boys," who want to fight sea battles the old-fashioned way, and men like McCain, who know that, with the advent of the aircraft carrier, sea battles will never be fought the same way again.)

McCain argues that you can never win a fleet victory unless aircraft carriers operate at a distance from the fleet, and that Admiral Bloch's flawed strategy will doom not only the carriers but the U.S. fleet too.

If an enemy's carriers destroy more U.S. carriers than the United States destroys of the enemy's, that alone can turn the tide of any sea battle and determine the outcome of a naval war. The results of the war games clearly indicate that carriers launching aircraft, and not battleships alone, will win a naval war. Anyone serving aboard the *Ranger* knows that once your carriers are knocked out, you have lost your chance to wage an offensive war.

If you disable a carrier, you disable its planes, and you compromise or knock out its offensive capacity. Knocking out the offensive capacity of a fleet, which relies primarily on the long-range bombing capacity of its aircraft, means you will be forced into fighting a defensive war with battleships. And if you fight a defensive war, you'll never be able to knock out your enemy's offensive capacity because the only way you can do that is by using aircraft flying long distances launched from mobile carriers.

But Vice Admiral Frederick Joseph Horne understands that the fleet problems carried on off the coast of Hawaii prove that the only way a carrier can protect herself, her planes, and her crew is to carry out evasive maneuvers, at high speeds, *away from the fleet*. Fleets move slowly; carriers can move quickly. Carriers should be used for offense, for attacking an enemy's aircraft carriers. Unless an enemy's carriers are destroyed—and U.S. planes launched off aircraft carriers could accomplish that mission—an entire U.S. fleet can easily be destroyed.

(Yet it took until January 1940, after my father's first discharge, for naval strategists to agree that carriers would operate independently of the fleet. And it was after the Japanese attack on Pearl Harbor in 1941—launched from Japanese aircraft carriers—that the aircraft carrier became the Navy's most important weapon, and the Battles of the Coral Sea and Midway in 1942 confirmed that sea combat in the Pacific would be dominated by the aircraft carrier, and by the offensive search-and-destroy warfare that Captain McCain and the pilots and crew aboard the *Ranger* insisted was necessary. To many, it was *this* strategy, together with superior carrier design, that helped win the sea war in the Pacific.)

1930–1934

Since the early 1930s, the naval high command knew that a Japanese attack with only 150 planes could destroy the entire Pearl Harbor fleet and force the United States into a defensive, rather than an offensive, war with Japan—they'd learned this through a series of battle simulations. But these findings were dismissed because it was considered too difficult for Japan to undertake such an attack so far from its home islands.

For Japan to attack Hawaii meant it would have to transport aircraft and pilots aboard aircraft carriers to within striking distance of Hawaii without the United States learning of that enormous naval operation. And because the United States itself was not yet capable of such a complex naval maneuver, and would not be for perhaps a decade, the naval high command dismissed the possibility that the Japanese could launch such an attack.

By 1934, the United States had determined that if the Japanese, as part of their expansionist strategy, were to attack the United States, they would first strike U.S. possessions in the western Pacific, such as the Philippines. Because international treaties forbade the United States from constructing military bases on Pacific islands, the United States would be at a strategic disadvantage if the Japanese decided to attack. According to the Navy's War Plan Orange, the Philippines and other western Pacific outposts would have to hold out on their own while the Pacific Fleet guarded against attacks on the Panama Canal.

After the fleet mustered more strength, it would sail to the western Pacific, to Guam and the Philippines. Then the fleet would engage the Japanese Navy near their home islands and blockade them.

Everything needed to wage war—troops, ancillary personnel, food and water, clothing, tanks, arms, ammunition, aircraft, pilots, repair supplies—would have to be transported more than 5,000 miles across the Pacific in seas notorious for their swells—thirty- to forty-foot swells were common during gales. The United States was not anywhere near ready to wage this kind of war.

"Did they expect the Japanese to wait for us to get ready to fight them?" my father said when he discussed his shipmates' frustration at U.S. unpreparedness to fight Japan in the western Pacific. He and his shipmates believed it wasn't a question of *whether* the United States and Japan would be at war but of *when* the war would start, and they feared that at the beginning it would be a bloodbath.

As early as 1934, Japanese military experts had crafted a strategy for war with the United States. Attack U.S. naval forces in the Orient. Harass the U.S. fleet. Try to provoke the U.S. fleet into an assault. Attack U.S. bases in the Pacific. Secure Japanese trade routes in the Pacific to ensure oil supplies. Defeat the U.S. Navy through a surprise attack on one of its bases in the Pacific.

When Pigs Can Fly

1938–1939

The *Ranger* participates in several more war games, fleet problems, training exercises, and submarine patrols during late 1938 and 1939: in Hawaii; off the West Coast of the United States; off the coast of California; in Panama; off the coast of Haiti; near the coast of Puerto Rico; off the coast of Barbados; near Guantánamo Bay; off the Virginia capes. And no matter how many training exercises my father participates in, he tells me that you could never let your guard down, you could never treat the events as routine, because every day presented a new problem and a new challenge, and nothing was ever the same.

"It was exhilarating," he said, "and it was terrifying."

The largest simulation is Fleet Problem XX, conducted in the Caribbean and the Atlantic, with President Roosevelt observing. There are 134 ships, 600 aircraft, and 52,000 servicemen involved in this large-scale game to coordinate maneuvers between aircraft and destroyers to defend against submarines and aircraft attacks; to use aircraft to attack enemy carriers; to use patrol planes to scout for and attack the enemy. The Fleet Problem demonstrates "the suddenness with which an engagement could be completely reversed by the use of air power."

This operation convinces my father that the United States is readying itself for war.

And it's not only my father who fears an outbreak of hostilities. Throughout this time, a serious case of "war jitters" prevails among the crew. According to Captain McCain, simulations have "demonstrated just how vulnerable aircraft carriers are"; there is a high "probability of air attack on carriers" if the carriers remain with the fleet after daylight. And it's become painfully evident to everyone on board just how perilous carrier operations can be, with the ever-present possibility of tragedy.

Off the coast of California, an SBU-1 loses control coming in for a landing during gunnery training. It flips over, descends, hits the water at an estimated speed of 100 knots, and breaks up upon impact, killing the pilot and his crewmember.

Off the coast of Norfolk, Virginia, the engine of an SBU2-1 stalls, plunges to Earth, and kills the pilot and his passenger instantly.

In September 1939, President Roosevelt, who has proclaimed U.S. neutrality, orders the Navy to organize a "Neutrality Patrol" that will report on "the movements of all foreign men-of-war approaching or leaving the east coast of the United States and approaching and entering or leaving the Caribbean," but the patrols are to avoid "creating the impression that an unneutral service" is being performed. The *Ranger* is put on reserve for this service. In the meantime, training exercises continue.

1939

It is near the end of my father's first tour of duty, and he contemplates signing up for a second tour. He suspects that, by the end of the next four years, the United States will be at war. Still he decides he'll do it if he can learn how to fly. Being around airplanes has only intensified his desire to become a pilot, not diminished it. And he knows that the service offers his only opportunity to learn how to fly. He was a poor man when he joined the service; he'll be a poor man when he leaves. He has no illusions about moving up the economic ladder. If he's lucky, he might land a good job that pays him enough to support himself and a wife in a place of his own.

"I thought maybe when they studied my record," he tells me, "they'd overlook the fact that I never went to high school."

My father is no patriot, not in the traditional sense of the word. Here, his Italian heritage clings fast. Your first, your only, loyalty is to your family. These are the people you make sacrifices for. Like most Italians he knows, he's deeply suspicious of government.

Still, my father has learned first-hand how defenseless his country will be if it's attacked, and he believes—no, he knows—that an attack is inevitable. It is his duty to do what he can: Men with his skills will be needed to help stop the aggression of ruthless war machines like those of the Japanese, who are already occupying land in China, and of the Germans, who are on the march. He knows how long it takes to train a good machinist's mate and he knows how many machinist's mates will be required for a navy dependent upon air power to help fight a war. If the integrity of the United States is jeopardized, his family will suffer. So he believes he has an obligation to do what he can to protect *them*. Hasn't the Navy been training off the coast of California and in Hawaii in simulated defense maneuvers against attacks because the high command has determined that such attacks might take place? And aren't German U-boats already plying the waters of the Atlantic?

One night, as the *Ranger* is cruising toward Guantánamo Bay, my father is on deck, and he sees a superior officer standing nearby, smoking. He approaches, salutes, asks for permission to speak, and it's granted.

My father asks the officer whether, if he reenlists, he might be able to attend flight school. But when my father tells him he hasn't attended high school, the officer says, "When pigs can fly, son, then you can fly."

"Thank you for your time," my father says, as he retreats, even though, he tells me, he wants to throw the man overboard. The dream my father has been quietly and secretly nourishing evaporates. He'll never be a fly boy; he'll never climb into the cockpit of his own plane; he'll never go through the routine that's required before takeoff; he'll never fly off the tilting deck of an aircraft carrier; he'll never be waved onto the deck by a signal officer for a landing; he'll never feel the snap of the wire as the hook secures his plane; he'll never feel the pride of a mission accomplished, of a job well done.

But when he tells one of the machinist mates about his conversation, his buddy says, "Why the hell do you want to fly? Do you remember how many pilots have already died? Do you know how many pilots are going to die if we go to war? Do you remember that the life expectancy for a pilot during the Great War was only eleven days? Eleven days!"

When my father protests, his friend interrupts him.

"Don't be an idiot," my father's friend says. "Finish your tour. Go home. Get a good job. Find a girl. Get married. Have babies. And forget about this old tub."

AUTUMN 1939

During the last months of my father's first tour of duty, Germany invades Poland and the world witnesses the first Blitzkrieg—how quickly heavily armed forces can take a country. Great Britain declares war on Germany, mobilizes her fleet, and evacuates citizens from London. The naval battle for the control of the Atlantic has begun.

The United States continues to profess its neutral status. Yet although vessels in the U.S. Neutrality Patrol are equipped to perform peacetime tasks, they aren't prepared to engage an enemy. The *Ranger's* hull isn't reinforced: A torpedo finding its mark would penetrate it and sink the ship. Nor can the *Ranger's* guns be maneuvered to fire upon enemy planes, a design flaw caused by a limited defense budget when the vessel was built.

Naval strategists predict that the Germans will be using U-boats to attack merchant ships bringing supplies to England and that the Atlantic will become a battlefield. After Britain declares war on Germany, U-boats sink the passenger liner *SS Athenia*, a British aircraft carrier, a British ship at anchor.

The U-boat gives the Germans an immense strategic advantage. Despite U.S. neutrality, many believe Germany will try to lure the United States into war early by sinking a U.S. ship in the Neutrality Patrol while U.S. forces are still no match for the great German war machine.

England now depends upon food, fuel, and materiel shipped across the North Atlantic. If German subs can sink enough merchant ships in the North Atlantic, and if sufficient supplies can't make their way through that dangerous corridor, England's lifeline will be severed and the British won't be able to stave off the German advances throughout Europe and the Germans will win the war. The fate of Europe now depends upon Great Britain alone. The U.S. military is unprepared to fight a war and the United States is still strongly isolationist.

Before my father leaves the *Ranger*, when she's docked in Norfolk, Virginia, it's unclear whether the *Ranger* will join the Neutrality Patrol in the North Atlantic.

This would be a high-risk mission because German U-boats intent on sinking merchant ships might regard a U.S. man-of-war as a target. My father is happy to be going home. But he feels like a deserter.

DECEMBER 1939

On the day my father is mustered out, there's no ceremony. As a parting gift, a shipmate gives him an advance copy of the ship's newspaper. My father reads that after years of preparation, the crewmembers of the *Ranger* are happy they will have the opportunity to show the nation that its confidence in its fleet as a first line of defense isn't mistaken.

APRIL 29, 1939

It's Saturday morning, and the young woman who will become my mother in three years' time hears from her best friend, Rose, that the *Ranger*, in New York for the opening of the World's Fair, is entering New York Harbor.

Rose and my mother work at Grant's on Hudson Street in Hoboken, a few short blocks from Hoboken Heights, overlooking the Hudson, the best vantage point to see the *Ranger* cruising up the Hudson. Rose and my mother have been given permission to leave work and they join the crowd on the Heights celebrating the carrier's arrival in New York.

The entire fleet was scheduled to sail to New York Harbor from Norfolk as part of the festivities for the grand opening of the New York World's Fair in Flushing Meadows on April 30. It was to have been the greatest concentration of naval vessels ever to visit New York.

But as the fleet set sail for Norfolk, Italy sent troops into Albania, and Great Britain began to gather her fleet in the Mediterranean for a show of strength against the aggressors. President Roosevelt had pleaded with Germany and Italy to pledge a decade of peace, but he'd been rebuffed. So after the fleet's brief stay in Norfolk, Roosevelt ordered all the vessels in the fleet—except the *Ranger*—back to the Pacific, fearful the Japanese would provoke an incident.

Less than a month before, Hitler's troops had taken Czechoslovakia. Most people in the United States believed that events in Europe wouldn't affect their lives. The Atlantic and Pacific oceans were vast natural barriers. Still, Hitler and his Nazis had annexed Austria, had taken the Sudetenland, had begun to persecute Jews, and had shown the extent of their madness with the horror of *Kristallnacht* and the reprisals against Jews thereafter.

My mother alone of all her friends envisaged a world at war. She hated the prospect of war, but she hated letting such violence go unchallenged even more.

The promised spectacular display of the entire fleet steaming up the Hudson had dwindled to the passage of one small aircraft carrier—the *Ranger*. No one could predict—and many weren't aware of—what might happen to the rest of the fleet in the Pacific. A war in the Pacific with Japan seemed inconceivable. But not to everyone. Not to the young woman who would become my mother.

Standing on the Heights, peering at the *Ranger*, with its sailors (among them, my father) standing at attention on deck, my mother thinks there is little cause for celebration. The *Ranger* might be a great ship, capable of launching many aircraft from its deck. But she seems so small, so vulnerable, so isolated and alone in the wide expanse of the Hudson. How can this ship protect the United States against foreign powers who've been arming for years while the United States has stood by, hoping that two oceans will shield them from the horrors in Asia and Europe?

Although it cannot possibly be true, after my father meets my mother, when they are courting, and after he learns that she's witnessed the *Ranger* steaming up the Hudson, he tells her, "I saw you there, standing up on the Heights, waving. I picked you out of the crowd. And I said to myself, 'I'm going to find that girl and marry her.'"

And my mother, by this time, is much too much in love with him to argue.

Two

"The Girl for Me"

1940

When my father returns home, he can't comprehend how much has changed.
There are so many more cars on the streets, more than he ever could have
predicted in the days when he worked as a car mechanic. Relatives in Brooklyn have a telephone. Some apartments have hot water, although his family's
doesn't. Some people even have electric refrigerators instead of iceboxes.

The friends my father left behind seem undisciplined and immature. He
believes he has nothing in common with them. They see how different he
is—the focus in his gaze, the seriousness of his behavior, the intensity in his
speech—and they make fun of him for it.

"I lost a lot of friends," my father says. "Frankly, I dropped them. They
imagined I'd been on an extended vacation on a ship in the Pacific that happened to carry airplanes and that I found eager girls in every port. They
didn't want to know, and I couldn't tell them, what I'd gone through. They
couldn't see we were headed for war. They had their heads in the sand."

The girls my father knows are wearing their hair longer and looser than
before, and their clothes are shorter and more form-fitting. A lot of them
just want to have a good time. My father isn't interested in these girls. He
would prefer to date a serious girl, and he wonders if there are any left.

My father thinks it's time for him to start looking for a wife. He wants to
marry, although he suspects it'll be a year, two years at most, before he's
called back in to the service. He wonders whether any girl will let herself fall

ove with a man who'll have to desert her. And he decides that if he finds a girl to love, he won't risk losing her by telling her he'll soon have to leave.

He's decided he'll say he's already been in the service so he probably won't be called up. He wants a chance for love, marriage, and an ordinary domestic life. He won't lie. But he won't tell the truth either. Still, maybe he'll meet a girl who'll love him even if she knows he has to go away.

My father has returned to his parents' apartment in North Bergen because there's no place else for him to go. A single man from an Italian family doesn't live alone. His family is now living in newly built government housing for the indigent, and although the apartment is new and bright and has electricity (though his mother still uses an icebox to store their perishable food), my father is ashamed of where they live. After all the time he's spent in the service, and after all the money he's sent home, he's hoped his family's situation would have improved. But everything costs so much, his mother says, that they're still just getting by.

His family is breaking the rules by allowing him to live with them: Only four people are supposed to be living in the apartment—his parents and two of his four sisters. My father doesn't want to risk his family getting evicted, so he sneaks in and out at odd hours so the super won't see him.

The apartment is barely big enough for his parents and two sisters, and my father is once again sleeping on two chairs pushed together in the living room.

"It was hard," my father says, "to come back to what I'd left four years before. Nothing had changed at home. My four years away and all the money I sent home seemed to count for nothing."

My father promises himself that he'll get a good job, find a woman to marry, and move out of the house as soon as he can. His mother now deals with his father by lapsing into stony silences whenever he's around. The household seems filled with as much tension as before, although his parents aren't fighting. But as uncongenial as his household is, he can't strike out on his own until he marries.

And then one day his mother surprises him.

"She took me into her bedroom, reached way back into her underwear drawer, took out a wad of bills, and told me she'd saved all the money I'd sent home. If I found someone to marry, she wanted me to have it as a little 'nest egg' to rent an apartment so we wouldn't have to live with the girl's parents."

This was unusual, my father said, an Italian mother hoping her son would marry and saving money to help him.

Because of his Navy training, my father soon lands a good job as a machinist at Keuffel & Esser, a prestigious Hoboken company manufacturing range finders, transits, compasses, slide rules, and drafting instruments. His plan of bettering himself by joining the service has worked.

K & E is housed in the Clock Tower, a beautiful industrial building located in the middle of an Italian neighborhood. My father hopes that one day he can get an apartment close by so he can walk to work.

The conflict in Europe is creating a huge demand for wartime equipment. Orders for range finders, transits, and compasses are soaring, and so K & E is hiring skilled machinists as quickly as they can be found. My father has been assigned to work on tooling parts for surveying equipment. The work he's hired for at K & E is important. A malfunctioning piece of equipment on a battlefield could mean the difference between life and death.

Although the work isn't as exciting as repairing airplane engines, it's a dream job with opportunities for advancement. My father is earning more money than ever before, more money than he ever imagined. Because of the war, his job is secure and he knows he can soon support a wife.

"But it was a hell of a thing knowing that I was earning good money because people were dying," my father said. Although he's not a religious man and doesn't attend weekly mass, doesn't go to confession, doesn't take communion, on his lunch break he stops at Our Lady of Grace Church close to K & E to pray for a quick end to the war and the safety of his former shipmates.

My father works long hours, doesn't have much time to socialize, and he wonders how he'll ever meet a girl. He knows he won't settle for marrying just anyone—he's seen too much strife in his parents' marriage for that, and he vows his marriage will be different from theirs.

Unlike his father, he will honor and respect the woman he marries. The two of them will work together to make a better life, and he won't squander money on himself. He spends almost nothing as it is and saves every penny he can. Since he's returned home, he's bought only one tie—ties are shorter and wider now. His mother has altered his one good suit—he's leaner now and more muscular—so he hasn't had to buy a new one. When he first tries the suit on, the trousers slide off his slim hips, and he and his mother laugh at the sight of him standing there in his underwear.

During the catastrophic year of 1940, before my parents meet, the Nazis invade Denmark, Norway, Belgium, Luxembourg, and the Netherlands. The British begin bombing targets in Germany. Holland, Belgium, and Norway surrender to the Nazis. The Germans take Paris. German U-boats attack merchant ships in the Atlantic. The Soviets occupy Lithuania, Latvia, and Estonia. The Italians invade Egypt. The tragedy at Dunkirk occurs. The Battle of Britain begins. And soon the British are living through massive, continual bombardments.

Like all other men between the ages of twenty-one and thirty-six, my father complies with the terms of the Selective Service and Training Act by registering. Each day he scours the newspaper for reports of the *Ranger's* activities or the fleet's maneuvers.

AUGUST 1, 1940

A few months before my parents meet, my mother decides not to celebrate her birthday. She relates this story to my father on their first date.

"Too many people are suffering," she tells her friends.

They mock her and say her she's a bleeding heart. She's so thin-skinned that everything affects her. She's terrified the war in Europe will involve the United States. She's the only one of her friends who thinks like this.

Her best friend, Rose, buys her a present anyway, a teal blue merino sweater from Grant's that my mother's admired but that she doesn't keep. She brings it to the local war relief agency, together with the suit she'd bought for the World's Fair, the suit she wore when the *Ranger* sailed up the Hudson River. Other people need them more than she does.

When, in September 1940, the United States passes a bill for military conscription; Germany, Italy, and Japan enter into the Tripartite Pact; and Italy invades Greece, my mother believes that war is on the horizon although President Roosevelt is still committed to neutrality despite the sale of bombers to England and France by the United States.

Whenever someone tries to fix my mother up on a date, she says no. She tells them this is no time to fall in love.

"Make hay while the sun shines," Rose urges. "Eat, drink, and be merry." My mother knows, but doesn't quote, another biblical line that says, "Let us eat and drink; for tomorrow we shall die."

She imagines falling in love and having her lover snatched away from her, put into a uniform, and sent to a faraway place to fight and die. Still she knows she'll soon have to marry. She's not cut out for spinsterhood, and life with her stepmother is becoming unbearable. Besides, she's tired of sleeping on a cot in the living room and having no privacy.

MID-NOVEMBER 1940

Franklin Delano Roosevelt has been elected president for an unprecedented third consecutive term. Newspapers report the German bombings of Coventry and London, the Greek defeat of the Italian Army, the British offensive against the Italians in North Africa. None of the Italians my mother's family knows supports Italy's belligerence. Yet members of her father's and step-mother's families live in Italy. Her father doesn't want Italy to be victorious. But he doesn't want his family to suffer either.

On one of my father's rare nights out, a friend tells him about a girl his sweetheart knows. She's Italian, like him, and movie-star beautiful, a dead ringer for Ingrid Bergman.

"Why is she single if she's such a catch?" my father asks.

His friend says it's because she's a good girl. She works hard, lives with her parents, and stays home except for an occasional evening out at the movies with her girlfriends. She's a serious, studious kind of girl, not a party girl, not frivolous at all, not inclined to date just for the sake of dating, so if my father is only out for a good time, he should forget it.

"I bet she just hasn't met the right guy," my father says.

My father learns that she works in the shoe department at W. T. Grant's in Hoboken, just a few blocks away from K & E. His friend tells him to walk over on his lunch hour to meet her. He'll tell his girlfriend to tell her to expect him.

"Do you think she'll go out with me?" my father asks.

"Hell, yes," his friend says. "I don't see why not. Who wouldn't want a hardworking guy like you?"

"And now comes the best part," my father says.

And then my father tells me the story of how he meets and courts and marries my mother. He tells me this story a score of times during the last years of his life, and I am left wondering why he relates it to me over and over again.

Is it that he wants me to learn that they once, although all too briefly, had a love that was as yet unsoiled by the detritus of history? Is it that he wants me to know that there was a time when he was a man capable of kindness, gentleness, and consideration? Is it that he wants to give me the tremendous story of that love to know the kind of marriage I was born into? Is it that my father wants me to know my mother in the way she was before she gave birth to me, that birth which so drastically changed her into the sorrowful mother I knew? Is it that he wants to give me his memory of my mother as consolation?

Every story my father tells me, I begin to realize, is a kind of elegy. An elegy for what he's lost. An elegy for the men he knew aboard the *Ranger* who died. An elegy for what he had with my mother for such a short time. An elegy for the time before my birth, that changed her. An elegy for the time before he left for the war, that time which changed him.

He came back from his first tour of duty chastened, grieving, still, for the men who'd died, and apprehensive about what was to come. Still he wasn't yet damaged in the way he would be. He had that demon of a temper, yes. But he'd learned to control it. That's what the military had done for him, among so many other things. Taught him self-control and given him a sense of worth although he still smarted at the thought that he couldn't become a pilot.

And yet I come to realize, too, that my father, by telling me these stories, is reclaiming a past that he's lost, a past that he wants to return to, a past that by the end of his life he wants to reside in. These are the moments he cherishes, these are the memories he returns to and inhabits during the grimmest of times, both during the war, and after, and at the very end of his life.

"Of Course I Will"

LATE 1940

When my father walks into the shoe department at W. T. Grant's, he recognizes her at once from his friend's description—her full figure, dignified bearing, elegant clothing, her dark hair caught in a snood at the nape of her neck. She has her back to him, and she's dusting the shoes on display with a feather duster, tidying them, adjusting the price tags, making sure everything is perfect. Tasks she doesn't have to do, he thinks, but wants to do because she takes pride in her work like he does.

He watches her, waiting quietly, not wanting to interrupt her. Should he stay? As he stands there, she seems so remote, so beyond his reach, so impossible to woo.

He's just a working man. And, yes, she's a working girl. But she looks like something more. In those first moments, even before he sees her face, he thinks she deserves someone better, that she deserves a better life than the one he could ever give her.

She turns and sees him staring at her. Her face is illuminated from above.

What she notices first, she tells me years later, are his eyelashes, eyelashes so long, they're wasted on a man. What she notices next is his handsome face, his dark, thick, wavy hair. She's heard him approach, has felt his penetrating gaze, but she's waited to discover who is standing behind her because men often stare at her as she works.

He smiles at her, a "There you are, and here I am" kind of smile. She smiles back, a shy, demure smile. She's more beautiful than he's imagined, a dead ringer for Ingrid Bergman just like his friend said, and he wonders why she's here dusting and straightening shoes, smiling at him, when she could have been an actress in Hollywood, and he thinks that if he's lucky, he'll get to look at her all the days of his life.

She blushes. Looks down. Drops a shoe. He rushes to pick it up. But she gets to it first. It was that blush, he tells me years later, that did it. And he tells himself, "She's the girl for me, if only she'll have me."

He moves closer now, but not so close as to frighten her. Introduces himself. She says she's heard about him, expected his visit, but she has to get back to work.

"Can you meet me for a cup of coffee at Schnackenberg's Luncheonette after work?" he asks. It's a bold move. But he can't let her slip away.

She doesn't answer his question. Instead, she asks, "Do you like pie?"

He doesn't yet know that she's dreamed of making pies in her own kitchen for the man she loves.

"Yes," he answers, "I love pie. Homemade pie. Blueberry pie. Peach. Pecan. Lemon meringue. Coconut custard. Almost any kind of pie but rhubarb. But chocolate cream is my favorite."

"Okay," she says. "Schnack's, then, at 6."

He's surprised she's agreed to meet him and as he turns to go, he says, "I'll see you sooner rather than later," words that become his ritual parting. And as he turns away, he discovers what it's like to walk on air.

But he doesn't wait for her at Schnackenberg's. He's afraid she'll get cold feet and go straight home instead of joining him. And he suspects she'll be starving after a hard day's work and want something substantial to eat right away, and he worries he's been inconsiderate in asking her to meet him.

Still, he's never been to a restaurant; doesn't know of any in Hoboken; can't imagine taking her to one; thinks she might construe his wanting to take her to a restaurant as too much of a date. So he takes off from work early and buys her a hot dog so she can eat something as soon as she leaves work, and he waits outside Grant's for her.

"I hope you like hot dogs," he says as soon as he sees her. "Because here's one waiting for you. I figured you might be hungry."

"For me?" she asks. She's amazed he's been so thoughtful.

"Yes, for you," he says.

She's happy to see him. She's been thinking about him since their meeting and is looking forward to the possibility of a happy evening, to some time away from home, away from her stepmother's hectoring, away from the anxiety of her family's nightly gathering around the radio with her translating the latest news reports to her father and stepmother, away from their fear that men from their villages in Italy might be fighting and dying in Greece. She hopes this might be an evening when she can put aside her worries about the war.

She tells him that she *loves* hot dogs. And that, yes, she is always hungry after work. Starving, really.

My father worries that he's done the wrong thing despite what she says. He's ashamed he's brought her a hot dog instead of something romantic like a bouquet of flowers. But the flowers would have been wrong, too, he thinks. They would have declared his intentions too soon.

He is new at courtship. During his years in the Navy, he hasn't been with girls, hasn't even been with prostitutes like so many of his buddies. He's seen a few girls since he's been home, but none seriously. And so he doesn't know how to behave and he worries that he's already ruined his chances.

But she eats the hot dog with gusto, not as demurely as he expected. So she isn't a shrinking violet, he thinks, the kind of woman who pushes food around her plate without eating it for fear of gaining weight. He imagines deep passion running beneath her proper exterior, and he is right, for he soon finds out that she feels things deeply. She rails against violence, injustice, inequity, and the state of the world. But physical passion? That is something else, again. And it will take him a long time to realize that here she feels more fear than curiosity, and this is something that will pain him for the rest of their life together. For while he will want her, utterly, she will consider desire a terrifying loss of control.

After she wipes her hands on the napkins he's provided and disposes of them in the trash, she takes his arm (to his surprise) and they stroll up Washington Street from Fifth to Eleventh to Schnackenberg's. This is the first time he walks arm-in-arm with a girl, and when he sees their reflection in a store window, he thinks that they make a fine young couple.

They settle themselves into a booth, and he orders coffee and lemon meringue pie, and she orders coffee and lemon meringue pie, and he is surprised she still has an appetite, and they talk and talk and talk, and years later, he can't remember what they say to each other, but he remembers that it is the most wonderful time he's ever had, and he remembers asking her if she's ever eaten deep-fried hot dogs like the ones they serve at Hiram's near Palisades Amusement Park, and he remembers her saying, no, but that she'd love to try them if he'll take her there, and he asks her if she'd like to try them soon, and she says yes, she would.

* * *

For my father, it was love at first sight. When he'd asked his mother how he'd know a girl was the right one for him, she'd said, "You'll just know." He couldn't imagine how his mother had come by this knowledge. Still, he now knew what his mother meant. And by the end of that evening at Schnackenberg's, my father knows that he will marry her, if only she will have him.

2009

All these years later, I imagine the two of them gazing at each other across the table with that first look of love. I imagine each of them hoping for, though not discussing, the possibility of a deep and abiding love that might bring them pleasure and that will be strong enough to endure what each suspects is to come.

I imagine my mother shrinking back from this love, telling herself to take it slow, to think it through, to not fall too fast, too soon. I imagine her thinking that falling in love with this handsome man might bring her sorrow. But I imagine my father deeply in love already, heedless of the consequences. And I imagine him feeling as exhilarated sitting across from her in that booth at Schnackenberg's as he was standing face to the wind at the prow of a ship in a dangerous sea.

LATE 1940

That night, she won't let him walk her home. It is too soon for that, she says. But she'll see him soon, on Saturday.

On Saturday they go up to Hiram's in Fort Lee for deep-fried hot dogs. She loves the food and Hiram's gritty charm, which pleases my father. It is the first of their many trips there, and Hiram's becomes their special place.

On the day they go to Hiram's, my mother decides it's simpler for my father to wait for her on the corner of Fourth and Willow outside Our Lady of Grace Church instead of having him call for her at home. They've only just met, and although she suspects her father will be pleased she's dating, for he wants her to marry, she doesn't want to endure her stepmother's censure.

Her stepmother has never welcomed any of her friends. She's never even greeted Rose, her best friend, when she comes to call for her. Instead, she stands in the kitchen and swears under her breath until they leave the apartment. Civilized people, she tells my mother, don't bring strangers into the house.

When my mother asks him whether he knows where Our Lady of Grace is, he says of course he does. She knows he works at K & E, a few blocks away from the church and a few blocks away from where she lives on Adams Street. They think it's remarkable that she lives on the same block as the place where he works. She wonders whether they've ever passed each other, and he says no, because if he'd seen her, he'd have remembered her, for he thinks, but doesn't say, "Who could forget a face like yours?" She doesn't seem to know how beautiful she is, and he likes that.

The day they went to Hiram's, they met, as planned, outside Our Lady of Grace Church. He was early. She was late. She'd run back to her apartment to get a pair of gloves because the day was cold. During those minutes when she wasn't there, he was in agony. Would she stand him up? Had this been an impossible dream of his? But when she turned the corner onto Fourth Street, she smiled and waved and ran to him and took his arm and they walked up Fourth Street on their way to the trolley that ran up Hudson Street.

They passed Church Square Park, where my father often ate his lunch on warm days. He liked spending time away from the din of the machines at work. He liked watching the old Italian men playing bocce, the mothers pushing their babies on the swings, the teenagers carrying on. As they passed the band shell, he pointed to the names of the composers—Verdi and Puccini—on its frieze and asked if she listened to opera, and she told him she didn't, and he told her something he'd never told anyone before: that he'd once dreamed of becoming an opera singer. This dream he'd harbored for ever so long, for far longer than his dream of becoming a pilot.

"I have a good voice," he said. For years, he'd listened to his father's opera recordings on the family phonograph. As he listened to arias from Puccini's *La Bohème* and Verdi's *Aida* and *La Traviata*, he memorized the tenor parts, and after he learned them, he sang along.

Listening to opera was the only thing he and his father shared. Singing gave him pleasure, and he wished he'd had the money and the education to train to become more than just a man with a good voice. But he was a working man, so it was best not to dwell on it.

They walked past Demarest High School, where my mother had gone to school, a yellow brick building trimmed with tile work in buff, gold, blue, and green, and with a balustrade around the roof and a decorative frieze. My mother thought it was beautiful, and she was proud she'd gone to school there. She'd won an award for her writing and a scholarship for college, but she couldn't attend because she had to work to support herself and bring money home for the family. Still, she loved to read. Poe. Dickens. Did he know they'd both lived in Hoboken for a while? Did he know Hoboken had a good library? It was right there, across Church Square Park.

He loved to read too, about the great explorers who traveled to distant shores without knowing whether they'd survive; about the planets; about the strata beneath the Earth's surface; about the world's great volcanoes; about the shift and movement of the continents through time. And he treasured an illustrated book about Michelangelo his sisters had given him one Christmas.

"So we're both readers," she said, and he could imagine them sitting together in the evenings, reading.

He wanted to give her the world. But he couldn't. The most he could promise was a roof over her head, enough food to eat, and a love that would last a lifetime.

On the ride home, when the trolley nears Hoboken, my father tells me, he slips off one of her gloves, takes my mother's hand, looks into her eyes, and sings "Che gelida manina" from Puccini's *La Bohème*, his favorite opera. Her hand is cold, just like Mimi's in the opera.

His singing makes her blush, and he's afraid he's done the wrong thing. But she's pleased, not embarrassed. The other passengers are charmed; some clap, and one man shouts, "Encore, encore!"

The next week, my father starts borrowing his father's car to pick her up from Grant's. First, he'd pick up a few hot dogs.

Each evening, he'd usher her into the car, and they'd drive up to Hudson County Park on Boulevard East in North Bergen. He'd park the car in a lover's lane, the only place they could have privacy, and they'd eat their hot dogs.

They said very little to each other at first. Just being together seemed pleasure enough. It was winter, and it was cold, and so they embraced as much from necessity as from desire. Sometimes they listened to music on the car radio, the lyrics of "You Made Me Love You," "These Foolish Things (Remind Me of

You)," "The Very Thought of You," expressing sentiments they hadn't yet spoken.

As yet, he knew so little about her. During ordinary times, he might not have rushed into wooing her with so little knowledge. But he believed the United States was on the brink of war and that he had little time to spare. If he had to leave before making her his own, he feared he'd lose her.

I can imagine her, still shy, still not saying much, still turning her head to the window to look at the skeletons of the trees outside, still looking down as often as she looked at him. I can imagine him, afraid he might say the wrong thing, afraid he might do something to scare her away. But I imagine them, like all new lovers, shocked at their good fortune, at the mystery and miracle that each of them is caring for someone who cares for them in return. And so I imagine them during this first blush of love hoping for an untrammeled life together that it will be impossible for them to have.

In late December, sitting in his father's car parked in lover's lane in Hudson County Park, they amuse themselves by writing their names on the windows fogged with love. She draws a heart and writes both their names inside. And he writes, "I love you."

During ordinary times, he might not have rushed so quickly into this declaration. But these are no ordinary times and this is no ordinary world. It is a world filled with death and destruction, a world torn by partings.

"Me too," she scribbles back. He teases her, tells her that what she wrote means that she loves herself and not him. She blushes. But later that night, in their season out of time, as the great engine of war grinds on to maul their future, after he again tells her that he loves her, she tells him that she loves him too.

The next night he writes the words "Will you marry me?" on the fogged window. He isn't sure whether "marry" has one "r" or two and he is afraid he's misspelled the most important word he's ever written and so revealed he isn't good enough for her. But in the next moment, her words, "Of course I will."

2014

The story I relate here about the early days of my parents' relationship, the good days they had together, lived on in his imagination, and now it lives on in mine. Since his death, I have thought about the circumstances of their meeting, their courting, their early lives together. I do this because I need them still. And when I think about them, I *see* them. See them meeting outside the church. See them walking past the park. See them walking past Demarest High School. See them eating Hiram's hot dogs. See him serenading her on the trolley.

I want them to have been happy in that first flush of love. I want them to have been very much in love. I want to tell their story as if each moment they were together was not blighted by what they knew was happening and what they must have known would happen to them, what would happen to all those men and women who risked loving at this time. I want to see them happier than they might have been, their lives filled with possibility rather than with the dread of a wrenching parting during a time when the world trembled from the sorrow of so many.

2005

I ask my father why she let herself fall in love with him if she knew he'd be snatched from her and put in harm's way. He tells me that he'd lied to her, that he'd told her he'd be able to stay home, until, one day, the look in her eyes told him he wasn't fooling her.

"How can you lie to me?" she said. "How can we make a life together if you lie to me?"

She told him that she considered ending their relationship, not because he might leave her to serve his country, but because by lying to her he imagined she wasn't strong enough to take the truth. And this reminds her too much of her father, how he watches her to make sure that she is okay. How he asks her how she's feeling. How he wonders if she will, again, descend into that difficult, sorrowful place where he can't reach her. But she knows she's fine, now. She has to be fine.

"After all is said and done, she stayed with me," my father tells me, "because I convinced her that if she loved me, I couldn't die."

Courtship

WINTER, 1941

During the frigid nights in the early months of 1941, my parents talked about when they should marry. In early March, they heard Edward R. Murrow's broadcast predicting that both the British and Germans would soon begin using more powerful bombs more frequently. They soon heard news reports of the bombing of Hamburg, Bremen, Emden, and Berlin, and about the reprisal bombing of London during which the British Museum and St. Paul's were hit.

President Roosevelt signed the Lend-Lease Act, committing the United States to aiding democracies in their fight against totalitarianism short of war by furnishing them with ships, planes, tanks, and guns. My father took this as a sign that Roosevelt was inching his way toward war.

My father believed their time together was running short, although he didn't tell my mother because he didn't want to scare her. But my mother knew their time together was precious; she understood that he'd be gone soon despite his protestations, although she didn't tell him because she didn't want to spoil the time they had left. My father hated himself for keeping up the pretext that he would somehow avoid going to war.

My father wanted to marry as soon as possible. But my mother persuaded him to wait until July so they could have a proper church wedding in her parish church, St. Francis on Jefferson Street, built by Italians at the end of the nineteenth century, and dedicated to St. Francis of Assisi. It was the church where she'd been baptized, received her First Communion and Confirmation, and where her father and mother and her father and stepmother had married.

She didn't want to be robbed of the pleasure of a white wedding because they were living in difficult times. She would wear a dress made by her friend Rose's brother, who owned a small bridal shop on Fourth Street. Rose would be her only bridesmaid. She wanted her father to walk her down the aisle and dance with her during the reception.

"I'm only doing this once," she told my father, "and I want to do it right."

She wanted to prolong their courtship; she wanted them to have a few months together without responsibility. And she knew they needed time to find an apartment and outfit it as a proper home and she knew this wouldn't be easy: Many of her married friends still lived with their parents or in-laws—vacant apartments were so difficult to find.

She wanted to travel to Maine on their honeymoon, so they agreed to rent a cabin in York. My father suggested driving through Connecticut, Rhode

Island, and Massachusetts in a car he'd borrow from a friend because, he told her, the journey was half the fun. But he didn't tell her he wanted to tour Revolutionary War battlefields on their way.

It was now time for my mother to bring my father home to meet her parents, for their marriage could not proceed without their blessing.

Her father had witnessed the welcome change that had come over his daughter since she'd met this man. Her face flushed with pleasure when she spoke of him, and she seemed happier than ever before. Her father had been urging her to marry for years, hoping that marriage would settle her. She was twenty-three years old, far too old to be unmarried according to his Old World standards, and he wanted grandchildren to indulge before he got too old to enjoy them. He'd come to the United States so life would be better for his descendants.

My father told me that when he met my mother's father for the first time, he liked him right away—his warm welcome, his gusto, his gnarled workman's hands—and he hoped that the man might become a father to him. He was nothing like his own dandy of a father who believed he was too good for hard labor. Her father had come to America to work on the Delaware, Lackawanna, and Western Railroad Company, but he was a longshoreman now, working on the docks in New York City. He was ruddy-cheeked from hours of work in the sun, burly, thick-chested, and strong-handed from grabbing and heaving cargo from pier to railroad siding. He was so red-faced, my father suspected he drank too much, although my mother never complained about it.

As a gift, my father brought him a growler of beer, a round tin can filled with beer on tap from one of the many saloons in Hoboken. My mother had told him that her father liked his beer, and the old man was grateful for the gift.

My father was a hardworking man too, and this would forge a bond between them. My mother's father knew this man would work hard to support the daughter he adored, the girl he'd almost lost after his first wife died, when the caregivers he hired to look after her almost starved her to death, the daughter he almost lost to a grief and sorrow that at times he thought would never leave her.

Her stepmother was another story. On the day they met, she was far from welcoming. She shook his hand and uttered the ritual greeting, "*Piacere.*" But then she turned her back to him and continued cooking. Under the same circumstances, his mother would have set the table with good dishes and linen napkins for a cup of strong espresso and a few biscotti.

"In time," he told himself, "I'll win her over and she'll come to like me." But all he would get from her was a grudging acceptance.

On this day, my father didn't ask for my mother's hand in marriage: He was too cowed by her stepmother's behavior. But he asked for, and received, permission to "keep company" and, a few weeks later, her father's permission to marry.

My mother didn't want an engagement ring. She didn't need that outward symbol of my father's affection. Besides, she wanted them both to save money for their wedding, honeymoon, and the furnishings for their first home. Instead, he bought her a gold locket, the first good piece of jewelry she ever owned, a locket that my father gave to me after my mother died.

While they were courting, my mother liked to sit across from my father at Schnack's and nurse a cup of coffee while he talked. He had more stories to tell than he had time to tell them. He was a good storyteller, and he told her about his life in Italy; how he and his friends played in the ruins of Pompeii; how his father had run them out of money and how his mother had to work in a canning factory to make ends meet; how his father stood talking with his cronies pretending to be a bigshot. How the five of them lived in two tiny rooms in a house without heat or running water perched over a rushing river so that it was always damp; how his mother cooked their food on a brazier outside. How he and his friends taunted the Blackshirts by singing the *Bandiera Rossa* and how they had to hide to escape being beaten. How he and his friends were molested by a trumpet player in a local band—he made little of it, laughing as he told her how the trumpet player was run out of town without his clothes. But he never told her about why he joined the Navy, his time in the service, and all the men who died.

She had less to tell, less she wanted to tell. She told him she'd led a perfectly ordinary life: She liked to work; she spent vacations with her stepmother's relatives in Rhode Island; she loved to swim in the ocean; she loved to go blueberrying; she adored her father. But she never told him about her mother's death, her childhood breakdown, her frequent depressions.

In the months to come, sitting together in a booth at Schnack's, on a bench in Church Square Park, walking on the promenade above the Hudson, exploring the castle on the grounds of Stevens Institute of Technology, or sitting in his father's car in the park on Boulevard East, my mother and father continued to share stories about their lives. When they agreed to marry, my mother didn't know about my father's ferocious hatred of his father, or about how he'd started working when he was just a toddler, buttoning the shirts his mother sewed piecework. He didn't yet know the most significant fact of her life, that her birth mother had died during the influenza epidemic when she was an infant, that her mother was buried quickly in a mass grave in an undisclosed location; that her father had sent her to a caregiver while he worked in upstate New York and that when he came home she was so emaciated that he sent for a woman from Puglia, his province in Italy, to come marry him and help raise his child; and that, at times, she wasn't altogether well. All this, they would learn during their season out of time while the great engine of war ground on to maul their future.

"Let's forget the past," my father said. "We'll make a life together."

As soon as they set the date, my mother started work on her trousseau. She looked forward to designing and sewing garments from Butterick patterns. She had a budget and she'd focus on quality, not quantity, but she wanted to be stylish in a quietly elegant way. She'd buy the best material she could afford and sew in the early morning before work and in the evenings when she wasn't seeing my father.

Her stepmother had been a seamstress in Italy, making clothing, embroidering priests' vestments, and crocheting *biancheria* for trousseaus, and she'd passed on her skills to her stepdaughter. The time they spent together at the Singer sewing machine was the only time they didn't argue.

My mother ran up a white topper and matching turban to wear on cool evenings. For daytime, she made a simple dark skirt, a pair of trousers, and a few blouses. She indulged herself by buying a polka-dot dress with a flared skirt, a pair of white pumps, and saddle shoes.

My mother convinced my father that he deserved a new wardrobe for their honeymoon.

"Once we're married," she said, "we'll be saving our pennies."

He'd spent so many years in the service and spent his workdays in coveralls so he'd never bought himself anything but a tie since he returned home, and the clothes he had were becoming ratty.

He hadn't yet seen this side of her—a woman concerned with appearance. Still, each time he saw her, she was beautifully dressed and well groomed. He'd assumed that she was a natural beauty. When he told her this, she laughed and said, "You have sisters. How do they look in the morning?"

She told him appearance was important, especially in sales, and that she liked nice things. She bought little, but she bought carefully. Before she purchased a garment, she inspected it, turned it inside out to look at the seams, crumpled the fabric to see how it would wear, rubbed her finger over the material to see if it would pill.

"I'm too poor to buy cheap," she said.

She shopped with him because he didn't know how to shop for himself, and she persuaded him to buy two new pairs of trousers, two shirts, a sweater vest, and a long sleeve lightweight sweater for evenings. She insisted that he buy a dapper, close-fitting, pinstriped, three-button suit with a narrow lapel, a white shirt, and a dark tie.

"Every man needs one good suit," she said, and he reluctantly agreed, and she persuaded him to buy a pair of spectator shoes—two-tone brogues—to wear with them.

"I'll look like a gangster," he joked. "Only gangsters wear such beautiful clothes."

As he tried on the clothes, he was amazed at how good he looked, and he imagined what a handsome couple they'd make on their honeymoon. For this one time in his life, he would be a dandy like his father, even though it wasn't easy for him.

Safe House

Finding an apartment seemed hopeless. They wanted to live in Italian City in Hoboken near my mother's parents and near their jobs. Italian immigrants felt comfortable there because the buildings were small in scale, close together, crowding the sidewalk, much like their villages in Italy. And there were open spaces and public parks nearby where people could gather, just like in Italy, too. But there were no apartments available because Hoboken was in the midst of a housing shortage.

When my parents had almost given up hope of living in Hoboken, my grandfather found an apartment in a tenement on Fourteenth Street, in the undesirable industrial north end of the city. A fellow longshoreman told him he had a friend who was the super at 109 Fourteenth Street, and he'd heard that an apartment on the second floor would soon become vacant.

On his way home from work, my grandfather met the super. The apartment was in a dangerous part of the city, but it was better than no place at all, he thought. His daughter knew a woman living there, so she'd have a friend nearby. He told the super about his daughter's impending marriage, asked about the apartment, agreed to the rent, and dug deep into his pocket for a deposit.

When my parents learned about the apartment, they weren't keen on the idea of living on Fourteenth Street, a busy, noisy place, with truck traffic rumbling up and down the street all day and night. The apartment was up the block from one of the largest shipyards in the country with factories and docks nearby, and there were saloons on every street corner. Still, my parents realized it was that or nothing. They didn't want to start their married life the way many of their friends had been forced to—living in crowded quarters with parents or in-laws.

The apartment was a three-room cold water flat with a parlor in the front with two windows facing the street, a bedroom in the center with a tiny clerestory window facing an airshaft, and a kitchen with two windows facing a courtyard in the back. The kitchen had a coal stove for heating and cooking, an icebox for storing food, and a shared toilet for all the tenants on the floor.

My mother was used to carrying coal up the stairs from the basement for the stove; lugging water from the sink to the coal stove to heat for washing; washing her clothes on a washboard in the sink, wringing them out by hand, and hanging them out on a line to dry. In winter, her parents closed up the front room from the rest of the apartment with a blanket tacked up in the doorway because the heat from the kitchen's coal stove wouldn't reach there, and she'd have to do the same. At first, they thought the smell of cooking from the restaurant downstairs would bother them, but they got used to it. Still, this apartment was no worse than the one she'd lived in for most of her life and she didn't expect more.

But in some ways this was a better apartment than either of my parents had ever lived in. The building was red brick with brown cornices decorating each window, and there was a decorative frieze at the top. Her parents lived in a wooden tenement, a notorious firetrap, especially in winter—there had been a spectacular fire on Harrison Street a year and a half before that had left many families homeless. Unlike her parents' apartment, this one had doors separating one room from another. My father, for the first time, would have a proper bedroom. My mother, for the first time, wouldn't be sharing a bedroom with her parents during the cold months when she couldn't sleep in the parlor. They both imagined their home would be a retreat from the perils of the war, and that they would feel protected and safe there.

My mother had pored over illustrations in women's magazines in the library, looking at furniture ads. She wanted her home to be beautiful, unlike her parents' austere, functional home. How she decorated her home would signify a transition from her parents' Old World ways to the modern way of life she and my father would create together. Since she'd started working, she'd saved money for a "nest egg" if she decided to marry, and there was the surprise of the money her soon-to-be mother-in-law gave her soon-to-be husband, so they had more than enough money to furnish their home.

"You only married me for my money," she'd often tease my father.

"But now I have some money, too," he'd reply. "And besides, I didn't know you had any when I started courting you."

In the months before their wedding, my parents fixed up their apartment. My father told me she decorated it as if it were in a posh brownstone on

Castle Hill Terrace instead of in a tenement on Fourteenth Street: "She made the place beautiful."

She used the pedal-driven Singer to run up a set of cotton draperies in ivory and beige stripes—she would have preferred silk or linen, but she knew the grime of the neighborhood would make delicate fabrics difficult to care for. She and my father installed a rose carpet with a stylized leaf design in the parlor. And they bought the best-quality furniture they could afford at Art's in Ridgefield, New Jersey: a sofa and a side chair and ottoman upholstered in a deeper rose than the carpet; a Chinoiserie side table (all the rage); another side table that opened into a small dining table for four.

They bought an antique bureau, a gilt-framed mirror, an Italian chiffo-robe to store their clothing (the apartment had no closets), and a bedstead from a used-furniture store in Hoboken catering to Italian immigrants. My mother bargained while my father watched, amazed to see his timid wife-to-be so determined to save a few dollars. "A penny saved is a penny earned," she told him. She would grace their bed with a quilted silk comforter and pillow shams, an engagement gift from Rose.

Hanging the leaf-patterned wallpaper in the parlor and bedroom was a nightmare, my father said, because the walls weren't smooth. But my mother insisted upon it.

"In the time it took to hang that wallpaper," he said, "we could have built the Taj Mahal."

They prepped the walls, persevering through the long hours it took in the evenings after work, and then hung the paper, making sure the seams lined up correctly. The wallpaper, he said, transformed the place.

Over their bed, they hung a wooden crucifix. After they were married, they would add a framed photograph of their wedding on the top of their bureau.

While they worked, they listened to radio reports describing the worst bombing raid over London; the fires raging through London because there was no water to fight fires; the British bombing of Hamburg; the German sinking of the *Hood*; the British sinking of the *Bismarck*; the Allied invasions of Syria and Lebanon; the German invasion of the Soviet Union and the capture of Minsk; the British plea to use the U.S. Navy to clear the Atlantic of German vessels; the destruction of the Italian fleet in Tripoli; the uncovering of a Nazi spy network in the United States and their plans to bomb the docks.

"When we heard that the Nazis were planning to bomb the docks, we knew the war was coming home," my father said. "From that moment on, I knew that the home we were making together might not be safe although we never talked about it."

They heard Roosevelt's speech declaring his retreat from isolationism: "To retire within our continental boundaries is to invite future attacks." They heard New York Mayor Fiorello LaGuardia's order to manufacture and issue 50 million gas masks in anticipation of a German attack. And they heard the report that the United States was freezing German and Italian assets in America. Their parents weren't yet citizens, and so the paltry sums they'd saved would now be unavailable. And if the United States entered the war, their parents might be considered enemy aliens.

Although they were both now sure the United States would be entering the war, no matter how horrifying the news, they continued to work each night on creating their first home. It was as if by laying carpets, papering walls, hanging draperies, and installing furniture, they could shut out the war and create a space where they would both pretend that violence could not penetrate.

But abroad, homes created with as much care as my parents lavished on their three small rooms were obliterated in a moment. In June, my mother pored over photographs revealing the devastation of Hamburg—gutted interiors, shredded wallpaper, smashed tables and chairs, demolished windows and mirrors—telling my father that if it could happen there, it could happen here.

"Those poor people," she said, "lost everything."

She didn't value material objects more than the lives of people. But she deplored the destruction of these sacred spaces, and the loss of the kind of life that ordinary people had created in those rooms. She was sure they cared about their homes as much as she had come to care about hers. She was sure that they, too, thought these places would provide them with shelter, safety, and protection.

But in this war, no one was safe, nowhere was safe. In this war, ordinary people living ordinary lives had become targets—twice as many British civilians had died in German bombing raids as British troops had died in combat.

"That's just plain wrong," my mother said.

Finally, they declare a moratorium on listening to the radio on the night of July 2 that will last through the end of their honeymoon on July 19.

"Let's try to enjoy our wedding and our honeymoon," my mother says. "Let's pretend the world isn't at war."

They are married on July 6, 1941, at St. Francis Church. My mother wears an elaborate silk gown with a high neck, long sleeves, and a cathedral train. And she insists that my father wear white tie and tails—it is the first, and the last, time that he wears a "monkey suit."

In their wedding pictures taken outside St. Francis, he looks exhilarated and she looks exhausted. His father is dapper, as always, in his double-breasted suit. His mother wears an austere suit but a festive hat and fancy gloves. Her stepmother wears a black dress and hat and refuses to smile. Her father wears his one good suit and a new tie, his unruly hair slicked back for the occasion.

They spend their first night as a married couple in their apartment on Fourteenth Street, and she's reluctant to leave for their honeymoon. He believes they need this time away, so early the next morning, he loads their luggage into the car he's borrowed from his best friend, and they begin their journey.

They'll be away two full weeks. My father has sat with maps and has plotted their route to Lexington, Massachusetts, where they'll stop for the night. He wants to tour Revolutionary War battlefields on the way to Maine. He doesn't consider how these wartime reminders might affect his bride.

The drive to Lexington takes the better part of the day, but they make the journey without incident, and without a blowout, for which my father is grateful. They've dressed "to the nines" for the car trip, an adventure for them both.

Early the next morning, they tour Lexington and Concord. My father is fascinated with the history of warfare, and he's read much about the first battles of the Revolutionary War. He wants them to awaken early to reach the Old North Bridge in Concord at dawn, where the first battle of the Revolu-

tion was fought. He wants to see it as the sun rises, the same time when mili-
tiamen against the king's troops fired the first shots. But my mother refuses.

"Enough," she says, "is enough." It's the first time they come close to
quarreling. He doesn't understand why she won't go.

Going to visit a battlefield isn't her idea of a good time. She's on vacation.
She wants to sleep until she awakens. And she wants to have a proper breakfast before she goes anywhere.

And here she is in a photograph, wearing her new coat and turban, standing on the brick walkway outside their inn, and she's not smiling. Maybe he's
told her to hurry along, as he does throughout their marriage. Maybe she's
told him she'll come along in her own good time.

And here she is in Lexington, again not smiling, gazing up at the statue of
the bronze Minuteman holding his musket, the hero who fired the first shot
in that war. Maybe my father has lectured her about how many steps it takes
to fire a musket, about how inaccurate a weapon it is, about how it's a miracle
that anyone ever hit their target, for he likes to tell her what he knows.

Is the stress of their new marriage telling on her? Is she thinking of her
new husband being handed a gun and put in the line of fire? Is she worrying
about the war news they'll hear when they return home? Is she uncomfortable
with the sexual side of her marriage?

And here he is in the picture she's taken of him in his new sweater, shirt,
and trousers, the trousers rumpled from their long drive and their long walk
across the battleground at Lexington, and he seems to be all male bravado.
And here they are, the two of them, in another photograph, sitting on a
stone wall on the Lexington battleground, and they're trying to smile for the
camera but they aren't, and he has his arm around her shoulder, and she's
placed one of her hands very tentatively upon his knee.

Their cottage in Maine has a screened-in porch, a window box, a field of
wildflowers out front, an Adirondack chair for two that faces the sea, a beach
easy to access and calm enough to swim in. And my mother swims, but my
father doesn't because it's too cold for him. He's astonished by how this timid
wife of his can venture so far out from shore, and he watches her and watches
her until she returns and scrambles up the rocky outcropping to the safety of
his arms.

"There were times," my father said, "that I thought I'd lose her in the waves offshore."

They take many photos to record this special time. Of him sitting in the Adirondack chair wearing his new bathrobe. Of her in a bathing suit sitting on the rocky beach penning postcards to family and friends. Of her standing in the entrance to their cottage. Of him standing astride a boulder at the shoreline. But there are no smiles in these photographs.

On the long journey home, they don't say much, my father tells me. They don't know what kind of life they'll be returning to. They've hoped against hope for one kind of life. But they're returning to another, unimaginable one.

"Some honeymoon," my mother says.

"What do you mean?" my father answers, bristling, although he knows what she means.

In less than five months, the Japanese will bomb Pearl Harbor. In less than five months, the United States will be at war.

On their honeymoon, they broke their promise to avoid the news. They'd learned—and they will learn even more when they return home—that there are U.S. Marines in Iceland, and my father now understands why the *Ranger* went on maneuvers in the northern Pacific. They've learned the Japanese have declared that the U.S. occupation of Iceland is a decisive step toward hostilities. That the Panama Canal Zone is on high alert. That a U.S. high official has declared "the time has come to act" against the Japanese in the Pacific. That there are plans to evacuate Hawaii's coastline civilians "in the event of an attack." That Roosevelt has declared the United States will defend itself outside of the Western Hemisphere if necessary. That Congress is preparing for a debate on war. That mines have been laid in the approach to San Francisco Bay. That the British have bombed Palermo, Sicily. That the Germans have broken through an important Russian line of defense and are driving toward Kiev, Leningrad, and Moscow. That Japan is gearing up for total war. That the U.S. consul in Italy has been called back to the United States. That the United States is nearly halfway finished with building an air base in the Philippines, and that patrol squadrons are already operating from it. That the entrances to bays in the Philippines are being mined by the United States as a precautionary measure against enemy attack. That the Russians have lost well over a million men so far, yet they have five million more men ready to fight the Axis powers. That after an RAF bombing using American-made planes, hundreds of acres of Düsseldorf lie in ruins. And that it seems as if Japan and the United States are moving toward a head-on collision in the Pacific.

In bed one night, with the lights off, after they return to Hoboken, he asks her whether she wants to have children. He's not getting any younger, he says. The last time they discussed this was in the early days of their courtship, and she had said, "Well, yes, of course I want children. Doesn't every woman?"

But now, in answer to his question, she seems reticent, and she says, "Well, yes, I'd like a child. But this isn't a world to bring a child into." And he agrees.

2004

When my father tells me about their honeymoon, when he shows me the photographs he took of my mother standing next to a war monument, I ask him why he's taken her there.

"Didn't you realize you were visiting a battleground?" I ask.

"I always wanted to see it," my father says, "and I didn't think she'd mind."

"Mind?" I respond. "You were on your honeymoon. And the first site you visit is where men were killed and wounded."

"But the colonists," my father replies, "died for a good cause."

I sense, but don't say, that this honeymoon marks a turning point in my parents' relationship, for from now on my mother will have to reckon with a man who is obsessed with warfare, and that from now on my father will have to reckon with a woman who despises armed conflict and who is far more fragile than he imagined.

And then I remember a trip our family takes to Lake George in 1959, the summer before I leave for college, one of many summer holidays during which my father drags us to one or another military site, and when, included in his agenda for the vacation, is an event during which he tried to toughen me up.

"Do you remember when you made me swim across Lake George?" I ask.

"I didn't make you do it," my father replies. "You wanted to, and besides, it showed you just how tough you could be if you put your mind to it."

Lifeboat

1959

"Gather courage."

This, my father tells me as I cling to the gunwale of a rowboat somewhere in the middle of Lake George. I'm sixteen years old; I'm swimming across Lake George; my family is vacationing at a cabin in Bolton Landing on the shore of Lake George; the cabin we're renting comes with this old boat my father rows beside me as I swim.

"Pace yourself," my father reminds me when I enter the lake from the dock. "A mile on water isn't a mile on land. A mile on water is longer, far longer."

I'm wearing a baby blue swimsuit with a balloon bottom, unsuited for a long swim. It's the only suit I own, so it's the one I'm wearing. The balloon bottom fills with water as I swim and drags me down with every stroke. I slap the water out of my suit, gasp for air, start to stroke, start to swim again.

No matter how afraid I am, because, by now, I'm near the middle of the lake, swimming in very deep water, I mustn't hyperventilate, so I'm paying close attention to my breathing. In, out, in, out. One, two, one, two. If I hyperventilate, my father's told me, I'll black out. I remember my father telling me that swimming in deep water is the same as swimming in shallow water. Still, I know if I black out, I'll drown, I'll die, and I can't count on my father to save me. So I'm trying to control my breathing, trying to slow it down, trying to plow my way through choppy water, trying to swim Lake George.

I've been doing the American crawl, the stroke my father swears by for long distances. But today the lake isn't calm, so when I turn my head to breathe, I'm smacked in the face with a wall of water. There are foot-high swells in the middle of the lake, high enough to make a rough swim even rougher.

The best stroke for this swim would be the breaststroke. The breaststroke would let me see where I'm going every time I surface to breathe. But it's the only stroke I've never learned, the only stroke my father couldn't teach me. I'd tried hard to imitate him when he'd demonstrated it to me, but I'd fatigue quickly. If I'd been born a boy, he'd said, he'd have had no trouble teaching me the breaststroke. So I gave up trying to learn it even though my father warned me that one day I'd need to see ahead of me while I'm swimming. And that day is now.

I'm spent. I'm angry. What am I doing here? I see a purple stain on the surface of the lake just beyond my reach. Is it an oil slick? A gathering of tangled grass I must avoid? A darkness indicating a deepening of the lake?

"Full fathom five my father lies"—these Shakespearean lines announce themselves. I can't remember what comes next—bones, eyes, something about coral.

"You're halfway there," my father says. Yet reaching the dead center of the lake unnerves me. The lake is 200 feet deep here, maybe more. If I go down, underwater currents will take my body through falls and chutes and rapids into Lake Champlain. Weeks, maybe months, from when I disappear, a local boy will cast a fishing line into the lake, snag my bathing suit, and reel in my bloated body long after my family has given up hope of it ever being found.

I panic, scissor over to the rowboat, grasp the gunwale, elude my father's gaze. Holding on to the rowboat means I'm cheating, means that even if I make it to the other side and make it back, I really won't have swum across Lake George. My father doesn't like cheaters; he doesn't like quitters; he doesn't like losers. He doesn't like people who take the easy way out. The only person you're cheating when you take the easy way out, my father says, is yourself.

But my father lets me clutch the gunwale, then tells me in his most serious voice to gather courage and move on. I keep myself from laughing. It's my father, playing to an audience, only out here, the only audience he has is me. I can't figure out why I've let him persuade me to undertake this swim, still wonder why I've given in to him this time, instead of resisting him as I so often do, and I hope that my giving in to him won't be my undoing.

I scissor-kick away from the boat. Now I'm moving through the water more easily. The wind has veered, or backed, terms my sailor father uses, terms I don't understand. But now the wind and waves urge me along as I slice a trail through water to safety on the other side.

My father teaches me the American crawl a few years before in the mud hole where we used to swim on summer weekends some miles away from our house in Ridgefield, New Jersey. When I turned thirteen, my father insisted that I learn the crawl—the stroke, he said, that distinguishes good swimmers from amateurs.

"Master the crawl," he'd say, "and you'll be a real swimmer."

My father would get into the water with me. I'd stand on the mucky bottom, and he'd show me how to move my arms, turn my head, and breathe.

"Stroke, stroke, stroke," he'd say, as I'd turn my head right, then left, then right, then left again. Then he taught me the flutter kick. He held me, first, around the waist, and after I got the hang of it, he'd hold me by my out-stretched hands, and I'd practice until he was satisfied.

Near the end of the summer, my father let me swim far out to the raft in the middle of the mud hole and back again to shore. Out and back. Then out and back again. He stood at the edge of the water and watched, too far away to help if I foundered. When I emerged from the water, my father would tell me what I'd done wrong.

My hands weren't slicing into the water at the right angle.

My head was lifted too high.

My kick was throwing up too much water.

Even though my technique wasn't perfect, I'd learned something hard, something my father wanted me to learn, maybe even pleased him. All that summer, my father reminded never to take chances in the water.

"The water," he says, "can be your friend if you understand it, but only if you know your limitations. It's an element that's impossible to control. But the crawl and the dead man's float could save your life."

Like my sister, my mother didn't venture into the water except to cool off, though she had been a fine swimmer as a young woman, my father told me. She sat on a blanket for most of the long summer's day, watching my sister during the morning, doling out sandwiches and drinks to us at lunchtime, burying her feet in the sand and flexing her toes, gazing out across the muddy water to the woods on the other side while my sister took her afternoon nap.

Before the end of the summer when I learned the American crawl, I was allowed to swim to the raft and back as many times as I wanted to without my father watching me. This was bliss, this swimming. My head nearly underwater, my vision blurred, my ears stopped against sound, the force of my arms and legs propelling me forward. In the water, there was no father, no mother, no sister, no doors slamming, no dishes shattering against the kitchen wall, no oaths and imprecations, no tyranny, no strangling of the heart's desire.

My father taught me the dead man's float, too, and I'd practiced it, though I never intended to get myself into a situation where I might need to use it, never wanted to do more than swim to the raft in the middle of the mud hole and back in deepest summer.

"Take a deep breath," he'd say. "Float in a vertical position. Relax. Dangle your arms and legs. Raise your head a bit above the surface when you need to breathe. Move your limbs as little as you need to. Don't waste your energy. Then return to the floating position." He said you could survive in the ocean for a very long time without fatiguing if you knew this skill.

"Swim clear of a sinking ship and other survivors," he'd say. "Do the dead man's float": my father's mantra for survival. Back then, I didn't ask why you needed to swim clear of a sinking ship and other survivors, or whether he'd ever needed to use the dead man's float to save himself. Back then, I didn't care.

"Oh yes," my father would say, "the dead man's float can keep you alive. Unless a shark gets you. Or an enemy plane swoops down and opens fire. Or a ship never comes by to rescue you."

Still, I thought there must have been a good reason why my father taught me how to survive in the deep. Did he think that one day I'd need his lessons? Did he imagine me jumping off a burning ship into churning water, stroking fast to get clear before a ship sank, creating a whirlpool to drag me down? Did he worry that one day I'd be alone somewhere on a vast body of water without him, and that I'd have to save myself?

Years later, when my father is very sick and I'm asking him about his life in the Navy because I want to know as much as I can about him before he dies, he tells me he learned the American crawl and the dead man's float when he was a sailor. The sidestroke, the elementary backstroke, the breaststroke, the shallow dive, too, he says. He learned to swim underwater; learned how to abandon ship; learned how to swim through and under debris, oil slicks, fire, and floating bodies.

Before he enlisted in the Navy, he couldn't swim, couldn't float, even. When you joined the Navy, you had to learn how to swim. But you didn't need to learn how to swim very well or very far, which my father thought was stupid.

"Imagine," my father said, "a branch of the military where you spend most of your time on a ship in the middle of the ocean and you only have to learn how to swim fifty yards! You only have to learn how to stay afloat hoping someone will come to rescue you! No wonder we lost so many men at sea. Typical Navy bullshit, not insisting you have to know what you need to know to survive. Men in war are expendable," he said, and shook his head.

Although my father knew sailors who never learned advanced skills (how to jump clear of a sinking ship, how to survive in cold water, how to inflate your clothes and tie knots in shirtsleeves, in trouser legs, so you could use them to float), sailors who never bothered to become more than third-class swimmers, my father believed it was his duty to learn everything he could to become a first-class swimmer, and he did. You couldn't count on someone else to help you in a dangerous situation. You had to be responsible for your own survival. "After the first shot's fired," he said, "it's chaos out there."

Out there in the ocean, once a ship is in danger, once you abandon ship, no matter what anyone says about following orders, about team spirit, every man is his own captain, and it's every man for himself. A man who doesn't know how to swim well will cling to you to survive, will push you under and drown you. Which is why it's best to swim clear of everyone, find your own piece of debris to cling to.

"Better," my father said, "to die alone than be dragged to the bottom of the ocean by someone clawing at you because he was too lazy or too stupid to learn what he should know to take care of himself."

But in the dreams I have about my father jumping off a sinking ship, I never see him in the water alone, far from others, holding on to his own piece of flotsam. I see him rescuing someone, see him towing a limp body to a lifeboat or to shore or to a waiting ship, see him performing mouth-to-mouth resuscitation, breathing life into a drowning man's lungs. I always see him casting his eyes about, looking for someone to save, looking for someone who, without his help, wouldn't have survived.

I'm now more than halfway across Lake George. I tell my father I'm tired, tell him I want to give up, tell him I want him to help me climb into the boat.

"You'll make it," my father says.

"I can't," I say.

"Can't?" he asks. "Or won't? You'll have to make it."

"Why?" I ask.

"Because I'm not letting you in the boat," my father says.

Is this some kind of test? Does my father want me to succeed? Or does he want me to fail?

The evening before my swim, during a cookout, my father decides I will swim from one side of Lake George to the other. We've helped the owners of the cabins make homemade peach ice cream. We're waiting for the ice cream to ripen, waiting for our first taste of homemade peach ice cream. We're finishing our hot dogs and hamburgers. This holiday isn't as bad as I expected.

My father's telling the owner what a beautiful spot this is. The owner tells my father that, here, the lake's only a mile or so across. From this point a good swimmer can easily swim to the opposite shore and back again. His guests do it all the time.

"My daughter is a fine swimmer," my father says. "I taught her myself. She could do it."

My father turns to me. "Tomorrow," he says, "you'll swim Lake George. It's not that far across."

"No," I say. "I don't want to." I have other plans for this holiday. I've worked the whole summer up until now, up early, home late, at a hard job in an office in New York City. I want this week to rest so that I can be at my best when I start college in September.

"Yes," my father says, "you will."

My mother knows this is the start of one of our fights.

"For once," she says, "will the two of you try to get along?" She makes it sound like a joke because we're not alone, but it isn't funny. Like always, she's not saying no to my father and I know he won't give up; I know that he'll keep bringing it up until he wears me down and gets his way.

Help, I think, *help.*

The day before my swim, we'd taken an excursion to Fort William Henry at the southern tip of Lake George. My father was big on exploring historical sites, especially battlefields and forts. He tells me that seeing Fort William Henry will be educational for me because *The Last of the Mohicans*, a book I've read, was set there.

I'd protested. I'd wanted to sit in an Adirondack chair on the dock, soak up the sun, and read. I'd been reading the Russians. For my holiday, I'd chosen Mikhail Aleksandrovich Sholokhov's *And Quiet Flows the Don*, about Grigori Panteleevich Melekhov's life as a Red Army soldier and a Cossack nationalist. I'd imagined hours of uninterrupted reading.

And Quiet Flows the Don is another in a series of novels I've read throughout middle school and high school about war, insurrection, and rebellion, subjects that fascinate me as much as they do my father, although, back then, I never would have attributed this obsession to being my father's daughter. That summer I'd read Ernest Hemingway's *A Farewell to Arms* and *For Whom the Bell Tolls*, Norman Mailer's *The Naked and the Dead*—boys' books, my best friend called them, when she made fun of me, and asked me what the carnage count was for the book I was currently reading. "Too many to count" would have been the right answer, if I'd deigned to give it, instead of shrugging her disapproval off.

My father gets his way and as we tour Fort Henry, he reads from the brochure about the battle that occurred there during August 1757—he'll add it to his collection of brochures when we get home.

"French guns pounded the fort for days, and each day, they came closer to the British inside." He pauses. "Imagine what it was like knowing you were surrounded, knowing the French would overrun the fort."

My sister wanders over to a wall. She picks up a twig, squats down, begins to dig. My mother follows. I'm left alone with him to listen, and I do, for as much as my father bothers me, I respect his knowledge of history gleaned from the many nights he's sat in his chair reading one hefty historical volume after another.

Montcalm sends Bougainville out of the fort to surrender to the French. He's holding a white flag. ("Bougainville, also the name of an important World War II battle in the South Pacific," my father says. "Remember that name when you study World War II in college." He's irate that we never got to World War II in high school.) The French accept, but as the unarmed British leave the fort with their women and children, the Indian allies of the French attack them, scalp them, slaughter them.

Men running. Women trying to escape. Children screaming. Indians in pursuit. War whoops. People thrown to the ground. Blood, blood, and more blood. Dismembered limbs. Piles of bodies. Scalps held on high.

"Filthy fighters, the Indians," my father says, "just like the Japanese. Didn't follow the rules of war. But whether it was their idea or the French's, who can say?"

Rules of war? How absurd! I think, and look away.

"You don't know any of this about the English? About the Indians? About the French?" my father asks.

"No," I reply.

"What the hell do they teach you in school?" my father asks.

"But what if it's raining hard tomorrow?" I ask.

"It won't rain," my father says. "Look at the sky, look west. You can tell by the western sky that tomorrow will be beautiful."

I see a red-stained sky. Red sky at night, sailors' delight. Red sky in the morning, sailors take warning.

"But it might rain," I insist.

"You can do the swim even if it rains," he says. "As long as we don't hear thunder."

"But I've never swum that far before," I say.

"Oh yes you have," he says. "At the mud hole, out to the float and back, all day long. Way more than two hours. Way more than two miles. Won't you feel proud if you can say you swam Lake George?" he asks. "Wouldn't you like to tell your friends you swam the lake?"

"Sure," I say. Being proud isn't a feeling I'm familiar with. And even though I get good grades in school, even though I've blocked some shots in basketball and won a game for my team, even though I've earned a lot of money for a girl my age, I've never felt proud. They're just something I've done; something I've had to do.

I don't want to swim the lake. But I don't want to argue with my father, either, don't want to ruin this vacation. I'll be leaving for college, soon. I want to come away from this week with the memory of us as a family, enjoying ourselves, without my father ruining it with one of his outbursts, without him telling me it's all my fault. I want us to have a good time like other families.

And so I decide to swim Lake George. I tell myself it's not because he wants me to, but because *I* want to. It will seem like my father is getting his way, but he's not.

Or maybe I *do* want to please my father. Maybe I've always wanted to please him but don't know how. It's been a long time since I've pleased him, so long ago that I can't remember.

My father wants me to develop mettle. Mettle isn't courage, isn't daring, which is foolhardiness. It's something like courage, but more, he's said. It's grit, determination, pluck, endurance. Mettle is what a good soldier, a good statesman has. He tells me about Winston Churchill's speech about "mettle."

"The only way you got through the war was if you had mettle," my father says. "Mettle. Plus a heavy dose of good luck."

Mettle, I think, *is what I need to survive having him as a father.*

I swim across Lake George. I swim back. I swim maybe two-and-a-half miles. I swim the American crawl. The sidestroke. The elementary backstroke. I tread water. I use the dead man's float a few times when I think I can't go on.

And just like my father says, I can tell everyone I swam Lake George. But I won't. Nor do I tell anyone that on the long swim back, when I cling to the gunwale of the rowboat for the second time, when I tell my father that I want to end this swim, want to climb into the boat, my father threatens to take the oar out of the oarlock and beat my fingers so I'll let go of the boat and swim free.

"That's what they did," he says, as we're pulling the boat up onto shore, "that's what they had to do when a ship went down, when one too many men wanted to climb aboard a lifeboat. Beat their hands until they slipped into the sea."

2004

"But do you remember," I ask my father, "how you told me you wouldn't let me climb into the boat when I was so tired I didn't think I'd make it back to the other shore?"

"Did I do that?" my father asks. "I don't remember."

"And you also told me that you'd hit my hands with the oar to force me back into the water," I say.

My father says nothing for some time. We've been talking about his honeymoon, one of his favorite subjects, only this time, I've told him I didn't think it was a good idea for him to take my mother to battlefields on their honeymoon. Our conversation has taken a turn he hasn't expected. I'm reminding him of something he doesn't want to remember.

"That doesn't sound like me," he says. "But if I did tell you I wouldn't let you into the boat, it was for your own good. It was to teach you that in a difficult situation you couldn't give up, you had to endure, even if there was no one around to help you."

And now I realize that for most of his life my father has been imagining himself clinging to the gunwale of an overloaded lifeboat out there somewhere in the middle of the vast Pacific, has been imagining someone not letting him aboard, has been imagining someone hitting his hands so that he'd let go, slip into the sea, and sink. He has lived in one time; I was born into that time, but I have lived in another. Only my father is preparing me for that other time, and he's doing this, not to torture me, as I always said when I was growing up, but because, in his own mind, he's trying to help me.

THREE

So Much to Lose, So Much Already Lost

THANKSGIVING, 1941

It's a little more than four months after my parents' wedding and they've prepared their first Thanksgiving dinner in their apartment on Fourteenth Street for my mother's parents—a simple pasta with tomato sauce; baked chicken and vegetables. My mother isn't comfortable in the kitchen; she's just learning to cook and the food is good—not great, my father says, but at least she didn't burn anything. Her father eats with relish; her stepmother toys with her food—this is the first time in her adulthood that someone has cooked for her.

For dessert, my mother has prepared a refrigerator cake made with store-bought chocolate cookies and whipped cream.

"Look at what I baked," my mother says, as she takes the cake out of the icebox and shows it to my father. She's proud of this concoction of hers that has been so easy to assemble.

"You didn't bake that cake," my father teases.

This upsets my mother and she begins to cry. She's tried hard to make something she thinks he'll like. She hasn't yet had the courage to bake a pie for him, and she's found this recipe for icebox cake in a women's magazine and thought it was the solution to the problem of what to make for dessert. Baking in a coal stove is tricky, her friend Argie tells her, and my mother hasn't yet had time to learn. My father doesn't understand how easily her feelings are hurt, and it takes a long time for him to calm her down. For a while, he fears he's spoiled their holiday.

After her parents leave, the two of them sit at the kitchen table for another cup of coffee. My mother has been brooding all day about Roosevelt's "1941 Thanksgiving Day Proclamation," declaring that U.S. "defenses against threatened aggression are mounting daily."

"Does this mean we're near war?" she asks my father. Since their wedding, she's felt more vulnerable than before because she now has so much to lose, and also because the war news has been so dismal.

In October, a few weeks before, a torpedo from a German U-boat hit the *USS Kearny* and killed eleven sailors. The *Kearny* had been tasked with releasing depth charges to try to stop a German U-boat wolf pack from destroying a convoy in the North Atlantic with much-needed materiel for Great Britain. The attack on the *Kearny* means the shooting war between Germany and the United States has begun although war hasn't yet been formally declared. My father has been a civilian for less than two years, but he still feels like a military man, and the loss of these sailors' lives affects him deeply.

He's started reading David Garnett's *War in the Air* to learn about how the Germans and the British are using bombers in this war. He's gotten it out of the library and it sits on the end table in the parlor where my father goes to read after supper on nights when the room isn't too cold. It's his duty to learn about this kind of warfare because he believes he'll be called back into the service. The fact that he is reading this book upsets my mother.

Even as he's preparing himself for war, he's vowed to try his best to stay home. His work at K & E, he thinks, might be considered vital to the war effort. Although he has an obligation to help keep his country safe, he has begun to think that he has an even greater obligation to his wife, this woman he's married. He's learned that she's far more prone to sadness than he realized. He sees his duty, now, as helping her see that the world isn't as terrifying a place as she thinks it is. Only he knows that, now, it's far more terrifying than anyone could have imagined.

Since they've returned from their honeymoon, the only time they've relaxed was in late August when they went to Coney Island. They swam in the ocean, sunned themselves, ate hot dogs, strolled on the boardwalk, and posed for photographs. During that fine summer day, they tried to block out the news that the Germans were winning the war on the Russian front; that the United States had frozen Japanese assets and had severed relations with Japan; that military strategists believed Japan might attack the United States before it could defend itself.

DECEMBER 7, 1941

Seventeen days after Thanksgiving, the Japanese attack the naval base at Pearl Harbor, as my father and many of his shipmates believed they would. Years later, when my father reads the news of what actually happened on that day (the United States kept the severity of the attack hidden for years), he tells me he can't understand why most of the vessels of the Pacific Fleet, except for a few aircraft carriers, were in Pearl Harbor.

"Having so many ships concentrated in one place," he says, "was like pasting a 'Kick Me' sign on your backside."

Years after Pearl Harbor, my father keeps trying to understand what happened. Was the Fleet gathering for an offensive against Japan? Did Roosevelt know the attack was coming and let it happen, as some believe? Did the United States discount the possibility that the Japanese could launch an attack so far away from the home islands?

DECEMBER 8, 1941

President Roosevelt signs Proclamation 2527, reviving the 150-year old Enemy Alien Act of 1798. German, Japanese, and Italian foreign nationals living in the United States are declared enemy aliens. Government agents can now raid the homes of enemy aliens to confiscate anything (radios, cameras) that might be used to help the enemy. Newspapers report the arrest of 165 Germans, 65 Italians, and 241 Japanese in the New York area: They've been rounded up and are being detained on Ellis Island.

That evening, after work, my parents walk to my grandparents' apartment to discuss what to do, for no one knows if there will be more raids into Italian neighborhoods. None of my parents' parents are citizens. My mother's parents are terrified they might be incarcerated or deported. They think they might go to Rhode Island to stay with her mother's relatives but they both need to continue to earn a living. They've also heard rumors that there are strategic checkpoints around New York, so they decide that it's now more dangerous to travel than to stay put and risk having their home raided. They've learned there will be a curfew imposed in Italian neighborhoods; that Italians will be fingerprinted; that travel permits will be required to leave their neighborhoods. They fear, of course, that they too will be rounded up and taken to Ellis Island.

"We decided to wait and see what would happen," my father tells me. "What else could we do?"

My parents and grandparents decide to avoid calling attention to themselves, to not speak Italian outside the house, to not talk about the war with anyone but family members. (Soon, menacing signs saying "Do not speak the enemy's tongue" appear throughout Hoboken. And from that moment on, my mother decides that should she have a child, she'll never speak Italian to that child.) They fear government agents might send them into detention on Ellis Island if they're caught speaking Italian, or, worse, deport them. The streets of Italian City in Hoboken, once filled with talk, become silent.

In California, government agents seize the homes and possessions of Italians and Italian Americans. Many near the coast are forced from their homes and sent to relocation camps. The boats of Italian fishermen are seized. The news is talked about in hushed whispers in Italian stores on Adams Street.

"Will we be next?" my mother's parents wonder. Hoboken is as vital to the defense of the United States as California's coastline. My grandfather works on the New York docks. Will he be considered a security risk and thrown out of work? Will my mother's stepmother be forced out of her job as a superintendent of her building? Will they lose their apartment? Will their meager savings be confiscated now that all assets of enemy aliens have been frozen?

MID-DECEMBER 1941

The shift from peacetime to wartime happens in the blink of an eye. Antisubmarine nets are strung below the Narrows leading into New York Harbor. New York Mayor LaGuardia orders air raid drills, regulations for the use of blackout shades, and gas masks. W. T. Grant's, where my mother works, mounts a display of blackout necessities, flashlights, and bandages. Families are urged to have emergency supplies on hand—tins of water, dried food, and first aid kits. My mother complies and lays in a store of necessities for them, and she urges her father and stepmother to do the same and even brings them some supplies from Grant's.

My parents read of the plan to evacuate women and children from around New York Harbor. My mother says that, afraid as she is, she'll refuse to go, she'll refuse to leave her husband. She would be far more worried away from him than she will be with him by her side. Newspapers publish a map of escape routes in the event of a bombardment. My mother clips it out and posts it in the kitchen in the event they're both ordered to evacuate.

"But how do they expect us to evacuate?" my father asks. "On foot?" Images of people fleeing European cities flood my mother's mind. My parents know that scores of people have tried to escape from danger in Europe and have died trying.

Still, my father tries to calm her fears.

"LaGuardia's a crank," he says. "The Germans aren't interested in us. They're too busy with the Brits and the Russians."

A few days after the attack on Pearl Harbor, my father, against my mother's protests, volunteers to be a civilian plane spotter. He can't stand on the sidelines, waiting. On his assigned nights, he stands on the roof of their apartment building, gazing at the night sky through a pair of binoculars, looking for the enemy aircraft LaGuardia insists will soon be bombing New York City.

My mother thinks that by standing on the roof and scanning the skies my father is trying to relive the excitement of his years in the service. He admits to me years later that civilian life, much as he'd looked forward to it, was boring and that he often secretly hoped that he could return to active duty, even though he didn't want to leave my mother, although not during wartime. His desire to rejoin the service is something he keeps from his wife; this is something she would never understand. He's vowed to her that if he *is* called back to active duty, he'll never volunteer for anything dangerous and that he'll try to keep himself out of harm's way.

(After his death, as I peruse his personal papers, I learn that he has tried to sign up for another tour of duty after he comes home from World War II, but for some reason he can't. And I wonder whether my mother knew this; I wonder whether the strain of living with us after the war was so great or whether the allure of that life was so powerful that he wanted to return to a life in the military.)

My mother is upset that he's volunteered to be a plane spotter. She has images of airplanes in the sky singling him out for harm, she tells him. He laughs at this image.

"Do you really think Hitler is interested in me?" he teases.

"Everyone during a war," my mother replies, "is in harm's way."

Still, upset as she is at his nighttime duty, she fixes him a thermos of coffee and brings it up to him. She doesn't stay on the roof long. She just gives him his coffee and scurries downstairs to the warmth and safety—she hopes—of their kitchen.

EARLY 1942

The Germans want to bomb New York City; they want to start a firestorm in the city like those that have raged in Germany. And although the Germans don't yet have the capability of bombing New York, British intelligence learns and informs Roosevelt that German U-boats are leaving bases in France and heading for the United States to attack targets up and down the coast; only 20 ships and 100 aging planes are available to guard more than 1,500 miles of coastline. In January 1942, a submarine is sighted off the coast of Nantucket moving toward New York City, and a German U-boat sinks the *Norness*, a 10,000-ton Norwegian oil tanker only 53 nautical miles south of Martha's Vineyard. The battle to control the Atlantic Ocean has taken a serious turn for the worse as U-boats come close to the United States.

Later that month, the Norwegian tanker *Varanger* is torpedoed 35 miles off Sea Isle, New Jersey, and six Allied ships are sunk in less than two weeks. German U-boats are now operating without intervention along the East Coast. There are oil slicks all along the beaches of the New Jersey coast; bodies are washing up on shore. In late February, the destroyer *Jacob Jones*, commanded to search for the survivors of a torpedoed ship, is attacked, hit, and burned; people stand on shore and watch the blaze; only 11 of the 150 crew members survive. And in February, too, the SS *Normandie* explodes in flames at Pier 88, West 49th Street. Was it an accident? Or sabotage?

A civil defense mania grips the metropolitan area. New York City and parts of New Jersey are on war alert. Mayor LaGuardia warns of "murder from the skies." The skies above New York City and New Jersey soon fill with naval patrol planes, and the beams from huge searchlights rake the night. A naval commander states that the North Atlantic Squadron is taking steps to protect New York from attack.

"With what?" my father asks, knowing how few ships and planes are available. It's soon announced that the Squadron needs the help of private yachts and planes manned by their civilian owners. This provokes an outburst from my father. Years later, when he tells me this, he's still outraged.

"Can you imagine a bunch of rich, untrained men in their yachts and airplanes being made responsible for the safety of our shores? That's how unprepared we were!"

After my mother hears one of LaGuardia's rants, she says, "You'll have to go back into the service soon, won't you?"

"I guess so," my father answers.

"You don't guess," my mother says. "You know."

2004

I want to know more about how my parents felt and what they talked about during these difficult days. When I ask my father, he says they talked endlessly about whether he would be able to stay home and whether they should have a child, that they tried to live a normal life for as long as they could, that my mother was a "nervous wreck" but that she tried to be brave, and that she tried to carry on although there were times when she seemed listless and uninterested in anything.

"What you do," my father says, "what *I* did, is focus on what's right in front of you and what you need to do next. You don't look back. You don't look too far forward. You don't hope for a world different from the one you're living in. You make the best of what has come your way. I learned that in the Navy and I tried to teach it to your mother. But she had a hard time of it. I think that for her it was impossible."

My father tries to quell my mother's panic while he tries to prepare himself emotionally to leave for war. My mother becomes so upset, she can't sleep. Her hands shake so much, she drops things and breaks dishes. Living so close to New York, living a block away from a major shipyard, makes her feel vulnerable, powerless, and terrified—she knows that docks and shipyards are primary targets. She considers quitting her job and moving in with her stepmother's relatives in Rhode Island for the duration of the war. But that would mean leaving her husband, and this, she can't, she won't, do.

"How long do you think we have left?" she asks him.

"I don't know," he says. And then they talk, again, about whether it's a good time to bring a child into the world, and they decide that it isn't.

But although my father agrees with my mother about this, what he doesn't tell her, and what he tells me years later, is that he thinks that if she had a child to take care of, she'd be less focused on him, less focused on the war, less fearful, less inclined to worry. And that he, personally, thought that their having a child was a good idea.

"You've got to be kidding," I say. "Didn't you realize that having a child never solves anything? It makes everything worse." And I wonder, for the first time, whether I was that child conceived in my father's misguided attempt to ease my mother's terror about the war.

Magic Bullet

2008

But when, a few years later, I begin to write what my father told me about how my mother and he decided it wasn't a good time to have children, I stop. I sense there is something I don't yet know, something my father hasn't told me.

I type the words "Calendar 1941, 1942" into a search engine. The calendars appear on the screen. And I count backward from my birth date, September 27, 1942. I count back 40 weeks, 280 days, the normal gestation period for a human being. I want to know when I was conceived. Was my mother already pregnant with me, although she didn't yet realize it, while she and my father had these conversations? Or was I conceived some time after? It becomes extremely important for me to know this.

I count back twice, three times, to make sure I haven't made a mistake. And what I learn astonishes me. For I discover that my parents most likely conceived me on or about December 21, 1941. Fourteen days after Pearl Harbor. Fifteen days after war with Japan, Germany, and Italy is declared by the

United States. Fourteen days after my parents discuss how sure they are that my father will go away to war. Fourteen days after my parents decide that this is no world to bring a child into. And having heard my father describe how panic-stricken my mother had become after Pearl Harbor, I can't believe—or rather, I can't understand—why my parents would have chosen to conceive a child who would be born during wartime, a child my mother might have to care for alone.

So I wonder what kind of an act of love this was, the one that made me, performed during the first gasp of our country's involvement in that terrible war. There was love, surely; desire, likely (on my father's part, if not my mother's). But could panic, despair, desperation, fear, and terror have also been hovering above that marital bed? And I am also forced to consider whether I was just a mistake. (My parents were Catholic, after all.) Or was I intended, despite their discussion about not wanting to bring a child into a world at war? Or was I, instead, to be the child who might keep my father out of the war or delay his deployment (for they were not yet drafting married men with children)? Or the one who would be the magic bullet my father imagined would help my mother forget her fears?

These are questions I can never answer. The answers to these questions must remain a mystery. My father is dead; he is not here to tell me the truth, if, in fact, he would have chosen to do so. But I do wonder whether my parents chose to conceive a child in wartime knowing how terrified my mother had become.

And how do I feel having learned this piece of my personal history? I do think that this small piece of the puzzle of my life—the timing of my conception—explains why, through the years, I have been obsessed with war, obsessed with finding out about my parents' lives at this time. I did become that child born into wartime, that child my parents originally believed it would have been better not to have.

WINTER 1941–SUMMER 1942

During the early days of my mother's pregnancy, the war news is unrelentingly gruesome. More than a thousand ships are lost in the Battle of the Atlantic. The Germans make steady progress in Russia and bomb the cathedral cities of England in their attempt to wear down British resolve. Thousands of

Italians together with Japanese and Germans are moved inland in the United States, although aliens on the East Coast aren't yet targeted. Japanese troops push U.S. troops back into the Bataan peninsula. German U-boats are torpedoing tankers off the East Coast.

"They were sitting ducks," my father says, "outlined against the bright lights on shore." Cities along the East Coast refuse to order blackouts, pleading they would be bad for business even though tankers are burning offshore and bodies continue to wash up on beaches.

Halfway through my mother's pregnancy, news of the Bataan death march appears, and atrocities committed by the Japanese against U.S. soldiers and people in the Philippines are reported—fingers cut off to take rings; people buried alive; women's stomachs cut open; beheadings. For the first time, my parents realize the extent of the brutality of this enemy that my father suspects he'll soon be facing.

Mayor LaGuardia, convinced an attack on New York City is imminent, orders patrol planes into the air all night long and they drone overhead. In the spring, blackouts, air raid drills, scrap metal and paper collections, and food rationing begin.

After Mother's Day, my grandfather plants a Victory Garden in old wine barrels on the fire escape outside his kitchen so the family will have fresh tomatoes, zucchini, and peppers all summer long. He and his cronies lug the barrels up to their apartment, then shovel soil into old pillowcases to haul upstairs. When the time comes to harvest his vegetables, they are small and covered with soot so they have to be washed well. But he is proud of his crop and the fact that the family can share some fresh food.

Unlike other women who empty their cupboards of pots and pans for scrap metal collections, my mother refuses to give hers up. They are new and precious to her and she has only a few. As a concession to the war effort, she cuts her hair short and gives away her bobby pins.

The air raid drills greatly affect my mother. When the siren sounds, my parents drop whatever they're doing, grab the bag containing their necessities, and go to the air raid shelter in the basement of their apartment building. As my mother's due date draws closer, she is terrified she'll go into labor during an air raid drill.

It isn't easy for her to move quickly, and she fears she will lose her footing and fall down the darkened stairs. It becomes impossible for my parents to relax in the evening because they never know when the siren will sound. Yet they are grateful that these are only drills; they know that the sound of a siren in Britain means something far different: that German planes are approaching and that there will be another night of bombardments, fires, destruction, and death.

During the summer months that precede my birth, there are servicemen everywhere in Hoboken, debarking from ships for a last fling in the saloons that are all over the city, several of them on Fourteenth Street. They get drunk and rowdy after a night of carousing and sometimes my father has to shout out the window for them to quiet down, but he understands the stress they're under, for they'll soon be leaving for combat.

My father believes he is destined to serve in the Pacific. So when finally, the good news comes that the Pacific Fleet has destroyed much of the Japanese Fleet at Midway, my parents celebrate. It is the first major victory for the Allies in the Pacific, and they hope it will turn the tide of the war there so that my father will not be deployed to an active war zone. Soon after, though, the gruesome reports of the battle on Guadalcanal dispel that hope.

On the Day I Was Born

1942

For years, I have known the circumstances of my birth. It was my father who had told me so very long ago that I was born on a rainy Sunday when Marines were enduring a ferocious assault on the beachhead they'd taken on Guadalcanal. Their target was Henderson Field, the only landing strip in the southeastern Solomons. Unless Henderson Field is wrested from the Japanese, the Japanese can prevent U.S. convoys from moving west, closer to the home islands.

I know that my mother was in labor for thirty-six hours—false labor, the doctor called it. The only good thing about being in labor, my mother told me years later, was that, throughout those long pain-filled hours, the war became insignificant. Still, my father continues to read the newspaper and listen to the radio when he leaves the hospital to take a break. He knows that unless Henderson Field is taken, the United States can never defeat the Japanese, can never move close enough to the home islands to extract a hard-earned victory.

Throughout my mother's labor, except for the breaks he takes to go home, eat a little something, wash up, and listen to the radio, my father sits in the waiting room perusing newspapers, smoking cigarettes, and napping, waiting, waiting, waiting, for his wife's long labor to end and for his first child to be born. It will be a boy, they're sure; they'll name him "Louis," after him.

Into her second day of labor, my father begins to worry. He asks the nurse if anything is wrong. No, nothing is wrong, the nurse said: This baby is just taking its own sweet time.

"Prepare yourself for a child with mind of its own," the nurse says.

And finally, after far too long, there I am, a girl, with a full head of hair, who looks just like my father.

I have known, ever since I can remember, that my parents were so sure I'd be a boy that they'd decided on the name "Louis," after my father. So that when I am born, they have no girl's name for me and decide to simply add an "e" to the end of my father's name. So, I am named "Louise." And whether he is disappointed at not having a son, he never tells me.

Throughout my life, my parents expected everything from me that they would have expected from a son: toughness, hard work, industry, success. Yet they also expected me to be obedient, caring, and gentle as a docile daughter in an Italian American family ought to have been. The daughter they got, though, perhaps because she shared her father's name, would have none of this. As far back as my father remembers, he tells me that I am willful, headstrong, obstinate, single-minded, purposeful, argumentative, and not the least bit docile. All this exasperates him, angers him, yet makes him proud.

"You were," he says, "you are, a chip off the old block."

But I don't remember the pride. All I can remember is the anger.

And I also learn, from my father, that my birth doesn't bring my mother joy. Whatever the reason—her long labor, hormonal changes, the inescapable war news, the likelihood of my father leaving her, my birth stirring memories of her dead mother and her own difficult childhood, the emotional difficulties that have been latent for a while—after my birth, whatever cheerfulness and competence she seemed to possess during my parents' courtship vanishes. I think it's fair to say, based on the stories I've heard, that after I am born, my father loses the woman he married, for she metamorphoses into someone he never imagined she would become.

I was one of many children born during wartime, and all things considered, my parents were more fortunate than many, as my father told my mother. My father was still home; the war was not being fought on our shores; our cities were not bombarded, although there were frequent air raid drills and fears that they might be bombed. And so my father thought my mother had no reason to be as morose as she became. He couldn't understand the change that had come over her; his four years in the military had led him to believe that it was simply a matter of her having the wrong attitude. She needed to toughen up, look on the bright side, and get on with it.

"Cheer up," he'd tell her repeatedly. "We have a healthy baby girl."

During the week my mother spent in the hospital, she cried without provocation. She had a difficult time feeding me, and she didn't want to hold me. For several of my feedings, the nurses gave me sugar water to calm me.

"Take her away," she'd tell the nurse who'd bring me to her.

The doctor assured my father that many women have a hard time adjusting to motherhood after giving birth, and that she would soon snap out of it. When my father expressed concern to my grandfather, he learned that when my mother was in her early twenties (the same age as when her birth mother died), she wouldn't see friends, she stopped going to work, she never went out, and she rarely got out of her nightclothes.

It took her six months to get better from that episode—she was institutionalized and shock treated. But after that, she seemed fine.

"Why didn't you tell me this before?" my father asked, angered at the fact that this important piece of information had been kept from him, although he told me it wouldn't have made any difference to him, that he loved her and would have married her anyway.

"We were afraid to tell you," her father replied.

＊ ＊ ＊

Despite the doctor's assurances, after my parents took me home to the apartment on Fourteenth Street, my mother wasn't any better. She tried to care for me. But after a few weeks, she couldn't get out of bed; she wouldn't feed me; I cried all the time.

"The baby's crying," my father would say.

"I know," my mother would answer, without moving. She'd lie in bed, staring at the wallpaper, wrapped in her pink chenille bathrobe, wasted milk leaking from her breasts, drying and crusting and making her nipples bleed (which was why she said she couldn't nurse), falling into a deep sleep that was not so much rest as oblivion.

"At first, she never knew whether she should feed you and comfort you or let you cry; whether to hold you or put you down," my father said. "Sometimes she'd stand over your crib and watch you cry, trying to figure out what to do. The doctor told her you should only be fed every four hours. But you were hungry all the time. When it was time for your feeding, you were so exhausted you couldn't nurse. So she gave up trying to figure out whether to nurse you or let you cry and she went to bed and didn't get up."

Sometimes my father said he'd get so angry that he'd wanted to drag my mother out of bed, pull her over to the crib, and force her to look at me. But he never did. Instead, he'd attack the pots and pans in the kitchen when he cleaned up after the rudimentary supper he'd prepared. And he'd remind himself that he loved her from the first moment he saw her in the shoe department at W. T. Grant's, and he'd tell himself this was just a phase that would pass, that my mother would soon return to her old self, the woman with the shy smile he'd fallen in love with.

During the days when he was at work, he made sure a friend or her stepmother came to help. But her stepmother made the situation worse; she wasn't fond of children, and because she believed it was my mother's duty to pull herself together, she would harangue her throughout the time she was supposed to be helping.

2004

All this I knew. All this I had known for years. But near the end of his life, my father told me something that I had never known before.

One day my father couldn't take my crying anymore. He left the apartment, went to a drugstore, and bought bottles, nipples, evaporated milk, Karo syrup, and a vitamin supplement with iron that the druggist recommended. If his wife couldn't feed his daughter, he said, he'd feed her himself.

"If you give her formula," the doctor had said, "she'll never take the breast." But the alternative, my father thought, was to let me starve.

He knew that my mother's life was hard. Every surface in the apartment, so near the factories and docks, became soot-covered as soon as you cleaned them. She had to scrub their clothes and mine and diapers, sheets, and towels on the washboard in the sink, then wring them out by hand and hang them to dry in fine weather on the clothesline strung from the kitchen window. In foul weather, she had to hang them in the kitchen.

She had to fetch coal from the basement for the stove, clear the ashes out from it, and dispose of them in the basement. To shop for food, she had to dress me, haul me and the carriage down the steep flight of stairs, and walk down Washington Street to the market, then haul everything upstairs a little at a time, hoping that whatever she left behind would be there when she came back for it.

My father would have been happy to stay home, but he had to work and he couldn't risk losing his job. Through this difficult period, he told himself he had to care for me as well as he could when he was home and that he couldn't give up hope. He didn't regret marrying my mother, not even when she wasn't being much of a mother to me, not even later in her life when she became so depressed she couldn't care for my sister and me and we had to be sent away to live with relatives until she recovered, not even during the times when she was hospitalized and shock treated.

"Everything I am, I owe to her," he told me, wiping tears. "We made a life together. She believed in me. She made me feel I was worth something."

The doctor had said to just give my mother time. But my father believed he didn't have much time. He'd received a notice stating that the United States would need 10,000,000 men in uniform to fight this war. He was classified 3-B, a man with dependents, and he'd filed the papers to prove he was their sole means of support. Still, there were news reports that because there soon wouldn't be any more eligible 1-A men left to be drafted, the Selective Service would start dipping down into the other categories, into 1-Bs, men with slight physical problems, and perhaps even 3-Bs, men with dependents, like my father.

Why, I wondered, did my father wait until the end of his life to tell me this? Why did it take him so long to tell me that he defied the doctor, and that he began to feed me with his self-made infant formula? Was it true? Or was it something he wished he had done for me but hadn't? Was it a story he made up at the end of his life to try to counterbalance all that had come before? His disapproval of me? His rages? His unpredictable violence?

Still, near the end of his life, I so needed the image of a nurturing father that I never once questioned whether the story he told me was true. Because the effect his story had on me was to unravel my hatred of him, a hatred that I had carried for years, even as, at the end of his life, I cared for him as a dutiful child should. And so this story—and another that he told me, too, that I will soon tell you—became a bulwark against the hard times that were yet to come, the times at the end of his life that were bearing down upon me, when he, again, showed the worst of himself, and chiefly to me.

1942

There are no photographs of my mother and me during the first months of my life. No pictures of her holding me, gazing at me, me gazing at her. My mother wouldn't pose for them; she didn't feel up to it.

In the first photo of the two of us, taken when I'm three months old, she looks toward me, bereft, and I look away from her, searching. In another, she's propped me up in my crib, and she stands beside it, looking down. But I'm not smiling at her; I'm scowling. And no matter how often my father tells my mother to smile for the camera, there are no pictures of her smiling, no pictures of me smiling until I'm eleven months old. And there are no pictures of her holding me.

My father believed he couldn't leave my mother and me, for he feared I wouldn't survive. This is a story he told me, with variations, years ago.

In one version, he gets a letter from the obstetrician and another from my pediatrician stating that my mother was ill, that I wasn't thriving, and that the chances of my survival were slim if he went into the service. His service is postponed a year and he agrees to re-enlist in the Navy after that year.

He tells my mother that, with luck, the war will be over by then or, if not over, then nearly over, although he suspected he was wrong.

The Germans were dealt a setback at Casablanca; the Russians stopped the Nazis at Stalingrad; the Japanese were stopped at Midway. But the war in the Pacific had to be won, much of Europe had to be retaken, and FDR announced that the United States would accept nothing less than the unconditional surrender of Germany, Italy, and Japan, which meant a long and protracted war, a war, my father feared, that might last for the next ten years. FDR announced that the United States would build ships, planes, jeeps, and weapons of war faster than they could be destroyed and that America would win the war. But this meant that many men would die.

In the version my father told me near the end of his life, he simply says, "I got to stay home with you until you were fourteen months old." And no matter how much I probe, he doesn't repeat the story he'd told me so many years before about how and why that was so.

1943

When my mother learns my father can stay home for another year, she begins to get out of bed to help care for me. By the beginning of 1943, although she isn't back to her old self, she's far better than she was before.

Throughout 1943, it seems that the Allies might defeat the Axis: The Germans are dealt their first big defeat at Stalingrad; the Axis powers surrender in North Africa; U-boats stop attacking ships in the Atlantic; the Allies invade Sicily, then began to move up the Italian peninsula, which is both good news and difficult news for my family.

Good news, because it means that the Allies have opened another front. Difficult news because it means my parents' relatives living in Italy will be placed in harm's way.

My father reads my mother the newspaper account of General George S. Patton's speech to his troops on the eve of the invasion of Sicily. He says Italian American soldiers should consider it a privilege to kill Italian soldiers.

"These ancestors of yours so loved freedom that they gave up home and country to cross the ocean in search of liberty. The ancestors of the people we shall kill lacked the courage to make such a sacrifice and remained as slaves."

So many years later my father can still remember his fury at Patton's speech. Patton was from a privileged family and couldn't imagine the suffering that had prompted the Great Migration; the sacrifices Italian families made to send someone to the United States who could earn money to send back home for the family left behind; the wrenching emotional cost of the Great Migration; or the horror Italian American soldiers who were fiercely loyal to the United States nonetheless felt because they would be fighting and killing their *paesani*.

In mid-September, the Allies bomb key cities in Puglia, my mother's parents' region. And in late September, my father reads a report that there is fighting at the bridge in Scafati, where he'd lived as a boy and where he still has relatives. My parents and grandparents won't know, until the end of the war, how their relatives fare, when they will learn how much their relatives suffered during the war and how many of them died.

"Hide Your Tears"

1943

As the day for my father's re-enlistment draws near, his boss at K & E announces that a few of the company's employees will be given service exemptions because the firm is doing essential war work. Men working in wartime industries with wives and children like him, my father learns, are being exempted from service.

One of his most important assignments is working with engineers to re-create a transit theodolite the Allies captured from the Germans. The instrument is used to measure horizontal angles and elevations, to understand terrain, to map and direct artillery fire, to track weather balloons, to measure high-altitude winds. It's used both aboard ships and on battlefields. They break it down, determine how it works, devise a plan to replicate it, make drawings, and my father helps produce a working model. After it's tested and refined, K & E puts it into production.

A telegram to K & E employees from an officer in the Navy later in the war praises their work. The transit theodolite on board his ship has been used throughout ten major campaigns in the war in the Pacific against Japan. It is still functioning well, the officer says, without once requiring recalibration that would have been impossible to undertake during wartime. Participating in this project makes my father proud.

2005

It is a heavy, cumbersome, beautiful, and wondrous thing, I learn, near the end of my father's life, when I locate a K & E transit theodolite on the Internet and purchase it on a whim. I display it on the top of the bookshelf next to the chair I sit in each day to write in my journal. I am proud of this work my father has done, and I'm happy to have it near me.

It is black-painted brass with brass fittings and stamped with a serial number and "K & E Co." on its base. It has two spirit levels, a compass, various wheels, and a sighting scope. It comes complete with a wooden carrying case, and I can't imagine the effort it must have taken for a soldier to carry it across a battlefield and set it up and use it. Nor can I imagine the places this particular transit theodolite has been, the action it has seen, and the carnage it has witnessed. Has it been used aboard ship? Perhaps one of the very ships that left for the Battle of Leyte Gulf from the base where my father was stationed in the Pacific? Has it been used on a battlefield in Europe, or North Africa, or the Pacific? Has it helped win a decisive battle? Is it the transit theodolite the naval officer writes about? And I can't help fantasizing that the very transit theodolite I now own is one of the instruments my father worked on before he reentered the military.

"What did you go and do that for?" my father asks me when I tell him I've bought it. "How much did it cost?"

"Seven hundred dollars," I respond.

"A terrible waste of money," he says.

I try to explain to him how important it is for me to possess this instrument. How thrilled my sons are to see an example of their grandfather's war work. How beautiful I think it is, quite apart from the essential functions it served during the war. But my father gruffly dismisses my reasons for buying it as ridiculously sentimental. What I don't tell him, and what I can't say, is that I want it as a reminder of the work he was doing when I was just a baby before he had to go away to war and before everything changed.

"Can you come over and show me how to use it?" I ask, not even knowing if it still functions.

"Of course," he says, "if you insist."

But he never does. A few days after I ask him, and before we can make firm plans, he becomes enraged at his wife, has a temper tantrum, goes through their home destroying things, falls down, hurts himself, and winds up in the locked psychiatric ward of a local hospital.

1943

My father never tells my mother that K & E keeps black widow spiders in the basement for the filaments used in the crosshairs of the transit theodolites and other sighting instruments. A woman dubbed "the spider lady" tends them, harvests the filaments from their webs, and places them into the groves on the lenses the machinists etch into glass. My father is afraid that knowing about the spiders will make my mother even more nervous than she already is. He thinks she might worry that a spider from K & E's basement will hitch a ride home on my father's clothing and bite one of us.

My mother now seems able to care for me and has an established routine—household chores in the morning, food shopping just before lunch, a nap for me and a rest for her in the afternoon, an early bedtime—that gives her some free time and the opportunity for a quiet supper with my father.

My father helps her as much as he can. He buys groceries on the way home from work. Washes the dishes and cleans the kitchen after supper. Takes care of me all day on Saturdays to give her some free time. Arranges an outing for us all on Sunday so she doesn't have to plan and to get her out of the house because if she stays home, she'll always find some chore to do.

But even though my mother seems so much better than she was after I was born, my father fears what will happen to her if he goes away. He'd rather stay home if he can. And he's convinced that his job is important to the war effort.

My father applies for an exemption from re-enlistment on the grounds that his work is helping the war effort and that he is a married man with a child. The foreman at K & E can select only one man for this exemption. But the exemption goes, not to my father, but to an unmarried relative of the foreman. There is no way my father can contest this decision, even though my father has seniority and the required qualifications. My father wonders whether the foreman wants to get rid of him because he's jealous and fears that my father will be chosen one day to take over his job.

"That's how it goes," my father tells my mother when he learns the news. He's angry, bitter, and disappointed, although he doesn't tell her. She's deeply upset. She now has to face the fact that her husband will soon leave, that her husband will see active duty in this horrible war.

"Who you know," she says, "is more important than the work you do."

Because my father knows he will be leaving in less than a month, he's determined to make my first birthday party memorable. He's gotten his orders; he'll be shipping out in eighteen days although he has no idea where he'll be stationed or what his duties will be. My mother is putting on a brave face.

He has treated himself to a movie camera because he wants to memorialize this special day. He wants to record us as a family before he enters the war so—and this, he doesn't tell my mother—we can remember him if he doesn't come back.

Although there are rationing and food shortages, my mother has stockpiled and collected enough sugar, butter, and flour to make a birthday cake. By now, she's mastered the art of using that pesky coal oven. My parents spend money they shouldn't on noisemakers, hats, and crepe paper decorations.

My mother will soon be living on less than $100 a month—my father will hold back a few dollars from his salary for himself, and he'll send the rest home, plus my mother will receive a government allowance for us of $40 a month. They've been living a frugal life in anticipation and saving as much as they can. My mother can dip into their savings if she has to.

Like so many other women living on a serviceman's salary, she'll have to make do, but my father is sure she'll manage. He's found her to be a woman who knows how to budget, how to live on a budget, how to strike a bargain, and how to save. When he gets paid, she portions out his salary in envelopes for rent, electricity, savings, clothing, food, vacation (although there won't be one for some time), and miscellaneous.

My parents invite our family—my two sets of grandparents; my father's sisters and their husbands; my cousins; my mother's best friend, Rose, and her husband—to the celebration. My mother buys me a new outfit—a plaid skirt and a white blouse—for the occasion. She does this because she wants me to look my best in the photos my father will take with him to war.

We all crowd into the kitchen on Fourteenth Street to celebrate. Although there are only four kitchen chairs and most of the guests must remain standing, everyone has a good time, my father says, for my maternal grandfather breaks out several bottles of his homemade wine for the occasion, and there they are, those bottles of wine, on the table, in the motion pictures my father takes on that day. And there are the guests, too, in my father's film, laughing and toasting me.

And there I am, now a chubby little thing with a head of curly hair, sitting in my high chair smashing my first piece of birthday cake. Then staggering across the living room rug with my hands held out toward a very large ball, a present from my parents, and my antics wrest a smile from my mother.

Years later, when we watch these films together, my father tells me my mother was trying hard to be brave and that she's hiding her sorrow. He's found her reading an article instructing wives to hide their tears to make sure their husbands' last days at home are pleasant. They're going to face grave dangers and it's essential to the war effort that they not worry about the well-being of the wives and children they must leave behind.

A wife's duty, the article says, is to reassure her husband that she'll be fine while he's gone. And to assure him that the war will be over soon and that he'll be coming home before he knows it. Being a good homemaker and a good mother and supporting the morale of her husband are her important contributions to the war effort. No matter how difficult life is for her, she must remember that the United States is not under fire, and compared with the wives of other Allied servicemen, her life will be relatively comfortable while her husband is away.

But this is not easy. For my mother has seen photographs of dead servicemen on a New Guinea beach, the first such photos from the war, and they are terrifying. The war is very real in Hoboken: Every family has someone in the war. Whenever my mother walks through the streets, she sees shrines in front windows bearing gold stars commemorating servicemen who have died. As the wife of a serviceman, she will be encouraged to place a banner in her living room window although she isn't sure if she will.

My father is grateful he's had this year with us and that all his hard work taking care of me has paid off, for I am thriving. Although he doesn't tell my mother, he's almost relieved that it's time for him to ship out. This, he admits to me near the end of his life. He tells me that the uncertainty of waiting to see whether he'll stay or go has been difficult.

Although remaining home was necessary, he has begun to feel guilty now that I am doing so well. He begins to think he's shirking his patriotic duty. This is no ordinary war. The Axis powers must be stopped; civilization depends upon it. And even though he wishes he might have gotten an exemption because of his war work, still he has come around to believing he can make an even greater contribution by reentering the Navy because of his skills.

My father knows that aircraft are essential to this war. He's read about the strategic missions pilots have flown off aircraft carriers in the Pacific, like the assault on Bougainville in the Solomons prior to the Marine landing. He's read up on Hellcats and Corsairs, the fighters used in the Pacific, so he'll be able to service them should he be assigned there. He's finished reading David Garnett's *War in the Air*, and he's thought about the strategic uses of aircraft in this war.

He's a seasoned sailor, and a good one, and he's skilled at repairing aircraft under the most punishing conditions. He's eager to do his share so that the war can end. Even so, he knows that serving on an aircraft carrier like the *Ranger*, as he imagines he will, will be an extraordinarily dangerous assignment.

For by the time he reenters service, my father has learned about the many aircraft carriers that have been sunk or destroyed. The United Kingdom's *Glorious*, sunk by the Germans, 20 aircraft lost, 1,207 dead. And then there are the carriers in the Pacific Fleet, some of which served alongside the *Ranger* in the war games my father participated in. The loss of these, my father feels deeply.

The *Lexington*, sunk during the Battle of the Coral Sea, 91 aircraft lost, 216 dead.

The *Langley*, crippled by Japanese dive-bombers, then scuttled, 34 aircraft lost, 16 dead.

The *Hornet*, sunk by the Japanese off the Santa Cruz Islands, 90 aircraft lost, 140 dead.

The *Liscome Bay*, torpedoed off Butaritari Island, 28 aircraft lost, 644 dead.

The *Wasp*, sunk off the coast of San Cristóbal Island, 76 aircraft lost, 193 dead.

The *Yorktown*, attacked during the Battle of Midway and sunk by a Japanese submarine, 90 aircraft lost, 81 dead.

But when my father learns of the loss of these carriers, and of all those who have died, he does not share the news with my mother.

House Hunting

1943

And this is the second story my father tells me near the end of his life that I have never heard before, a story that also changes my feelings for him. It's about how he tried to find us a better place to live.

After I hear this story, I hold the memory of it close. Here is a father who wants me safe, who wants to protect me, who doesn't want to leave me, who still isn't sure my mother can care for me, and who feels certain that if she lives elsewhere, closer to her family, perhaps, all will be well.

My father tells me that in the months before he leaves for the war, he now believes that Fourteenth Street, which he has taken to calling "the asshole end of Hoboken," is no place for a wife and child to live without a man to protect them. Fourteenth Street has become even busier, noisier, filthier, and more dangerous than it was when my mother and he married.

Though my parents were grateful to find this apartment before they wed, my father becomes determined to move us away before he leaves. There is the smell of coffee from the Maxwell House Plant on Hudson Street (the largest coffee roasting plant in the world) that never abates. The stench and the smoke from the factories nearby manufacturing metals, chemicals, food, leather, furniture, technical equipment, and foundry products for the war effort pervade the air and make my mother nauseated. The smells from the restaurant downstairs that seep into our living quarters. The racket from rivet guns at the shipyards that never stops, day or night. (Just one of the many docks—the Todd Hoboken Division—handles close to 8,000 ships and 34 million tons of goods during the war.) The blasts of the steamships leaving or entering port that startle me out of a sound sleep. The clickety-clack from the five railroad lines serving the city that can be heard day and night. The noise of the trucks that continually transport wartime supplies down Fourteenth Street to the docks where cargo is loaded onto ships. The tramping of the stevedores' and longshoremen's heavy boots that are heard late at night when the shifts change—the shipyards now operate twenty-four hours a day. The shouts from drunken revelers in the saloons on every corner that are heard until late-night closing.

My mother worries that one of the trucks carrying munitions will get into an accident and explode on our block. Although the U-boat menace in the Atlantic is supposedly contained, and although my father reassures her, my mother worries that a German U-boat will slip undetected into New York Harbor and torpedo one of the ships berthed at the piers at the end of Fourteenth Street. She worries the explosion will start a fire that will quickly spread down Fourteenth Street to our apartment.

My mother knows about the deadly 1900 fire at the piers near River Street—everyone who lives in Hoboken knows this story. A contemporary account published in the *Graphic* on July 21, 1900, reported that "in nine minutes the four piers, alongside which had been moored the pick of the North German lines, were aflame from end to end. Crowded with merchandise of every description, the dock buildings, light wooden structures, burned like tinder. Barrels of oil and spirits exploded, and spread the fire. . . . So sudden and startling was the outbreak that scores of the crews were imprisoned under the decks of the burning steamers. Comparatively few escaped."

The *SS Bremen, SS Main, SS Kaiser Wilhelm der Grosse, SS Saale,* and 27 other ships were destroyed in the conflagration that killed more than 200 people, some below deck; some on deck because of the fierce heat; and some by drowning. That day, the sky over Hoboken turned black with smoke. There is no reason why such a deadly fire, my mother reasons, can't happen again.

There is a saloon on the corner of Washington Street and Fourteenth, and another on the corner of Garden and Fourteenth, where servicemen on shore leave have a last fling before departing for battle. Beneath our apartment is an eatery frequented by dockworkers and servicemen, its location announced by a blinking red neon light that can be seen through the curtains of our living room windows, unlit, only, during blackouts. (And my first memory is of looking through the slats of my crib and seeing this light blinking on and off, on and off.)

All through the night, my parents can hear the sounds of carousing and brawling soldiers and sailors. And even during the day, Fourteenth Street is thick with servicemen on shore leave, awaiting the departure of their ships. They pour off vessels at the docks, looking for a place to drink away their pay, drink away their fears. They spend their money in the saloons and dancehalls that Hoboken is famous for.

"Fools," my father calls them. They are fools to be spending their last days of freedom so drunk and out of control.

Staggering down the street, several abreast, arms locked, they hawk every woman they see, looking for a goodbye fuck before sailing to Europe or the Pacific, places where men are dying in great numbers, places from which they fear they will never return. It has gotten so bad that my father doesn't want my mother to leave the apartment without him.

My father wants to move us south and west, away from the piers, the factories, and the city's major thoroughfares, and into Italian City. There, my mother will be closer to her parents, food stores, parks, and the Free Public Library on Park Avenue, where she takes me almost every day for some peace and quiet away from Fourteenth Street. She borrows books for herself to read, and some to read to me before I go to sleep. She settles me on the floor with a picture book while she reads the latest magazines. The first book she reads to me is *The Little Engine That Could* and it's a message of steadfastness and resilience that, I later think, she wants to convey as much to herself as to me.

But my father knows that finding another apartment during wartime will be almost impossible. Vacant apartments are scarce. Residential building was stopped when construction companies started building factories for the war effort. Not many people are moving: Women whose husbands are at war want to remain in a familiar home; they want their husbands to return home to the same place they've left.

On Saturdays and Sundays during these last months before my father leaves, he takes me with him as he searches for a new apartment. He figures he'll stand a better chance of persuading someone to rent a vacant apartment to him if he is holding me in his arms.

And although my father doesn't tell me all the details of his long and fruitless search for a better place for us to live, this is how I imagine it.

My father lugs my stroller down the stairs, comes back up to get me, carries me back down, and settles me in the stroller. He makes his rounds, staying away from neighborhoods beyond his means: the mansions on Castle Point Terrace near Stevens Institute of Technology, the exclusive Eldorado Apartments and the Yellow Flats on Washington Street where Hetty Green, one of the richest women of her day, has lived.

Instead, he searches through Hoboken's working-class neighborhoods, up and down First Street through Tenth, then up and down Garden Street, Park Avenue, Willow Avenue, Clinton Street, Adams Street, Jefferson, Madison, Monroe, Jackson.

He climbs stairs, knocks on doors, stops people on streets, talks to women in shops.

"Do you know anyone renting an apartment? I need a safe place for my wife and child while I'm in the service." Each query receives a negative reply.

Some people are polite and patient. Others are impolite and rude.

"What makes you think you're so special?" one superintendent peeking from behind a doorway snaps at him after he tells her where he's living and why he wants to move. "These days, you take what you can get, and thank the Lord for it," she says. My father doesn't blame her. He figures that, during a single day, there are many people like him disturbing her as they make their own rounds looking for a place to live.

When we come to my grandparents' apartment on Adams, we stop for a short visit. My grandmother is the superintendent there, and my father hopes someone will decide to move. This is his biggest hope. The widow who lives next door to my grandparents is hanging on to her apartment even though her son, who's exempted from the draft, is putting her up in his apartment a few blocks away for a few days a week and on weekends. But my grandmother can't evict her and she can't figure out a way to make her move.

After a cup of coffee for my father, and a glass of water for me, we move on. As the day approaches for my father's departure, in desperation he starts looking outside Hoboken. He pushes my stroller up the steep viaduct at the west end of Fourteenth Street and looks for places on Palisade Avenue, New York Avenue, and on Second, Third, Fourth, and Fifth streets in Weehawken. But his heart isn't in it, for he knows that if he finds an apartment up there, my mother and I will be too far away from her parents. And although Weehawken isn't really that far away, he can't imagine my mother pushing my stroller up the viaduct's steep incline after a visit to Hoboken, and he realizes that she'll be far more isolated and alone living there than she is on Fourteenth Street.

Whenever we pass Church Square Park between Garden and Willow on my father's peregrinations, no matter the weather, he takes me out of the stroller, lets me totter around and crawl up and down the steps of the bandstand while he smokes a cigarette, this park that he loves, so filled with memories from when he courted my mother. If there is anyone in the park, he asks the question he's been asking all day long, even though, by now, he knows what the answer will be.

"Do you know anyone with rooms to spare? I need a safe place for my wife and child to stay while I'm in the service."

He pushes me on the swings, but not long enough to satisfy me. Then he puts me back into my stroller and searches through a few more blocks before heading home.

Four

Secret Code

1943

On the day my father went to war, he decided it would be important to record his leave-taking in pictures. He tried to joke about it, telling my mother that if he "kicked the bucket," then she would have these photographs as reminders of their last day together. . . .

2004–2013

And this is as far as I get each time I write a draft of this book, and then rewrite it and revise it, one, two, three, four, five times, and more.

The day my father leaves for war.

Each time I come to this point in my father's story, I tell myself I need a break before I can move on. And so I pack up everything I've written. Make sure it's organized and labeled so that when I pick it up again, I'll know exactly where I am. I tell myself that I'll take a week off, or a month off, or two. It's the summer, after all. Or the dead of winter. Or spring. Or fall. A good time for a break from writing. And then I put the book down.

And then, for one reason or another—another book which compels me that I tell myself I must write, and do write; a valued reader who tells me she doesn't like what I'm doing and insists that I take a new approach to the work (I should get myself out of the work entirely, let my father speak for himself, she says); a major illness requiring a prolonged period of recuperation; or quite simply, a reluctance to begin again—time passes, and then more time.

And then, when I take up the book again, I begin, not with my father's leave-taking, but with doing more research or revising or rewriting from the beginning again.

I change the voice. I take myself out of the story. Or I put myself back into it. I decide that this is my father's story. I decide that, no, this is my story, too, the story of the child of a sailor, left behind when her father goes to war. I decide that I don't yet know enough about my father's tour of duty during the 1930s, or the war in Europe, or the war in the Pacific, or the home front during the war, or the effect of the war on the women and children left behind, or what the men were like when they came home, and that I need to read even more, take more notes, make more timelines, fill and file many more manila folders.

But no matter what I do on this round, no matter how hard I work, no matter how much I transform the narrative, no matter how much I learn, when I come to writing this very moment, the day my father leaves for war, I stop again.

This is the halting point.

This is the moment I cannot write beyond.

And, for the second or third or fourth or fifth time, I ask myself why.

Well, why *would* I want to recount (or perhaps even relive) the moment that I experienced as sheer abandonment? That moment when I was thrust by historic circumstances into the care of a woman who was unable to nurture her child? Why would I want to let the father who *had* taken care of me leave me? Why would I want to write of his leave-taking? Or about what happened to him during the war? And why would I want to write about what happened to my mother while he was gone? Or what I felt? Or what happened to us, to our family, when he came back? For these are the stories that I have lived with for nearly a lifetime, and perhaps they are the ones I am reluctant to write down, for in writing them, I will be forced to let them—and let him—go. And I don't want to let him go. At least, not yet. Not until I understand something more of the man. And the only way I can understand him is to move forward, plod on, and write those words that I haven't, yet, been able to write.

Still, I must and I *will* write beyond this moment. For this must be a work, not only of the *before*, but also of the *during*, and the *after*. And so, on this round, I tell myself, no matter what, I will push the story forward. I will write the leave-taking, the absence, and the return. For if I do not do this now, I have promised myself, I will put this book down and not return to it. I will, I insist, abandon this book if I cannot make it right. Still I know that what happened to us—and worse—happened to many other families. And this, finally, is what impels me to continue, for this is not only our story.

"It's time," my husband says, "for you to let this book go. We've been living with your father's corpse in this house for too many years. And it's beginning to stink. It's time that you bury him."

2014

And so, I begin, again . . . .

1943

On the day my father goes to war, he decides it's important to record his leave-taking in pictures. He tries to joke about it, telling my mother that if he "kicks the bucket," she will have these pictures to remember their last day together. And so he plans an outing to Castle Point in Hoboken. He plans to ask a passerby to take a photograph of my mother, and him, and me—the three of us, a family.

"Oh, Lou," she says, unable to say more. She can't fend off the terror of his leaving, as he can, with a witticism. She's never found herself able to tell jokes under the best of circumstances, although she usually does her best to laugh at his so he can feel good about trying to cheer her up, even if she doesn't think they're funny, and she rarely does.

Today, though, she can't laugh. All she can bring herself to do is inspect his uniform for pieces of lint that she brushes off in her final attempt at being the brave and supportive wife she's read she's supposed to be at this difficult time.

It's just like her, he thinks, tending to him in these last few moments, making sure he looks his best. And he *does* look his best. More handsome than ever in his dress blues. White sailor hat crushed at the brim precisely as it should be. The hat, though, cocked ever so slightly to one side in what might be construed as the defiant gesture of a man who will wear his uniform in his own way rather than strictly adhering to regulations.

"Don't be so sad," he says. "When I come home, we'll find a better place to live, I promise." As if her sorrow is because she'll be living on Fourteenth Street while he's gone and not something else.

They both think, but don't say, not "When I come home." "If . . . ."

"And don't you worry," he continues. "You'll be fine. I'll be home sooner rather than later. Sooner than you think, and then we'll see."

She turns away. These words echo his parting words on the day that they met.

"I'll see you," he waved and then said, "sooner rather than later."

But he knows, even as he tells her she'll be fine, that an ordinary day when he's away at work can be an agony for her, as she worries her way through her day's chores and tending to me, wondering whether, by the end of the day, he will return to her safely and unharmed.

And now? How will she stand it? What will she do during all those long months she'll have to spend alone? Listening to radio reports of faraway slaughters. Reading newspaper accounts of carnage too horrible to describe. Hearing gossip about the latest neighbor's husband who's died. How will she survive? And how will she stand not even knowing where he is?

But he'll worry, too, although he doesn't say so, he tells me years later, for she needs him to appear strong, needs to believe she's the one who worries enough for both of them, and that he can take whatever comes his way, no matter what. Yes, he *does* worry, he tells me, not about himself or what might happen to him, because he doesn't care about what might happen to him, but about her. About how she'll manage without him. About whether she'll be able to take care of me. About whether she'll get sick again. For she's fragile, this wife of his. Breaks down easily. Takes to her bed often. And he won't be there to make sure that everything is all right.

Still, she assures him she's fine now, and he hopes she's not pretending. His daughter is more than a year old and thriving. And he hopes she'll continue to grow sturdy and strong while he's away. And then his wife reminds him that long ago, when they first fell in love, they decided that nothing bad could happen to him because of how much she loved him, of how much they loved each other.

My father tells my mother, and he tells himself, that he'll be safe repairing aircraft. But he knows—and she knows—that there is no safety in this war.

Even if he's stationed, not on a aircraft carrier, as he suspects he will be, but on an island in the Pacific, there is all that ocean to cross before he gets there, all that time in open water when any Japanese submarine, any Japanese aircraft, can blast the ship he's traveling on to kingdom come.

And neither realizes, until he's long gone, that they hadn't gotten around to taking that last picture, that photograph of the three of us that will remind her of their last day together in case anything happens to him.

Instead, there is only this picture. A photograph my mother has taken of my father and me outside a stone building on Castle Hill, near the parapet where my mother once stood and watched the *Ranger* make its way up the Hudson. Near the place where my father told my mother he'd singled her out of the crowd as he stood, in review, on deck.

"She only has eyes for you, Lou," my mother always tells him. "When you're around, she acts as if I'm not there."

But on this day, I don't. On this day, a force field pushes me away from my father. No one has told me what is happening. And even if they had told me, I was too young to truly understand. So I experience this day before and beyond language. And to reproduce this moment, I can only imagine what it must have been like for a very young child to know that something was amiss, but to have no way to express or to understand what was happening.

My father is wearing his dress blues, and he's kneeling behind me, smiling his wide, handsome smile. I'm wearing a camel hair coat, hat, and leggings, a new outfit my mother has bought for me, together with the sailor dress I wear underneath, one of many my mother dresses me in throughout the war.

He's trying to hold me close. But I keep pulling away. And no matter how hard my father tries to get me to smile, I refuse.

This is the only photograph my father will have of the two of us throughout the first long months he'll be spending on an island in the Pacific. My mother will send it to him in one of her first letters. It shows me standing awkwardly in front of him. I look as if I suspect—no, as if I know—that something important and terrible is about to happen.

And there I stand, gazing into the far distance, unable to imagine a future without him.

* * *

A week or so before he leaves, my parents decide—and my mother suggests it, and this astonishes him—that they should work out a code he can use in his letters to let her know where he is.

"Why do you want to know?" he asks her.

"Because then I only have to worry about what's happening in one place," she responds, "and not about what's happening everywhere."

This task, devising a code so his wife will know where he is, comes as a welcome relief from the last few days they've spent together.

During the long nights before, they sit in silence at the kitchen table while I sleep in the next room. Not wanting to sleep, for sleep will separate them. Not wanting to talk, for in speaking they might name their worst fears that now must remain unspoken. Not wanting to plan for a better time after the war, for in so doing, each feared, but did not say, they would invite disaster.

Yes, figuring out a secret code will be a welcome diversion for this silence between them that has become unbearable. Still, it's not like her to want to know where he is, my father thinks. He assumes she would want to be left in ignorance, left to hope that he is safe wherever he is, rather than know for certain that he is, say, in the midst of a terrible battle. So, at first, he balks. But then he realizes that she won't hope he's safe; she'll fear he's lost.

Before they decide on the code they'll use, they buy a globe and a detailed map of the Pacific. This is a gamble, their focusing on the Pacific. But my father feels sure he's headed there.

On the day they purchase these items, they leave me with my grandparents and they travel into New York City to a map store on the Lower East Side that my father has heard about. The place—a dusty shop that before the war has done very little business—is filled with servicemen and their wives, intent, or so my father believes, in setting up secret codes of their own.

The journey home is difficult, for the globe they select is large, and the set of maps unwieldy, and they struggle their purchases onto the ferry that returns them to Hoboken. Still, these objects are necessary to ensure my mother's well-being while my father is away.

The code they devise refers to articles of my clothing and the price my mother has supposedly paid for them. They will communicate where my father is or where he thinks he is going.

My father will indicate the latitude of where he is in the first number he uses in his letter; the longitude in the second. The numbers will ostensibly refer to the price my mother paid for an article of my clothing or the amount my mother saved on it.

Because my father knows that referring to the exact longitude and latitude of where he is will be picked up by censors and blackened out, or worse, my mother and he decide to use a constant—the year of my birth, 1942, written "19.42" or "1942," depending—to disguise the number. The latitude and longitude my father is indicating will be the number subtracted from either number as he pretends to talk about the price of the item. If my father uses the words "grand total," the constant should be "1942." If my father is south of the equator, he will speak about the garment being on sale. If he is north of the equator, he will wonder whether my mother had paid too much. And they will refer, too, to their bank account—but no matter how many times my father explained this to me years later during those afternoons we talked about the war, I can't understand how this number figures into their secret code.

It is a simple enough code they feel sure will escape the censors. For what censor will care about a man asking his wife about the price of his daughter's clothing and telling her he thinks she paid more or less for something than she should have? And anyway, my father thinks, this will give my mother something to do besides worry.

Some time later, after my father leaves home, he writes the following.

Dearest Mildred, I cannot stop thinking about how adorable Louise looked in her brown winter coat on the day I left. I can't believe you found that outfit on sale for only $17.35, that is, if you're telling me the truth! Darling, you don't have to lie to me about how much money you spend on our little girl. On another note, I forgot to tell you that I deposited my last paycheck into our bank account before I left. So we have already saved the grand total of $1794.58 since we married! Dip into our savings if you must.

Love, Lou.

This message signifies to my mother that my father is stationed at latitude −2.07, longitude 147.42. At a dot on the map called Manus Island. In the Admiralties.

* * *

Beginning in August 1943, about two months before my father reenters the service, Pacific Fleet Commander Chester Nimitz and others devise a radical new strategy for fighting the Japanese in the Pacific. By now, the U.S. Navy is the most powerful in the world. And this strategic change will determine where my father serves.

The plan is to attack and conquer islands in the central Pacific, and to move, island-by-island, closer and closer to Japan. Attacking every island held by the Japanese would be impossible. Rabaul, for example, the most important Japanese base in the Pacific, is so heavily fortified that conquering that island will be far too costly in terms of lives lost. Instead, U.S. strategy now calls for capturing islands in a ring about Rabaul, thereby isolating it and rendering it ineffectual.

Once these strategic islands are captured, the United States will build forward bases—secure military bases from which tactical operations will be launched—on them. Teams of Seabees will dredge harbors and build airstrips and facilities (dormitories, hospitals, desalinization facilities, mess halls) large enough to support the huge number of men and machines it will take to launch offensives in the island-hopping strategy that, it's hoped, will drive the Japanese back across the Pacific and that will bring the Allied forces closer to and, finally, within striking distance of Japan.

The first targets in this bold strategic plan are the Gilbert and Marshall Islands straddling the equator. Another target is the Admiralty Islands. One of these forward bases will be built on Manus Island in the Admiralties, where my father will serve. From that forward base, a year after my father enters the war, General Douglas MacArthur's 7th Fleet will depart for the Battle of Leyte Gulf, in the Philippines, the largest naval battle of World War II.

The war against Japan in the Pacific is a war unlike any other. Troops fight on islands that seem to be nothing more than tiny specks in an azure sea, islands so far away from the U.S. mainland and separated from it by so many miles of ocean that ships can take months to reach them.

Amphibious landing vessels disgorge fighting men onto beaches, often without cover, where the Japanese often command high positions or are dug into bunkers underground. The Japanese are a formidable foe, skilled at fighting in impassable jungles, accustomed to subsisting on few provisions, committed to fighting to the death, and to the very last man.

Men fighting on these far-flung islands have to be supplied by vessels ferrying to and from supply ships that are subject to bombardments from both land and air. These ships transport everything necessary to supply a fighting force thousands of miles away from the mainland—construction equipment, food, medical necessities, airplanes, repair kits, clothing, as well as all the weaponry, ammunition, and supplies necessary to wage war. Often, because of high seas or heavy enemy bombardments, it is impossible for supply ships to reach these islands; then, the men fighting there are left to their own resources.

This is a war where men fight under the most difficult conditions—trying to gain ground from a beachhead devoid of cover; inching forward through jungle in intense heat and in pouring rain; trying to blast an enemy out from underground tunnels. This is a war where men fight for weeks at a time without relief from the scorching sun; where crews carve airfields out of jungle while they are under fire and pave them with crushed coral taken from surrounding reefs so that the control of the skies can be wrested from Japan. This is a part of the world where islands are covered with tropical rain forests and dense vegetation, filled with stinging and biting insects, and servicemen are often sickened by dysentery or malaria or wounds that will not heal.

And the war in the Pacific will become the largest naval battle in human history. By the time my father enters the war, there have been, among other naval engagements, the Battle of the Coral Sea, the Battle of Midway, the Battle of the Komandorski Islands, the Battle of the Eastern Solomons, the Battle of Santa Cruz, the Battle of the Bismarck Sea, the Battle of Kula Gulf, the Battle of Bella Gulf, the Battle of Horaniu, the Battle of Empress Augusta Bay, the Solomon Islands Naval Battles, and the Java Campaign and the Guadalcanal Campaign Battles.

When my father is called back into the service, the need for airplane mechanics is critical: The war in the Pacific has moved into a decisive stage. Airplanes launched off aircraft carriers to attack Japanese ships and bases unreachable by land-based aircraft, and airplanes deployed from forward bases on conquered islands, have become essential to winning the war in the Pacific.

* * *

My mother's knowing that my father is stationed in the Admiralties was good in one sense, for she was spared worrying about every other battlefield. But it was not good in another sense because it forced her into combing the newspapers she clambered down the stairs to buy each morning in Albini's Drugstore on the corner for news reports about the Admiralties. She'd sit with her cold cup of coffee, the sun streaming through the kitchen window onto her downturned face, and search its pages for a shard of information about what was happening in that remote place on the globe where the man she tried to keep alive by the sheer force of her love and of her need was stationed.

Had the Japanese bombed any transports a short distance away?

Had there been an attack on a nearby island?

How close were the Allies to invading Japan?

Were any Japanese still hiding on that island?

Would the westward movement of the Allies reverse itself?

And, what she worried about the most: Would he be moved from land to sea duty on an aircraft carrier where he would be in great danger?

If she gathered enough information, she hoped she could judge just how secure or how exposed her husband was and she could estimate just how many more months or years of this agony she would have to endure before he returned home and they could resume their life together. Still, she told herself, she was so far better off than so many of her friends whose husbands or sons had died, or whose husbands and sons were in combat zones.

Her husband was repairing airplanes. He was well away from the fighting. He wouldn't see action. He would make it through the war unharmed.

Still, when I imagine my mother during this time, I think she must have known there was no safe place for a sailor during that war, during any war. There was no way to outrun fate if it chose him, instead of the next man, to deliver a message from a commanding officer to the captain of a ship loaded with ammunition docked in the middle of the bay, a ship that would explode just as he was arriving, incinerating everyone on board and everyone nearby, leaving no remains for burial, nothing but a sea bag packed with your loved one's personal effects transported to your front door across a vast ocean and an entire continent, with a condolence letter signed from President Roosevelt

hand-delivered to you by a sailor in full dress uniform to place into an empty
coffin for a burial of a body that no longer existed.

"I am very sorry . . . line of service . . . entire nation . . . together with
you . . . proud of his . . . your grief."

Except for these moments in the morning when she inspected the newspapers, my mother tried her best to shut her ears to any conversations about
casualties and disasters and deaths that she encountered in her daily round
of chores, and to think, only, about what she had to do. It wasn't that she
didn't care about the war, my father said when I asked him about what he
knew about how my mother behaved during that time. It was that she cared
so very much.

It was easier, my father thought, for him than for her. She was so sensitive
to violence that, to endure the war, she made a rigorous schedule to give her
days form and substance. Early mornings: breakfast, straightening up the
house, dusting, reading the newspapers. Late mornings: food shopping,
lunch preparation. Early afternoon: excursion with me to visit a friend or to
the park. Late afternoon: a rest for us both. Early evening: food preparation
and cleanup, preparing us both for bed, reading me my story, putting me to
bed. Late evening: writing my father her daily letter, reading.

Throughout the time my father is away, my mother is one of the few
women in her circle who know where their husbands are serving, although
she can't say she knows where he is and there is no certainty that he'll remain
there for the duration of the war. And so as the battles progress westward
through the Pacific toward Japan, my mother worries that my father will be
plucked from what has been a relatively safe island and moved to an aircraft
carrier and, so, closer to the front lines, and so, at risk from the new Japanese
strategy of *kamikaze* warfare. His skills are necessary, for the invasion of every
island is preceded by aircraft bombardments, and the servicing of aircraft is
necessary in this war.

Still, as the battles in the Pacific move farther and farther away from the
Admiralties, and my father continues to serve there, my mother tells my father after the war that she privately rejoiced. But that she had to keep her
happiness to herself.

My father tells me that, in my mother's letters to him, she says that she
was grateful that she was far better off than so very many other wives who'd

lost their husbands, brothers, sons. But she confessed that she was living in a state of terror. She knew she was supposed to be brave. But she had to share her feelings with him. Did she have a right to her feelings because she was safe, she had enough to eat, had a roof over her head, parents to help with her child? Nonetheless, she said that even though she worried about him, she felt herself eroded by the grief of others, the grief of all the women she knew who'd lost their husbands, their brothers, their sons.

"The whole world," she wrote, "is awash in universal agony. Will it ever end?" And then she would apologize, for she wrote that she knew it was her job to keep his spirits up, not his job to reassure her.

On the day my father leaves for the war, my mother turns away from him. I remember standing between them, tugging at his trousers, peering up at him. I won't let him go. If I'm strong enough to hold on to him, he'll stay.

I'm wearing a sailor dress, the one my mother has bought for me for our last day together, turning her terror at her husband leaving during these last few days into a mad hunt for just the right outfit for our goodbye. And she's found the dress, after some searching, in New York City, at Macy's, where she's gone to shop a few days before, leaving me alone with my father.

He can't understand why she has to spend the day on such a foolish errand—for he doesn't care what I look like and to him I always look just fine no matter what I'm wearing. He can't understand his wife's concern with appearance, her need to shop instead of spending the time with him.

Can it be that she's practicing what it's like to be away from him? Or is she trying to show him that she's completely capable of crossing the Hudson River on a ferry without him, of taking the subway to Macy's, of finding the perfect outfit for their daughter, and of finding her way back home? Can it be that she's trying to prove to him that she will be just fine while he's away?

He's packed his sea bag with the only personal possessions he's permitted to take with him. A razor. A toothbrush. A change of underwear. Some extra linen handkerchiefs. There is nothing from his civilian life that he needs in the Navy. He has no favorite book. No well-thumbed family Bible. He has no totemic object—a coin, a pebble, a piece of ribbon from a special present, a lock of his wife's hair—like other sailors carry that they believe (wrongly, he thinks) will shield them from harm. And so he takes nothing from his

Hoboken life but the memory of my mother's lips pressed upon his in their last moments of her sorrow, and the memory of my hands grasping at his trousers, not wanting to let him go, wanting him to stay.

(And although my father insisted that he was not a religious man, and although the only time he attended mass regularly was years later when he joined a choir and became a soloist, he might have been wearing a scapula with St. Simon Stock on one side, and Our Lady of Mt. Carmel on the other. This scapula was, I later learned, given to servicemen to "shield them in time of danger" and to ensure that, if they died, they would be saved. And also, a sterling silver cross—a going-away present from my mother or his mother, perhaps—with the inscriptions "St Christopher protect us," "St Joseph pray for us." This, attached to one of his dog tags with a piece of wire. The dog tags with the attached cross and the scapula, I find after my father died, in a little box of his war memorabilia. But whether he wore these on the day that he left, or after, I don't know and can't say. Still, they tell a story different from the story he told me about not being afraid he was going to war.)

"Sooner rather than later," he tells my mother once again. He is, now that the day has come, eager to be gone. His wife, his daughter, belong to another life, a life filled with possibility, hopes, and plans. Once he dons his uniform, he is mired in the present. He will do what must be done. He will not hope for the best. He will, rather, hope that the worst will not happen. But not hope, really. For hope is something that belongs to another time. And then, what, if not hope? Resignation, perhaps.

He pries my fingers from his trousers. Opens the door. Walks through it. The door closes.

And then he is gone.

Command Center

2009

When I'm halfway through writing this book about my father, when I'm not sure I want to continue, not sure whether I want to revisit all my father's stories, I have a dream. By now, my father's dead. He's been dead for four years.

I'm lost and dazed and wandering through an island in the South Pacific. I've seen palm trees dotting the shoreline, an azure bay, a string of pulverized coral beaches, a stand of mangroves, and then a thicket of vegetation where I've been caught for hours. I don't know why I'm here, don't know what I'm searching for, but I know there's something important for me to discover on this island.

I'm sweating. I'm attacked by swarms of mosquitos. I bat them away, fearful of a dangerous bite. My body is lacerated from the knifelike leaves. My feet are sore and swollen. I've forgotten to put on sturdy shoes. My throat is parched. I need water. I look behind me to make sure no one is there, make sure no enemy is hiding. But how could I know there's an enemy hiding? I don't know where I am, don't know what to do, don't know how to take care of myself in this place, don't know if I can take care of myself here.

As I fight my way into a clearing, I see a score of old World War II veterans standing in a line to my left. They're in front of what I recognize as a mess hall, gathered there to eat their supper. But first they must take their quinine. A doctor stands before the entrance, dispensing tablets. He must ensure that the men ingest them before they can enter the hall: This is the only way to ensure compliance.

These vets aren't young. They seem to be in their nineties, my father's age just before he died. Have they been stuck on this island for more than sixty years? Did they choose to stay? Or have they been forgotten, overlooked, by those in charge of sending them home? Still, they seem in good enough shape; they're wiry, muscular, and tanned, though also craggy, scarred, and hunched over. Their uniforms—or what used to be their uniforms—are tattered. A few are bare-chested, wearing only shorts, the kind my father wears in a photo of him taken when he was stationed on his base (this base?) in the Pacific during the war.

One GI sees me, calls me over, asks, "Are you looking for your father? Your father is over there." He gestures toward a dock and a boat some distance down the beach from the mess hall.

"Go to him," the vet says. "He can help you. And maybe you can help him too."

I'm not surprised. Somehow I've expected it. Perhaps this is why I've come here: to find my father.

I walk down the beach, following the narrow sweep of sand. There's not much distance, here, between water and jungle, so I'm careful to hug the edge of the sea. I don't want to get lost, don't want to lose him now when he's so close, and the way to him seems clear enough.

As I come closer, I see that my father is at the helm of a PT boat. But he's not old and wizened like the other sailors. He's young, bare-chested, and beautiful. He seems to be about thirty, the age he was when he reentered the Navy during World War II for his second tour of duty after I was born.

This boat is heavily armed with torpedoes, machine guns, cannons, and rocket launchers like those I've seen in documentary footage of the war. I didn't know my father saw combat. So what is he doing at the helm of this boat?

"Climb aboard," my father says when he sees me. He doesn't say hello. Doesn't say he's missed me. Doesn't embrace me. Doesn't seem surprised to see me. Doesn't act as if my presence here on this island in the Pacific is out of place. Doesn't wonder how I've gotten here. He doesn't acknowledge that I've grown, doesn't think it's out of the ordinary that I'm now far older than he is. Doesn't tell me to go home. He seems to want me with him, and that's good enough for me.

"Make it quick," my father says, and none too nicely, his temper surfacing.

I stand by the boat, not sure I want to join him. Will it be more of the same? Him, commanding? Me, expected to follow his orders without complaint?

He tells me he's on a mission to attack some Japanese soldiers who hold defensive positions on a nearby island; it's important to flush the enemy out of their hiding places so an airfield can be built there. Once the airfield is built, he can do his job—fix damaged airplanes so they can return to battle.

My father is the only sailor aboard. I wonder how he can carry out this dangerous mission all alone. I've never thought of him as a hero.

When I tell him he's a machinist's mate and not a combat soldier, he scoffs and says, "They know I'm the man for the job." When I ask him where the island is located, he gestures at the horizon. But if there's an island out there, I don't see it. Like always, he's impatient; like always, I'm supposed to do as I'm told and not ask any questions.

I know I can't help my father: I don't know how to steer, how to fire a gun, how to launch a torpedo. I'm a timid creature, worried about what I'll see when I get to wherever we're going, afraid of what might happen to me, but more afraid of what might happen to him. I don't want to lose him, I don't want something to happen to him, although I fear it will. Still, I want to be with him, need to be with him, so I have no choice but to go.

"Are you coming or staying?" he asks.

"Coming," I say.

I start to climb aboard. But my father shoves the throttle and takes off full-speed-ahead before I'm safely inside. I don't fall into the water but cling to the gunwale of the boat. My father doesn't look back, doesn't know or doesn't care that I'm imperiled. It's hard for me to hold on, but I can't let go.

I've done my homework. I know what can happen to me if I fall off; I know what can happen to a sailor adrift alone in a waste of water in the Pacific. Men forced to abandon sinking ships could be lost at sea, attacked by sharks, go crazy, get shot by enemy aircraft, even if they have a life raft, so I know I must hold on.

I grip the gunwale firmly, shout to my father that I'm here, shout that I'm in danger, shout that he has to stop so I can climb aboard.

My father turns his head, nods. He hears me but doesn't slow down.

"I can't stop now," he says. "I have a job to do. You'll be fine," he says. "You can take care of yourself. You're a chip off the old block."

2010

I'm stopped at a red light on my way to teach in New York City. A bus pulls up next to me. On its side, a huge ad featuring war-weary Marines in jungle combat announcing a new TV series about the war in the South Pacific.

I've read about the series in the paper. I know I should see it. But by now I've looked at all the documentary footage about the war I could find and I don't want to watch any more. I don't want to view this series, no matter how excellent it might be. This one is based upon World War II memoirs I've read so I think I know what it will be about.

The truth is, I'm tired of this war. My husband has become so used to the sound of bombardments and explosions emanating from my study that he's started to call me Admiral Halsey. When he comes home from work one day, he comes upstairs, pokes his head through the door to my study, greets me, and asks me whether we're winning or losing the war, asks me whether my battle plan has been successful.

"There's nothing funny about what I'm doing," I say. "I'm trying to find out all I can about my father's war."

My husband apologizes. But his calling me Admiral Halsey strikes home.

I've set up my study as a kind of command center. Arrayed around me are books on the history of warfare. Topographical maps of strategic World War II battles. Books on air combat and on submarine warfare. Treatises on the effective use of tanks and flamethrowers. Illustrated articles about the most effective strategies for employing aircraft carriers in sea battles. Books about the war in the Pacific. Manuals on how to set up forward bases there. Reconnaissance photos of Japanese bases in the South Pacific. Lists of YouTube videos of the invasion of various islands, among them the one where my father served after the island was secured.

Whenever I've learned about a new battle, read about it, viewed the footage documenting it, I've thought about the battle and wondered what I would have done if I'd been in command, wondered how I would have strategized, wondered whether I could have foreseen what might have gone wrong.

I never picture myself in combat. I see myself, instead, in some command center, trying to find a safer way, faster way, to win this war.

"The Allies shouldn't have bombarded Berlin before the invasion," I tell my husband. "Bombed-out cities are easier to defend by the enemy. They provide all kinds of hiding places for defenders. Invading forces trying to flush out the enemy from bombed-out cities endured the worst form of hell."

"Eisenhower should have pursued his advantage after the landings in Normandy," I say. "The Allies lost time, lost countless lives that could have been spared."

"Why did they send men into winter combat wearing summer uniforms?" I ask. "The French did it. The Germans did it. And the Americans, too. Only the Russians understood how to fight a winter war. The French had boots with nails that conducted the cold from the frozen ground to the feet of those poor soldiers. The Russians wore felted boots, best for warmth and wet, best for snow. So many men froze to death. A waste of lives, and unnecessary."

"Why did the French think the Maginot Line could protect them from the Germans, especially because they never finished it? What hubris, what folly! And you'd think the Allies would have learned the first time the Germans invaded through the Ardennes that they might push through there again. But they didn't. They put their least effective troops there, assuming the Germans would never come that way again and then were surprised, and unprepared, when the Germans invaded through the Ardennes a second time!"

"Are you learning about the war or are you fighting the war?" my husband asks.

I don't answer.

"I think you're trying to stop the war," my husband says.

I've made a timeline, studied the progress of the war in the Pacific and elsewhere. My father's service as an Aviation Machinist's Mate on Manus and Los Negros in the Admiralties is but one infinitesimal piece of a gigantic narrative. I've written pages and pages of his story. But I have so much more to learn. There's no end to this war. And until I know everything (I know I can never know everything), I feel I can't continue.

My husband comes up behind me as I'm watching footage from the siege of Leningrad.

"Can you believe that Stalin arrested the very leaders who saw that city through its 900 horrifying days of siege by the Germans?" I ask. "They were accused of acting as mini-tsars and not communicating sufficiently with Moscow."

"I didn't know your father served in Russia," my husband says.

"He didn't," I say.

"Then why study Leningrad now?" he asks.

"Because it would be irresponsible not to," I reply. "All those people; all those deaths; all that time."

Yet the more I know, the more my father's story slips away from me even though I want this to be his story, and not someone else's.

My husband wants me to finish this book. He wants me to be finished with my father. He wants me to let my father go. He wants me to let this war go.

I know this. But I also know that he had his father with him during the war and so he can't really understand my obsession with finding out about what my father experienced while he was away so I can better understand him.

My husband knows that I want to—have to—write this book. But he thinks it's harming me. He's afraid I'm caught up in the past and that I'm not appreciating the present, my present, our present. We are at a good time in our lives; our children are grown and have made fine, happy marriages with admirable women; we have grandchildren we adore; we enjoy being together doing the simplest things—cooking, eating home-cooked meals, listening to music, watching one or another of our favorite TV series in the evening.

"Haven't you paid your dues by just being his daughter?" my husband asks me one morning after another of my restless nights.

"This is what I have to do," I tell him. And he's patient enough to dig in and wait it out.

The Sailor Who Flew Home on Wings of Air

1943–1945

On our kitchen counter in the apartment on Fourteenth Street, and later in the apartment on Adams Street where we move while my father is away (my grandmother, the superintendent of her apartment, having finally succeeded in evicting a tenant) there is a formal photograph of him in his dress blues, smiling and leaning into the camera, his clasped hands resting on one knee. On the coffee table in our living room, there is a photograph album with pictures of our family before my father ships out and the ones he sends home from the Pacific that my mother shows me every day. On my mother's bureau in a tin are the letters my father writes and sends to her as often as he can that she reads each evening after my bedtime story. At the end of each letter is a special message to me that my father prints in block letters. So that during the war, my father is not really home but he's not really gone. He is a phantom father who lives with us in the form of his photos, his letters, and my mother's stories about him.

There is the father I remember. And there is the father I stop remembering. There is the father in the photographs. There is the father in my mother's stories. There is the father I make up. But there is no real father.

"Do you remember the time we went to Lake Hopatcong with Daddy and you held onto his back while he swam?"

"Do you remember the time Daddy pulled you on your sled?"

"Do you remember your birthday party and how Daddy cut your cake?"

"Do you remember . . .?"

Each night before I go to bed, my mother presents my father's portrait to me to kiss. I like the feel of the cool glass that covers his portrait against my lips; I like the look in his eyes when I get close to him.

Sometimes, though, I resist. I can't remember my father; can't remember what it was like to kiss him, or for him to kiss me. And when I resist, my mother says that although my father is very far away, he can feel my kiss no matter what he is doing, and that when he feels it, he stops whatever he is doing and thinks of me. But if he doesn't feel my kiss, he worries about whether I'm all right. He might think that I'm hurt or that I've forgotten him, which isn't a good thing, because a man in the Navy working on airplanes is doing important and dangerous work, and it's work that must be done perfectly because men's lives depend upon it.

Each night before I go to bed, my mother spins the globe that stands on the kitchen counter next to my father's photograph and she points to the tiny dot in the middle of the Pacific Ocean where my father is stationed.

Each night before I go to bed, my mother reads to me or she tells me a story. And each night before I go to bed, I repeat the question I have asked my mother several times each day: "When is Daddy coming home?"

Like every other child whose father has gone to war, I am always asking my mother when my father is coming home. And like all other mothers, my mother has no way to answer that question truthfully. My father's tour of duty is for the duration of the war, plus. And there is no way she can tell whether he ever will, in fact, come home.

"Maybe by Christmas," my mother would say. And then Christmas would come and go.

"Maybe by Easter."

"Maybe by the Fourth of July."

Late in the war, worn down by worry and waiting, my mother stops answering my question. Instead, she makes up a story. She calls it "The Sailor Who Flew Home on Wings of Air." She invents it, I think, to ease the pain of my father's absence. But it doesn't ease the pain of his absence at all.

I cannot now remember precisely how my mother's story went. But when I think back to this story, and I try to re-create it from what I do remember, what strikes me now is how hard it must have been for my mother during those years. How hard it must have been for all those wartime women with children, missing their husbands, caring for their children, trying to make a safe space for them in a world gone mad with war. And so here is the story that stands for the story that my mother told me each night before I went to bed late in that war when my father was still away and when she couldn't be sure that he would ever come home.

My father, my mother would say, was far, far away on an island in the Pacific. An island so small, that from the sky it looked like a tiny leaf floating in a vast bowl of deep blue water.

The island was washed by waves, stung by rain, blown by whirlwinds. And it was hard to live there, even for the natives, because it was so hot and wet. There were mosquitos the size of hummingbirds. And scorpions everywhere. And in the water there were crocodiles. But my father knew how to take care of himself, so none of these scary things bothered him.

On the shores of this island were palm trees. And the people living there, who had lived there long before the war started, fished in the sea, hunted for wild boar in the forest, and grew everything they needed: sweet potatoes, coconuts, and bananas, and something called taro that my mother was sure I wouldn't like, and something called sago that could kill you unless you knew how to prepare it correctly, but the natives knew, so they didn't have to worry. And the natives from one part of the island traded with the natives from the other parts of the island. And those who lived on the land traded with those who lived on the water. And so all of them could always get whatever they needed.

The soldiers and sailors stationed on the island called the people who lived there "Fuzzy Wuzzies," although that was not their real name and it wasn't a very nice one. But they were called that because of how they combed their hair so that it stuck out in all directions.

It was very hot, so the people who lived there didn't wear many clothes. But they wore jewelry and other ornaments, some in their hair, and some through their ears, and others through their noses.

The children on the island learned how to swim when they were very young because some of the houses were built on stilts above the water. And they learned how to navigate the waters of the island in very small boats built just for them, even before they could walk. They were "water babies" and if I lived there, I wouldn't be afraid of the water either, and I would swim and sail a boat too, and cling to my father's neck and lie on his back as he swam through the water (like I did when we went to Lake Hopatcong before he went to war) like the little children did on this island.

My father missed us, my mother said, as much as we missed him. And he was as sad as we were that we couldn't be together. He wanted to live with us in our cozy little home with our coal-burning oven where he loved to bake potatoes until they were crusty on the outside and soft on the inside, and did I remember when he pulled pieces of the blackened skin off the potato to give to me as a treat?

And even though my father couldn't come home to us yet, my mother said, he dreamed that he could come home to us all the time, and in my father's dream, nothing could keep him from coming home. Not the war that wasn't yet over. Not his superior officers. Not the broken airplanes it was his job to repair that his crackerjack crew could take care of without him. Not the gigantic distance between us—an entire ocean pleated with waves, and the width of a continent ridged with mountains and crisscrossed by rivers. Not the violent storms of the Pacific that could blow a little boat way off-course. No, in his dream, nothing, nothing could keep my father from coming home.

And, my mother said, this is what my father dreamed.

Early one morning, my father awakened during a storm with the rain falling so hard from the sky that there was a river running through the Quonset hut where he lived. That morning, my father realized he was not just a sailor but also a man. And not just a man but also a husband. And not just a husband but also a father. And so he decided that he would find a way to come home to us for just a little while. For just long enough so I wouldn't forget him, just long enough so he could give me a kiss and tell me a story. Just long enough so he could have a home-cooked meal at our kitchen table and sleep in his own bed with his own wife for one night.

There were no airplanes for him to borrow because the ones on the base were always busy trying to find Japanese airplanes to shoot out of the sky, Japanese bases to bomb, Japanese boats to blow out of the water, Japanese submarines to destroy so that the war could end and my father could come home once and for all. And even if there was a spare airplane, he couldn't use it because the island was so far away that no airplane could fly all the way home. So, my father knew he would have to find another way.

My father knelt on his cot (there was too much water for him to kneel on the floor), clasped his hands, bowed his head, and prayed. My father was not a man who prayed for anything, my mother said. But this one time, he asked for God's help. And he vowed that if he got his wish, he'd never pray for anything again.

"Please, God," my father prayed, "give me wings so I can fly home to see my wife and little girl."

While he slept, my father dreamed of the great eagles that circled the sky above the island, and he dreamed of one of them swooping down from the sky, landing outside his hut, and waiting there for him. He would climb on the eagle's back, and they would soar over the sea and over the land, all the way to our apartment in Hoboken. The eagle would land on our fire escape, and my father would hop off, open the kitchen window, and climb through it to see us.

But when my father awakened, there was no great eagle awaiting him. So my father knew that his prayer had not yet been answered and that he would have to find another way to get back home.

One morning, a few days later, when my father got up from his cot and took off his tee shirt and stepped outside to enjoy the morning air, he heard a very loud rushing noise behind him. It was very early Sunday morning, well before "Reveille," and all his buddies were still fast asleep. My father "hit the deck" when he heard it because, at first, he thought it was the sound of enemy gunfire. But then he turned and saw a set of huge iridescent multicolored wings unfolding on his back like those on the archangels in the Michelangelo paintings he'd told my mother he loved so much.

Yes, these were the wings he had prayed for. But he never dreamed they would be so huge and so beautiful. And he thanked God that he had been granted his wish. But when my father reached back and tried to touch them, he couldn't feel them, because, my mother said, they were very special wings. They were wings of air.

Before anyone could awaken, my father ran away from his Quonset hut, out of his compound, and down to the slip of sand near the sea. He was wearing only his skivvies, my mother said, because it was so hot on this island, and he looked a sight, what with his uncombed hair, his morning beard, and all. And he ran down the slip of sand, and the wings flapped all by themselves. And before he reached the end of the beach, an updraft of air caught them and carried him skyward, high, high, into the sky. And he soared over the base, and over the landing strip, and over the hundreds of ships and seaplanes in the harbor.

With very little effort on his part—and this surprised him—just a tilt of his head up or down, or to the right or to the left, my father discovered that he could navigate through the atmosphere at speeds that were faster than the fastest airplane.

Down below him in the ocean, he could see aircraft carriers, battleships, and the trails of submarines skimming the surface of the sea. And he could even see airplanes below him, he was flying so high in the sky. And sooner than he thought possible, he saw land below him, and now he could see mountains and valleys and rivers and cities and towns and villages. And his journey to us, my mother said, didn't take very long, just a few hours, because he was flying so quickly.

My father was happy flying, for he had always wanted to be a pilot, not just a man who fixed airplanes that other men would fly. And the day my father flew home from the war on wings of air, my mother said, was the happiest day of his life. Not just because he was coming home to us. But also because he was flying.

My mother told me that my father would land on our fire escape and that he would open the window to our kitchen and climb in. Before he came into our apartment, though, his wings would disappear until he needed them again to fly back to his island because, she said, he couldn't stay with us very long.

She told me my father knew that after he had supper, and after he kissed me good night, and read me a story, and after he slept that one night in his own bed, he would have to fly back to where he came from, and that he would have to leave before I awakened.

He was a sailor, and there was a war, and his job was to fix airplanes, and that was what he had to go back and do. But we had all been given this great gift, this one journey, this journey home, and we were to be grateful for it, because no one else's father ever flew home from the war on wings of air.

At the end of the story, my mother reminds me that although the events in her story couldn't ever happen, and although they wouldn't ever happen, my father wished that they could happen. It was what he imagined all the time. Coming back home to us. And although my mother's story ensured that I couldn't forget my father, neither did it help me to remember him. Because remembering that he was once with us but that he was now gone was far too hard.

A Knock at the Door

1944

Nine months after my father ships out, he receives a letter from my mother. She tells him that, one night, after she puts me to bed, as she is sitting having a cup of tea in the parlor, writing her daily letter to him, she hears a commotion on the stairs.

At first, it doesn't concern her. She's used to servicemen mistaking the apartment's front entrance for the restaurant's next door. Usually, she just opens her door, leans out, and shouts down the stairs to set them straight. They thank her and leave, the ruckus stops, and she carries on with writing her letter, or putting me to bed, or doing her evening chores.

But on this particular night, the voices are so many and so boisterous that my mother is afraid to open the door to see what's going on. She hopes— wishes—that the servicemen will discover for themselves that the place they've stumbled into is not where they want to be.

But the noise doesn't stop. The men don't go away. They clatter up the stairs to our landing. Knock at our door. And then pound their fists on our door when no one answers.

My mother has no telephone, no way of communicating with anyone outside the apartment, except for throwing open the parlor window and calling down to passersby below. She hopes her neighbor on the same landing hears what's going on. But she's a woman living alone, her husband is away at war, too, so what could she do to help?

At first, my mother decides not to open the door. But the pounding gets louder, and she's afraid the commotion will wake me. So, she takes a deep breath, calms herself, and opens the door a crack to tell whoever is there that they're in the wrong place.

"There were a group of drunken sailors outside the door," she writes my father. "Five or six, I couldn't tell. Someone told them there was a whorehouse in our apartment."

Her tone is cool, measured, contained. No need to worry, my father tells himself, as he reads her letter at night in his Quonset hut by the light of a kerosene lamp. But here he is, thousands of miles away from her, on a tiny island in the Pacific, where he's powerless to protect her. And besides, whatever has happened is over and done with.

"I told them they were mistaken," she continues. "But they were so far gone they thought I was teasing them. And there were so many of them that they pushed their way into the apartment."

I can see my father putting down my mother's letter. Taking out a cigarette. Lighting it. Taking the smoke deep into his lungs. Exhaling. This is what he always does when he doesn't know what else to do.

"It took me a while to get rid of them," she says. "I pointed to your picture. I told them I was a respectable woman, married to a sailor. I said our apartment was most definitely not a whorehouse! I think it was Louise's crying more than anything I said that got them to leave. You know what a racket that little girl can make!"

And except for a few more lines about her father not feeling too well, and her stepmother's feud with the woman who lived next door to her parents, and her signature, "Yours faithfully, Mildred," at the end of the letter, that is all.

She has written nothing about whether or not she was afraid. Nothing about whether or not she's been harmed. Nothing else about what happened. Nothing to alleviate his fear for her; nothing to dampen his worry. And I wonder if he wonders whether the story she tells him is the whole story, if he wonders whether she's keeping something from him, if he wonders whether the unspeakable has happened to her.

2009

Years later, when I tell my husband what my father has told me about my mother's letter, he asks, "How old were you? Do you remember what happened? Do you think your mother was raped? Did you see her raped?"

All I can remember, all I think I remember, is a pounding on the door, a table overturning, a red light blinking through the parlor window, a cry, my crying, and that is all. But what my husband suggests makes sense. For how else can I explain that the sight of a blinking neon light fills me with terror; that every time some excursion takes me to the area around 42nd Street in Manhattan, I become agitated, can't wait to leave; that after one of my favorite cafés installed a blinking red light that said "Open" outside, I stopped going there.

1944

The next letter my father receives is devoted to the plans my mother is making for leaving Hoboken for an extended holiday. She writes that she is taking me to visit her stepmother's relatives, who live on a small farm in Rhode Island. And she is going without her parents. Her father can't take off work. Her mother can't leave the tenement where she's superintendent. My mother writes that it will be fun for me—feeding the chickens, harvesting the vegetables, playing with the animals, going for a swim at the beach. And it will be fun for her, too—getting out of Hoboken and away from all that dirt and noise.

She tells him the dates she'll be there, tells him not to bother writing her there because she doesn't know how long she'll stay, but not to write to Fourteenth Street, either, because she doesn't know when she'll return. She tells him to send his letters to her parents on Adams Street. They will send them on to her, or keep them, and she'll read them when she returns to Hoboken. Meantime, she'll write him every day.

I suspect that the plan my mother is making tells my father that my mother hasn't revealed everything in her earlier letter to him. Everything she won't say. Everything she can't say. Everything he needs to know but doesn't want to know. But maybe my father can't read between the lines. Maybe he doesn't understand that something far worse than what she described has happened. And there's nothing he can do to help her.

Because her trip doesn't make sense. He's been to Rhode Island with her. He knows she doesn't like her stepmother's relatives. When he's suggested taking me there for a summer holiday while he's away she's said she'd never think of visiting them without him. She's never traveled so far with their daughter on public transportation, not even as short a journey as visiting his mother in North Bergen. The trip to Rhode Island is a difficult and costly one on a bus, a ferry, a taxi, a train, and then another taxi to get to the farm. He's made it with her before so he knows. And now she'll be traveling alone with a suitcase and a little girl.

She doesn't want to get out of Hoboken for a holiday. She *has* to get out of Hoboken. This journey, he knows, is propelled by fear and fueled by terror. Isn't it that whatever happened to her makes her feel she must get out of Hoboken, no matter what? That she just can't stay in that place? That staying there is too much of a reminder?

Had one of them dragged her into their bedroom? Thrown her down on the bed? Torn her clothing? Had she cried out and punched his chest, scratched his arms, bitten his face? Is this what awakened their daughter? Her mother's cries?

What kind of a world is this? Where a man is forced to leave his wife and child to travel halfway around the world to help make the world safe? While his wife is left alone to fend for herself and their child?

But what I never know and never learn is whether I read more between the lines than my father has. And whether my father suspects, as I do, that something terrible has happened to my mother.

After my mother and I leave for Rhode Island, my grandfather decides that, when we return, it will be to another apartment, nearer to where he lives, and well away from the piers. And I deduce that the reason he does so is that he suspects something has prompted my mother's unlikely journey.

He enlists his wife's help. Together, they canvass all their relatives and friends. Do they know anyone who has an apartment for rent? Anyone who is moving?

My grandfather thinks my mother and I should live in the same building as he does. This way he can keep an eye on her, he can watch me on weekends, and they can share meals.

Through the years, I have heard the following story from my grandmother or from my father. But each time I hear it, it's different.

Next door to my grandparents lives a woman my grandmother can't stand. In one version, the woman next door has a son who lives nearby and she lives with him on weekends. My grandmother thinks she should vacate the apartment and go and live with him all the time so my mother can move next door, and she tells her this often.

This woman has nothing but contempt for my grandmother. Sneers at her on the landing. Throws the rent money at her when my grandmother collects. She doesn't believe a poor Italian woman should be superintendent. Intimates that my grandmother got her job because she's connected. And, no, she'll never leave her own place to go live with her son.

She and my grandmother get into a vicious fight. After, the woman smears shit on my grandparents' door. My grandmother takes the woman to court for harassment. My grandmother wins the case. The woman is forced to move out.

In another version, my grandmother is the instigator. "You know what a bitch she could be," my father says. He tells me my grandmother decides she'll force the woman to move. In this version, she's the one who smears shit on a door. In another, my grandmother does whatever she can to make the woman's life a living hell. My grandparents and the woman share a toilet, accessible only from each of their kitchens. When you use it, you lock the other person's door from the inside so you can have privacy. Unwritten rules stipulate that you do your business quickly, flush thoroughly, clean up after yourself, unlock the other person's door, leave, close your own door, and lock it from the inside of your apartment. But, my father says, the shared toilet was often used as a weapon in disputes between neighbors.

My father thinks that on a weekend when my grandmother knows the woman will be home for most of the day, she locks the woman's toilet door from the inside. Then she and my grandfather go around the block to my grandmother's relatives for the day.

All day long, he imagines my grandmother sitting and crocheting and drinking cool glasses of water. She imagines the woman, back at the apartment, desperate, breaking down the toilet door. She hopes this happens because then she can get the woman evicted.

What my father knows for certain is that the woman moves out and that my grandmother claims the apartment for my mother and me while we are still in Rhode Island. She writes my mother to tell her the good news. She says that she and my grandfather will move everything from our old apartment on Fourteenth Street to our new apartment on Adams Street while we're away.

"But," my father says, "what doesn't make sense is why your mother de-cided to move next to her stepmother. Because she and the old woman didn't get along."

On the day my grandparents move us, my grandfather borrows a truck and gets some of his stevedore friends to help him. My parents don't have many possessions so it doesn't take long to pack them and move.

After my grandparents set up our apartment, they travel to Rhode Island to accompany us home, or my grandfather travels there alone. My mother, it seems, is not up to making the trip home by herself. There is a photograph in our family album of my grandfather and me standing on the sidewalk in front of the house in Rhode Island just before we begin our long trip home. He wears his one good suit, his good pair of shoes. I am dressed in overalls and I am clutching a teddy bear. It's a gift from my grandfather, I think, for this is the first time it appears with me in a photograph. My grandfather is gripping my hand, pulling me close. He holds a large suitcase in his other hand, and he looks like a man who is determined.

In another picture, I am sitting atop the suitcase. My mother stands be-hind my grandfather and me, one hand on my shoulder. She is trying to smile. She is wearing an overcoat even though it's August.

Through all the years we live in Hoboken after we return from Rhode Is-land, my mother avoids Fourteenth Street. After my father comes home, whenever we return to Hoboken from a holiday, or a visit to my father's par-ents in North Bergen, my mother insists that my father drive down Willow instead of taking a left onto Fourteenth Street and a right onto Washington Street.

When I reach back in memory to that Fourteenth Street apartment, I don't recall much. The blinking of the neon light that shone in our parlor win-dow from the restaurant downstairs. The sound of laughter on the street late at night. The moan of a ship's horn as it leaves the dock. The clanging of a trolley as it makes its turn from Fourteenth Street onto Washington Street. The shouts of men in uniform carousing and dashing up and down the street. A plume of smoke from a ship berthed at a dock at the end of the street.

But there is this, too.

I remember grasping the sheet in my crib and sucking it. I remember clutching at my father's trousers as he walked out the door. And I remember awakening startled from sleep one night long after my father is gone.

There is a banging at the door. The sound of men's voices. My mother's screams. My crying. And I remember coming home from Rhode Island to an apartment that was entirely familiar but utterly strange. I did not know, but somehow sensed, that we moved because my mother and I had been exposed to great danger.

After we move to Adams Street, my mother has help caring for me from her father and stepmother. They help my mother shop. And they often cook supper for us all.

I want to believe that my mother regains her sense of safety by living next to her father. I want to believe that she no longer feels overwhelmed and overburdened. Perhaps my grandparents' help allows her sufficient time to rest when she needs to. Perhaps now that I am a toddler and speaking, and well on my way to reading, my mother feels more comfortable caring for me. Perhaps my father sends her letters reassuring her that he is safe, and so she feels she doesn't have to worry so much about him.

But how could it have been this way? There was the war, always the war. Whenever my mother bought a newspaper, there were photographs of the war. Whenever we went to the movies, there were newsreels of the war—men pouring off landing barges, wading chest deep through churning seas, guns held aloft; cities bombed to obliteration; hungry children holding their small hands out to beg.

Whenever we ventured out of the apartment, we would pass little shrines to the men at war. They were inside a shop window, or pasted on a wall, or hung on a fence. Rows of pictures of men in uniform, some bordered in black; photographs of battles; headlines torn from newspapers; lists of names. In front of them, little bouquets of flowers, crosses made from pieces of palm, votive candles. Affixed to them, little messages, some in English, some in Italian. "Johnny, we love you." "Nicky, come home soon." "Angelo, we're proud of you." "Luigi, we miss you."

And there was, too, what had happened to my mother. Although for years I told myself that my mother was fine, just fine when my father was away, and that we got along without him, what I didn't let myself see was that from then on, there would come a time when my mother would lapse into silence. When she stopped speaking, there would be quiet tears, burned food, long stares out the window, arms bleeding from her scratching.

"Are you all right?" my grandfather would ask her.

"Yes, I'm fine," she would answer.

But she was not fine. She was never fine. During the best of times, she was a woman who went through the motions of life, keeping a house clean and putting some food on the table and running an errand or two and reading a few pages in a book to a child and putting that child to bed. During the worst of times, she couldn't walk from one room to another without banging into the side of a door, or cut up a piece of toast without slicing a bit off her finger, or tell her father what she wanted him to buy at the store across the street without wringing the handkerchief she held so tightly in her hands, or tend to her child except in the most distracted way. And this is the wife that my father came home to.

Just a Very, Very Few of the Many, Many Who Have Died

2003–2005

Through the years, when my father talks about the war, he dwells not on what he did, although I learn something about his duties, and not on what he experienced, although he tells me something about what life was like for him, but on the deaths or disappearance of the men who served on the same base as he did on that small island in the Pacific. These stories, he repeated to me often. It was as if he could not get free of what he'd witnessed; as if he'd never moved, and couldn't move, and wouldn't move beyond those losses. It was as if he needed to recount the stories of other people's tragedies to preserve their memories, to honor their sacrifice, and to act as witness to what he had seen.

So every time I tried to steer the conversation around to his experience, he'd bristle, insisting he'd played only a minuscule part in a gigantic saga, and, instead, he'd tell me a story about someone else, even a story I'd heard before, or he'd talk about the carnage on other islands in the Pacific, or what the war in the Pacific cost in lives lost.

"If you're going to write about this," he said, "write about them, don't write about me. Write about all the men I knew who died. Write about all the people who died. But you have to remember," he said, "that the men I knew personally were just a very few of the many, many men who died."

1944

My father had arrived on Manus Island in the Admiralties in the Pacific some time after the initial American invasion on February 29, 1944, just as the fighting to take control of the island from the Japanese was ebbing. The invasion was called "Operation Brewer," and it was a part of the Allied island-hopping strategy—taking strategically important islands from the Japanese, ignoring others, and isolating some. Securing the Admiralties isolated Rabaul and rendered it relatively useless in Japan's attempt to stop the westward advance of the Allies across the Pacific toward Japan. Taking the Admiralties meant that the Allies would not need to defeat the Japanese on Truk, Kavieng, Rabaul, and Hansa Bay. The operation saved lives and shortened the war in the Pacific, for it meant that the defeat of Japan could take less time than had been previously anticipated.

A video of the initial invasion of Los Negros in the Admiralties that I have watched shows what my father himself did not participate in: B-24s and B-25s bombing the island; the first fighting force landing on the shore of Hyane Harbour near the Momote airstrip without casualties; the Japanese returning fire on subsequent landing craft and landing forces, killing two men; the Allies advancing toward a native house that has been destroyed; wounded men being treated in the field; the fighting force advancing toward the airfield.

After the fighting was over, 3,280 Japanese soldiers had been killed, 75 captured and 1,100 reported missing. Three hundred sixteen Americans had been killed, 1,189 were wounded, four were missing in action and 1,625 were evacuated. Twenty-two native people were killed and 34 were wounded.

Even as the fighting continued, the Americans began to establish a base of operations at Seeadler Harbor, situated between Manus Island and Los Negros, a 20-mile long fleet-sized harbor, where an island settlement had been—islanders had lived in habitations on stilts in the harbor. Soon after the invasion, the Allies improved Momote Airfield, the existing landing strip and airbase where my father sometimes worked. At first, there were only rudimentary lodgings on the base, only canned and dehydrated food available, a "pit latrine" and "Pee-Tubes," no laundry facilities. Seabees then built a gigantic harbor complex, military base, and forward station housing as many as 110,000 people on the jungle island, complete with pontoon dry dock, wharves, a seaplane repair base, a ship repair base, a landing craft repair base, wooden barracks, Quonset hut settlements, mess halls, movie theaters, a recreation center (that could accommodate 10,000 men on shore leave), hospitals, fuel and arms storage depots, a desalinization plant, a water treatment and supply system, a radio station, a POW stockade.

The weather was brutally hot (it could be 135 degrees in the sun), horrifyingly rainy and humid, with mosquitos, my father said, the size of bumblebees. More than a million bats would take to the sky at sunset and even the least squeamish man would cover his head. It was, my father said, far from paradise. Inhabitants of the base worried about contracting malaria, dengue fever, yellow fever, elephantiasis, and Scrub Typhus.

Seeadler Harbor provided anchorage for scores of ships (on October 8, 1944, for example, 621 ships of the Pacific Fleet were at anchor, carrying some 100,000 troops) and sufficient space for hundreds of aircraft (on October 8, 1944, 444 aircraft were on the Pityilu airfield where my father sometimes worked).

My father was a member of an ACORN (Aviation, Construction, Ordnance, Repair, Navy) unit, responsible for servicing PBYs, the aircraft sent out on "Dumbo hops" to rescue downed pilots and their crews, and B-24 Liberators, the most important bomber at the time.

The Admiralties were strategically essential to the defeat of the Japanese. The airfield on Pityilu Island alone averaged seventy reconnaissance and bombing flights a day. And the base was used as a launching point for many attacks on Japanese forces throughout New Guinea and the Philippines, including the Battle of Leyte Gulf in the Philippines. During the war, a million or so Allied servicemen came through this base on their way to operations in the Pacific. Scores never returned, for the fighting in the Pacific was brutal.

After my father dies, I find a set of photographs in his jewelry box I've never seen before from the time he served on Manus and Los Negros in the Admiralty Islands. They aren't pasted neatly into our family photograph album but shoved into an ordinary envelope and kept in a private place. These are the photos my father had never sent home, that he'd never shared with my mother and me. These are his private, and perhaps most meaningful, mementoes from the war. Thumbed through, it seems, many, many times. Taken out, during or after a day's work, and stained, on their edges with the ever-present grease on his hands. Photos of the men my father served with: bunkmates, pilots, crewmembers, acquaintances, friends.

Group photos of the men my father lived with and worked with. On the edge of the bush. In a clearing. In front of the commissary. Drinking beer. Chowing down. Clowning around. Relaxing next to a piece of heavy equipment. A few photos of him alone. One, shirtless, in the cockpit of an airplane he's working on. Another, of him peering out at the camera from behind dense foliage. Another, of him standing, wearing shorts, in front of his Quonset hut. Another, of him in a jeep.

A view of the Momote Airfield landing strip, taken from the air. A view of a ship in dry dock in Seeadler Harbor, again taken from the air. One, of the habitations of the indigenous people of Manus Island. One, of the interior of his Quonset hut—cots, mosquito nets, photos of naked women pasted on the ceiling above some of the other sailors' cots.

A photograph of seventeen men—my father's bunkmates, a note says. Most are shirtless and hatless; the island's heat is searing. A few smile for the camera. The rest of the men look grim, war-weary. Their names are printed carefully on the back of the photo. And a note penned in my father's hand stating that he has heard that the man in the second row all the way on the right is missing in action (and presumed dead), although he might not have been the man who died; it might have been his brother, for he, too, was serving in the Pacific. A photograph of three pilots standing before a U.S. Navy aircraft; on the back, the inscription, "three friends of mine."

* * *

The sailor in my father's Quonset hut who bunked right next to him had gotten married just before he shipped out. One night, he wanted to write a letter to his wife, only there weren't, as yet, any lamps to write home by.

So, like the other men in the hut, his buddy goes outside, puts sand in a bucket, pours gasoline onto the sand, sets the gasoline ablaze, and sits and writes to his wife, using the light from the gasoline fire. But the flame sputters and the man isn't thinking and he pours more gasoline onto the fire. And it flares, and the flame follows the trail of gasoline back up into the container the man is holding. And the container of gasoline explodes. And the man goes up in flames.

My father is outside, at some distance from him, smoking. When the container explodes, my father ducks for cover. Then he dashes back into the Quonset hut, grabs a blanket. Smothers the flames. Carries him toward the hospital. Sees a bus passing by, stops it, fights the driver and commandeers it. Drives the bus fast to the base hospital.

My father tells me his buddy survives, he is badly burned, but his genitals are so disfigured that he can never have sex again.

I think about this buddy of my father's, who, if he had not been serving in the military, if he had not set himself on fire writing a love letter to his wife, would have returned home to a woman who loved him and missed him. Who would have sired the children my father told me he hoped to have after the war. Who would have set up a little fix-it shop in the small town in Vermont where he came from. Who would have made enough money to live the quiet life he'd dreamed of, sitting on his back porch on warm summer evenings drinking iced tea, going hiking on Sundays in autumn, teaching his kids how to ice skate on a local pond during frigid winters.

In my father's nightmares, there is this man, this fire, this explosion, this man on fire, the smell of his burning flesh, the sight of this man's skin falling off his body.

"I probably should have let the poor bastard die," my father says. "After the war, his wife left him. What he had after the war was absolutely nothing. I didn't hear from him much and then I didn't hear from him at all, so I can't tell you what else happened to him stateside. And all because we didn't have lights to use when we wanted to write home."

* * *

My father tells me of a squadron of pilots sent out on a nighttime reconnaissance training mission in obsolete one-seater fighter planes, all but one without radios. The plan was that the plane with the radio would lead, and that the others would follow.

"A fool's plan," my father said, "and it was a fool who gave the orders for the plan." Everyone knew this was dangerous, but everything during the war was dangerous. But they knew it was more than dangerous, it was stupid. Knew the order should never have been given.

Still, the men were sent out. It was hard, my father said, watching these men climb into their planes, knowing they were bound to die because they didn't have the right equipment, and that they would be dying for no good reason. He knew he couldn't stop it, although he'd tried to stop it, tried to tell those responsible that sending those planes into the air without a way to communicate was just plain wrong.

When the pilots took off, the weather was clear. But when they returned, the airstrip was fogged in, which often happened at that particular time of year. Without radios, they didn't know where to land. In the fog, it was impossible to follow the lead pilot who had the radio.

When the fog set in, my father and some of his buddies didn't wait for orders. They lit the runway with flares. Set a giant flashlight at the end of the runway to light the pilots' way home. But the pilots, all but one of whom were rookies, panicked.

One pilot came in too fast and smashed his plane into the ground. Other pilots turned their aircrafts over, unhooked their safety harnesses, fell out of their planes, and parachuted out before their planes crashed into the bush or dove into the sea. After, there were search parties and crews sent out to find and pick up the pilots and any debris they could find. Some of the pilots were found. But not all of them.

"I think about those men all the time," my father said. "I think about the good they might have contributed to the war had they survived. And what they might have done had they survived the war. I don't know what their families were told. Probably some dumb ass thing like 'killed in the line of duty.' I think about what it must have been like to have been married to one of those men, and to have gotten that telegram, and to not know that your husband's death was useless."

And there were all those men my father told me about who went out on bombing missions and didn't return. Missions to Woleai in the eastern Carolines. To Biak in the Schouten Islands.

A plane carrying a new kind of bomb with a proximity fuse explodes in the air soon after takeoff.

A pilot's plane is hit by gunfire from a Japanese Zeke fighter plane.

On a bombing run to Yap Island in the western Carolines, two planes collide and fall into the sea, all men aboard presumed dead.

A photograph of two palm trees. Two fighter planes on a tarmac. Five men in the distance, standing. They are looking at a mushroom cloud in the middle of the photograph. A photograph taken by my father on November 10, 1944, a dreary day, while he is working in an open hangar, fixing an engine.

He hears a stupendous blast, turns, and sees a mushroom cloud in See-adler Harbor just across the bay from where he's working. He grabs his camera, takes the photo, one of very many taken by men stationed there that document this tragedy.

Within seconds of the blast, the cloud reaches thousands upon thousands of feet into the sky (7,000 feet, my father later learns). He thinks, at first, that the Japanese have dropped a new kind of bomb into the harbor. At the time of the explosion, the harbor is a docking station for more than 200 ships, although a month before, in October, there had been close to a thousand ships there, preparing for the Battle of Leyte Gulf in the Philippines.

My father learns much later that the *USS Mount Hood*, an ammunition depot, moored in the midst of the Seventh Fleet Service Force and carrying more than 3,800 tons of ammo—bombs, projectiles, rockets, depth bombs—has exploded, killing all 350 men on board and killing and wounding many more, some thousand in all, who were on other vessels in the harbor or on shore. Other ships were also destroyed and many others were damaged.

Some of my father's buddies think a midget Japanese submarine has tor-pedoed the ship. That the men on board should be awarded Purple Hearts. An official report rules out the enemy submarine and determines that the explosion was an accident, the cause of which could not be determined. My father, who hasn't seen the official report, wonders whether all these men have died because someone has been careless.

"People get lazy," my father says. "They don't follow regulations."

My father has seen crews loading and offloading ammunition haphazardly on other ships in the harbor. He's seen napalm stowed in shacks on decks. He's even seen men smoking in boats alongside ammo vessels. (And the official report, which my father doesn't read, but which I do, lists unsafe practices that the board of inquiry discovered: boosters, fuses, and detonators stored together; napalm gel stored in open wood and tar-paper huts on deck; fire hoses not laid out; smoking in the vicinity of flammable materials.)

My father worries that my mother will read about the explosion in the newspaper and worry about him, so he writes her a letter and tells her he's fine. Until she gets the letter, she will be terrified, he knows. But there's nothing he can do about that.

(There is a news item, and my mother does read it, and she tries to keep herself from worrying. But she knows that my father sometimes swims in the harbor when he gets overheated, that he sometimes takes a boat out to a supply ship to get supplies, and she's sick with fright until the letter from him arrives.)

And my father thinks, too, about the families of all those who have perished who will also be awaiting word. But the news they get will not be good news.

For a time, my father and his buddies wait for human remains to wash ashore. They hear that pieces of bodies have landed on the deck of the liberty ship *William McGuffey*. And if the body parts float ashore, it will be their duty to collect these remains and give whatever they have recovered a dignified burial. But none are ever found.

The only thing found, my father hears, is a badly damaged signal book. In time, everyone realizes that the force of the blast has been so great that there couldn't be any remains of the men on board the ship.

"Incinerated," my father said. "Nothing left of any of them. I stopped what I was doing, and stood there, and watched as hundreds of men died in an instant. The only good thing you could say was that they didn't know what hit them."

When my father is ninety-one and beginning to slip into dementia, and I am trying to collect his wartime memories before they disappear into the ether of forgetfulness, this is the story my father tells me every single day. That he stood and watched helplessly as hundreds of men like him turned to smoke and ash.

Rage

2005

On a sunny spring day during the last months of his life, I arrive at the nursing home where my father is now living and I'm told he's in the garden playing checkers with one of the aides. The garden is his favorite place on a warm day. It's in a courtyard bounded on three sides by the brick buildings where the elders live, some in apartments, and some, who need more care like my father, in hospital-like rooms. I find him there often, either sitting alone, appreciating the newest blossoms, playing checkers with an aide, or talking war stories with another World War II veteran, a man he calls "The Admiral," who always has a map of an important Pacific battle splayed on the table before him.

The aide he's playing checkers with today knows how to handle my father. Whenever he won't take his medicine, use his walker to get to the dining room, or change his clothes, she's the one who's called, and he does what he's told, "just for you," my father says. During my meetings with her, she tells me how delightful he can be. How he makes the other patients laugh by pretending to jog in place while holding on to his walker. How he proposes marriage to the nurses even though he's still married. ("My wife doesn't count," he tells them. "She never comes to visit."). How he's the first to volunteer during afternoon karaoke sessions and how he still has a fantastic tenor voice. And I think, "Delightful to you, yes, but not to me."

This reminds me of how, when I was a girl, I was always told that my father was a charming man. And he was always charming to others when people outside the house admired him. Admired him because he sang well. Because he helped his friends fix whatever was broken. Because he risked his life as a fireman. Because he was a good worker.

I pause for a moment outside the door to the garden and watch my father playing checkers. I want to go to him but I want to delay my entrance, too. I like seeing him happy and I don't want to interrupt his good time. But neither can I tell which father awaits me. The story-telling father I had for such a short time. Or that other father, the one for whom I can do nothing right.

My father smiles at the aide. He picks up one of her checkers and shows her how to beat him. I am astonished that he helps her. I am baffled by his joy, knowing that nothing I can do will elicit such a smile. Where has this man been hiding? Why have I never known him? Why did he keep this man hidden from me? Is this the man my mother married? The man I knew before my father went to war?

"After you see him," my husband says, "you look like a beaten dog that's sidled up to its master trying to win his love."

I gather my courage, walk into the garden, go over to him, and kiss his blotchy cheek.

"Can't you see I'm busy?" he asks, brushing me away.

I go to his room to wait for him there. The aide stays with him, neither of us wanting another scene. When I see her later that day, she says, "Honey, it's got nothing to do with you. It's just his disease," although no one at the nursing home can figure out what that disease might be.

"It has everything to do with me," I say. "It's not his disease. It's him."

When he returns to his room, my father says, "You still here? I thought you'd gone home." The aide tells him she has to tend to another patient. Asks me to settle him in bed for a rest.

I reach for him.

"Don't touch me," he says. "You get out of here. You kidnapped my wife. You put me in this motel where they're starving me to death. I know what you want. You want my money."

My father grabs me. He's old. He's weak. He can't hurt me. But when I try to push him away, when I try to get away from him, I can't.

"Nurse," I shout. "Nurse."

The nurses and aides know about how my father can turn on me so that it takes three people to pry him off me. Three of them to wrestle him into his bed. Three of them to hold him down while another nurse, a very strong woman, evades whatever he might have in his hand (a pen, a fork, a knife), takes the syringe and sticks the needle into his arm or thigh, presses the plunger down, and sends him on another trip to oblivion.

"Has he been like this often?" a nurse once asks.

When things don't go his way in the nursing home—and they rarely do—he pulls the sheets off his bed. Upsets his tray. Rips up his flowers. Throws a framed photograph across the room. But after one of his "moments," as the strong nurse calls these episodes, he becomes contrite and tractable, "the sweetest of sweets," she says, and he stays that way until his next "moment."

"Worse," I say, remembering smashed crockery, overturned furniture, broken clocks, days of my avoiding him, days of silence, days of his trying, and failing, to repair what he'd destroyed. To the nurses, it's a case of senile dementia. But to me, it's more of the rest of my life.

1949–1963

It begins with a litany of swearing.

"God damn it to hell."

"Son of a bitch."

"Jesus fucking Christ."

And then an outpouring of rage.

"Nobody appreciates me."

"Everyone takes advantage of me."

"What am I? A piece of shit in my own household?"

"Why is it always me who doesn't get any appreciation? I work my balls off, and do I get any thanks for it? No. Only disrespect. Ingrates, the lot of you."

By now, my mother is hovering. I have found a safe enough hiding place behind the couch, under the kitchen table, in the corner of the dining room behind a chair.

The shouting becomes louder. It's time to plan my escape. Up the stairs to my bedroom, where I tug the bureau in front of the door—by now there are no locks on the doors in the house, even the bathroom door, for I've tried to protect myself behind a locked door one too many times for my father. And although he always threatens to break down the door to get at me, and I know he could, and I know he would, still it seems far simpler for him, I suppose, not to have to put forth so much effort, and so he pries the locks off our bedroom doors, one at a time, and then, the lock off our bathroom door, for that's where I go to climb out onto the sloped roof outside the window where he cannot get at me.

Sometimes he's satisfied with throwing things. Plates. Knives. Forks. Saucepans (with or without their contents). Sometimes he turns over all the chairs in the house. Sometimes he opens dresser drawers and tosses all the contents on the floor. Sometimes he is satisfied with breaking things or ripping things apart. Crockery. Chairs. Books. Magazines.

Sometimes it goes on for minutes. Sometimes, hours. Sometimes, as in the time before he went into the hospital near the end of his life when he went on a rampage no one could stop, for two days. Two days, never more, as if his rage has an internal time clock and two straight days of oaths, threats, imprecations, and the heaving of furniture and breakable objects satisfy some inner need or compulsion or because, by the end of that time, he's exhausted himself and unleashed all the rage he's trapped inside, at least for now.

If I'm not quick enough, he catches me, tries to wrestle me to the ground, punches my arms, my hips, my legs, but never my face. As out of control as he seems, he's not *that* out of control, for he knows that if he punches me in the face he'll be found out. After, for a week, two weeks, maybe three, depending, I wear long-sleeve shirts and dungarees, even in summertime.

The only one who tries to stop him is my grandmother, my mother's stepmother, who lives with us in the suburbs where we move after my grandfather dies. Does my mother not try to stop him because she's not strong enough? Or does she know that if he comes at me, he'll leave her alone?

Each time he catches me, I vow it will be the last time. Each time he catches me, I vow I'll kill him before I let him get his hands on me again. I plan how I'll do it. I'll wait until he's asleep. Get a knife. Creep into his bedroom. Slash his throat. Thrust the knife into his heart.

Once, he comes at me with a knife. I think it is the end. But my grandmother tugs at the back of his shirt. Distracts him. He turns. And I sprint away, out the door, down the street, not knowing, or caring whether he's plunged the knife into the chest of my protector. I am too out of my mind with terror to care.

When he becomes a fireman, soon after we move, every time there is a fire I hope he'll die. I see him standing on the roof of a building, burning. I see him cowering inside a building, burning. I see him crouching behind a building, burning. I see him die a thousand deaths and more. But still, he does not die.

After his outbursts (for this is what my mother calls them), he is quiet for a day, a week, a month, or more. After, my mother's nervous hovering. After, my grandmother's agitated watchfulness. After, my numbed exhaustion.

After, no one talks. After, a preternatural silence settles onto our house. After, my mother and grandmother clean up the mess he's made. I am asked to help. But I refuse. For after, I am free, at least temporarily, to be by myself, go my own way, to read without interruption, but whether I really read or whether the words only pass beneath my fingers as I move them across the page without making their way into my brain, I cannot say. For after, it is as if I am not there.

It is hard, this setting of things to rights in our household. Sometimes repairs are necessary, to crockery, to furniture, to a handrail yanked off a wall, to a deep gouge in the top of a coffee table, to a clock that has ticked the seconds of our lives. My mother and grandmother work and work. My father tends to repairs as calmly as if my mother has asked him, say, to fix a handle that has come loose on a kitchen cupboard.

And after, my grandmother puts her finger to her lips to tell me that now is the time for silence unless I want it all to begin again. For even she seems to believe that it is all because of me. That if I don't do something, or that if I *do* do something—and what those somethings are, I never can figure out— then it won't start or then it will stop, then it won't happen again, then our lives will be normal, like other people's lives. Then there will be no shouting, no hurting, no breaking, no setting things to rights, no repair, and no need to buy cheap plates at yard sales or 5 & 10s every few months or so.

After a period of silence lasting a day, a few days, a week, or sometimes longer, my father begins answering some of the questions my mother asks. "What would you like for supper?" "Can I get you a cup of coffee?" "Are you sure you wouldn't like a scotch and water before supper?" "Would you like me to set out a fresh pair of pajamas before you go to bed?"

For a time, my father's rage is spent, and it will take him a month, or two, or three, to build up another, or the same, store of abuses. For a time, I am safe. Or as safe as I can be. For a time, he will leave me alone, or ask me what might be innocuous questions. "Did you help your mother clean?" "Are you doing well in school?" "Did you deal with the mess in the basement like I told you?" Questions he wanted the answers to, not questions that would elicit answers that would become the provocation for a flung cup of coffee, an overturned chair, a knife plunged into a tabletop.

Still, there was no telling how long it would take before it started all over again. During the best of times, life felt like trying to balance on an ice floe that was racing toward a waterfall.

Then would come a time—and these were also unpredictable—when, exhausted by the concentration it took to fathom her husband's whims, to anticipate his desires before he even knew they existed so he would have no cause for displeasure, to tend to her family's needs for food, clean clothing, attention, which, no matter how hard she tried, she couldn't provide, at least not always, or rather, not very often, my mother would lapse into one of her periods of silence. Which would sometimes precede one of her periods of depression. Which would sometimes precede one of her periods of catatonia.

Was this particular silence only a prelude to quiet tears, burned food, long stares out the window, arms bleeding from her scratches? Or a more serious silence when, if it was summer, we would be gathered up with some of our clothing and driven, by my father, to our relatives in Rhode Island? Or if it was winter, and we were attending school, and if my mother's depression was a bad one, we would try to ride it out, like a bad storm that kept us inside the house without much food to sustain us.

My life in that house, at that time, from the outside, looked ordinary enough, I suppose. I left the house at regular times to go to school and returned predictably, at the end of the day, to see if my mother's condition was the same, or better, or worse. I could not stop along the way to linger ("Did you come home right after school to see how your mother was doing?"), except for a few moments when the horse chestnuts fell to the ground and I smashed them open and tried to pry the shiny nut from its green protective coating.

But if you looked more closely, you'd have seen that my progress to school was slowed by hot tears. Or that on a day of torrential rain, I wasn't wearing boots or carrying an umbrella, for I had neither, because my mother hadn't bought them and we had to "make do" with what we already had in the house, which didn't include appropriate outerwear, for my mother believed we shouldn't leave the house when it rained, or if it was going to rain, or if it might rain, even if we had to go to school.

After, when I returned, I would find her where I'd left her. Sitting in her rocking chair, clutching her cup of coffee, rocking back and forth, back and forth, staring off into space, wrapped, still, in her old pink chenille bathrobe, which she'd take off to put on a housedress just before my father came home. For no matter how bad she felt, my mother would force herself into proper clothing before his return, for she knew that if she didn't there would be trouble.

She might try to put a meal on the table at the end of the day if she wasn't really bad. A can of Campbell's soup, diluted with water (the milk was sour). Two freezer-burned sausages for the four of us. Frozen TV turkey dinners barely heated through. My grandmother, though, made us bread or pizza that we would eat for breakfast, lunch, and dinner. The bread, plain. Or with butter and jam. Or with tomato smeared on top. Without my grandmother's bread and pizza, we would have starved.

2009

The night after I pen this description of my father's rages, I awaken from a dream in the middle of the night, heart pounding.

My father, dressed in a black fireman's uniform, is attacking me. I am throwing the pages of this book I am writing before him to protect myself. But the pages, small white things with scratchy, barely legible writing, can do nothing to protect me.

He continues his assault. I continue to mine the ground between us with my words. Still, they don't stop him. Still, he keeps coming. Until, at last, I decide that though these words of mine are not now, and perhaps never have been, sufficient to ward off his blows, they are my words, not his, and I will not throw them his way as a defense or to try to please him.

"Whatever you do," I say, "won't stop me."

When I stop ripping the pages from my book, stop destroying my work, stop trying to defend myself against him, my father turns and lumbers away.

It is not that I am free of him. It is not that he won't hurt me again. It is, instead, that I have decided that, harm or no harm, I will write beyond him. I will not take what I write and offer it up to him in peace, protection, rage, or honor. No matter what the price, I will continue. And he knows that he cannot stop me.

1945

When my father comes home from the war, he worries that this rage in him that has been mounting throughout the war will show itself when he gets back home. It seems to come from nowhere, and it turns him into a man he doesn't recognize and can't control. Can't control, he sometimes admits to himself, because he doesn't want to. This other man, unlike him, is invincible. He takes no shit. He clears the room. He scares the living hell out of people. This other man's rage is so great that it sends a mushroom cloud into the sky, obliterates all those around him, or makes those around him hit the ground or run for cover. And it's gotten him into trouble a few times during the war. When he raged that the supplies he and his crew needed that were stored in a ship's hold weren't being offloaded fast enough. When he stormed at a superior for sending men into the sky without radios when, by the time they returned, there would be fog thick as scum covering the landing strip. When he attacked the driver of a bus who wouldn't let him commandeer it to bring a buddy of his to the hospital. And he got away with it each time, but, each time, he came closer to not getting away with it.

My father tells himself that once he gets home, there will be no reason for him to be angry, that the rage that gluts him will disappear. He tells himself that he's bringing his old self, the man he was before the war, home. And he's leaving the other man behind, back in the Admiralties, along with the rotting carcasses of ships, acres of rusting cranes, and all that other detritus of this hard-fought war that the Allies are leaving behind. At least he hasn't hurt anybody. At least he hasn't killed anybody. At least he doesn't think he has.

Chasing Ghosts

1943–1945

Each day after my father leaves for the war, my mother tells me stories about the island where he's stationed. Stories about how, if he could, he'd come home to see us. Stories about how he spends his days. Stories about what we'll do together when he comes home. About how brave he is. About how, without his work, we couldn't win the war. I'm still very young, too young to understand. But by the time my father comes home, I do understand my mother's stories because by then I'm reading and I'm writing because my mother has spent so much time teaching me while my father is gone.

Until I'm a grown woman, I don't understand that my mother makes up most of the stories about what my father is doing on that island in the Pacific. I don't know that the censors would blacken out anything about where my father really is and how he spends his time.

And my mother tells me how my father can't wait to come home to live with us again. About how, when he does come home, we'll go swimming at the old swimming hole, we'll go on vacations, we'll buy a new house and live there, a very happy family.

Each day when my father is away during the war, my mother picks up the globe that she keeps on the kitchen counter, spins it until it shows the vast blue of the Pacific Ocean, locates a tiny dot, and says, "Here, your father is here." Each day after my father leaves for war, my mother brings out the photographs he has sent home and shows them to me. There he is on a swing he and his buddies have rigged up outside the Quonset hut where my father lives. There he is crouching down beneath a palm tree. There he is standing with his buddies on the sand. But although the man in the photographs looks something like my father, he also doesn't look anything like my father and I wonder, to myself, where my father is and where he has gone.

During the war, my mother dresses me up and poses me, takes a photograph of me, and sends it to my father. There I am dressed in a sailor dress, standing in a corner of the kitchen on Adams Street, next to a chalkboard with my mother's words "WE LOVE YOU DADDY" inscribed upon it. There I am standing in front of a tiny Christmas tree in my new pajamas holding one of my Christmas presents. There I am outside our apartment trying to roller-skate—I am never very good at it.

During the war, my father writes me little notes telling me to be a good girl and he signs them, "Your loving father." Notes telling me to help my mother. Telling me he misses me. Telling me he'll come home as soon as he can. Telling me to eat my vegetables, to brush my teeth, to make sure I go to sleep when I'm supposed to. Sometimes he comments on the stories my mother writes to him about me. About how my knees are always scratched and bruised because I'm always running too fast, or away from her, or down the stairs, or falling down when I try to rollerskate. About how I decide the way I should pose when she takes pictures of me to send to him. About how I'm becoming a handful and won't take no for an answer.

He tells me to be more careful. To do as I'm told. And that when he comes home, he'll make sure I toe the line. This is something I don't understand, so I ask my mother what my father means and she says that it means that my father will make sure I behave when he comes home. He prints his messages to me in big block letters. And then he signs them, "Your loving father." At first, I can't read what he writes. But then I can, and by the time he comes home, I'm already reading and writing and talking "a blue streak," as my mother has warned him.

During the war, my father writes my mother every day, and she writes to him every day. When I ask her what my father has written, she tells me it's private. When I ask her what she writes to him when she sits at the kitchen table after my bath, she tells me it's private. But if I pester her long enough, she'll read me the parts of my father's letters that she thinks will interest me. About how special men came to the island and build the Quonset huts where the sailors and soldiers live. How he has to put the legs of his cot in buckets of water so that snakes can't crawl into his bed while he's sleeping. How he has to put gasoline on top of the water in the buckets so it won't breed mosquitos. About how he has to sleep under a mosquito net so he won't get bitten because the mosquitos where he is are as big as bumblebees. About how, at first, the food isn't so good, but how, now, it's quite good: homemade bread and canned fruit and vegetables and sometimes even fresh meat.

After a while, even though my mother and I talk about my father all the time, I can't remember him. I can't remember what he looks like even though I see what he looks like in his photographs. I can't remember what he sounds like; I can no longer hear his voice. I can't remember what he feels like; I can no longer remember what it was like when he picked me up and carried me down the stairs and put me in my stroller. But even though my father is away, he is a presence in my life *because* of his absence.

There is the father who lived with us.

There is the father in the photographs that line the top of my mother's bureau, the top of the kitchen cabinet.

There is the father in my mother's stories.

There is the father in my father's letters to me.

There is the father in my dreams.

In one of these dreams, my father is coming home. He awakens me while I'm sleeping on my cot in the bedroom I share with my mother, that I used to share with my mother and my father. He bends down, kisses me, tucks me in, and then leaves. Every time I dream of my father coming home to me, and kissing me, he leaves. He leaves even though I want him to stay.

In another dream, my father comes home; my mother opens the kitchen door to let him in; but the man who comes home isn't my father. It's another man, a man who looks something like my father but who isn't my father. I wonder where my father has gone; I wonder who this new man is. This man sounds something like my father, but he sounds different from my father, and he smells different, he is different. In this dream, my father comes home and doesn't leave again. But in this dream, my father isn't really there.

There is, though, another father. The father in the stories I tell myself about him. I tell myself these stories when I'm playing under the kitchen table. My mother sets me up to play under the table by throwing an old red blanket over it, and putting a table lamp beneath it, so that I can read to myself while she does her chores. I pretend to read to myself even before I can read to myself. She gives me a pile of books and a few pillows so I can lean back and be comfortable while I'm reading. Unless I'm under the table, or with my grandparents, I interrupt my mother's work and I get in her hair.

Under the table, in the rosy glow of lamplight, instead of reading my books, I tell myself stories about my father.

In these stories, I have a father who plays with me, who smiles, who never sits in the rocking chair and cries the way my mother does. In these stories, my father never ignores my requests for water, or a snack, the way my mother does on the days she mopes around our apartment, especially when she hasn't had a letter from my father for a long time, or when she's read the newspaper, or seen a newsreel when she's taken me to see a movie.

In my stories, my father doesn't go away, he hasn't gone away, he isn't away, he isn't one of the men in the newsreels wielding a weapon, storming a beach, killing an enemy. No, my father is a man who takes care of me, a man who has taken care of me, a man who takes care of my mother, a man who takes care of me when my mother can't, and a man who fixes things when they are broken.

2005/1945

When my father is living in the nursing home and before he starts becoming abusive to me again, he tells me that when he came home from the war my mother had prepared a list of the names of his friends and the men in the neighborhood who had died. She hadn't written to him about any of this while he was away because she didn't want to upset him. The list of names was very long and included men who'd died in Europe, in Africa, and in the Pacific.

I wonder about this. I wonder what it must have been like to come home and to learn that so many of your friends and neighbors didn't come home. To have to remember, each time you saw their families, that their sons were dead or missing. That they were gone, gone, gone.

Once, my father said, years later, one of the guys down at the firehouse, also a war veteran, told him that he didn't go out much anymore.

"The noise? The airplanes? The cars backfiring?" my father asked, knowing how these sounds continued to startle men he knew, to make them sweat, even duck and run for cover.

"No," the fireman said. "Not that. Everywhere I go, I think I see a man who didn't come back walking down the street. Sometimes I'm so sure it's him, so sure he didn't die, that I run up behind him and tap him on the shoulder. But of course it isn't him. Sometimes all I see on the streets are men who aren't there."

About the list my mother made, my father said, "She didn't want me to walk into the bakery and ask about the baker's son. She didn't want me to ask any members of their families about these men. You have to understand that the whole world was mourning."

But the list was too long for my father to memorize. And besides, my father said he started getting the names of all these men my mother had written down confused with the names of the men he himself knew had died or the men who'd never come back from missions who were presumed dead, and even the men he'd seen die during his first tour of duty when, unbeknownst to so very many people, the United States was preparing for war. There were, my father said, so many, many names.

The trouble was that when my father went into the bakery, or into the drugstore, or into the barbershop, he told me he sometimes thought he saw the dead man or the missing man standing behind the counter, next to the man's father or his mother or the cash register.

"When I thought I saw these men, I thought I was going nuts," my father tells me. "But now I know I wasn't going nuts. Now I know I just wanted them to be back home like I was."

"What did they look like, these ghosts?" I ask.

"Not like the living dead," my father says. "More like the dead who didn't die."

And I can't imagine what it was like for my father to live in such a world, a world of the dead who didn't die, even while my father was trying to tend to the demands of the living, the needs of a woman who'd been brave enough during the war but who, when my father returned home, didn't seem to celebrate his return but acted, instead, as if he weren't really there. And a daughter who was so angry at him (at least that's what I think now) that she wouldn't do anything he said, wouldn't kiss him, wouldn't let him hold her, and ran away from him and to her mother or her grandparents whenever she could, so that my father said that he sometimes felt like he wasn't even there, or that he shouldn't have bothered coming home.

2005

Once, when I go see my father before he goes into the nursing home, he greets me with a cup of tea. He's been reading yet another book about the war.

"Do you know," he asks me, "how many people died during the war?"

"I don't," I admit.

"Jesus," my father says. "What the hell did they teach you in college?"

And then my father tells me that 16 million servicemen and -women from the United States participated in the war. Of that number, anywhere from a quarter-million to nearly half a million died in combat, from accidents, or illness, and did not return home. More than half a million men from the United States were wounded or maimed. Still, the far greater burden of the war fell on other nations. More than 24.5 million soldiers from other countries—Allied and Axis—were killed during the war. As many as 55 million civilians died, including those who died from disease or famine. And untold numbers became displaced persons who had no homes, for they could not return to what once had been their homes, for their homes had been destroyed, their cities ravaged.

My father learns the names of places where innocent people died. Babi Yar. Belzec. Chelmno. Majdanek. Mauthausen. Odessa. Sobibor. Treblinka. Belgrade. Jasenovac. London. Stalingrad. Nanking. Bataan. Manila. Singapore. Buchenwald. Katyn. Berlin. Dresden. Haburg. Hiroshima. Nagasaki. Tokyo. Yokahama. Bleiburg. Datong. Leningrad. Warsaw. Manila. Kryzwolka. Komorowo. Ponary. Gross-Rosen. Breslau. Rumbula. Sook Ching. Pforzheim. Moscow. Kiev. Kursk. Okinawa. Normandy. Budapest. Manchuria. Sicily. Naples. Rome. Scafati. Milan. North Africa. Greece.

All these places, my father learns about, and then I learn about, and so many, many more.

The next time I come to see my father in the nursing home, he's reading a book about the war in the Pacific, one of the few I've brought to him from his home.

"Can you tell me the names of some of the battles in the Pacific?" my father asks.

"I can name a few," I respond. I'm ready for my father to say what he always does when he asks me about the war—"Jesus, what did they teach you in college?"—but he doesn't, and so I say, "Iwo Jima, Midway, Wake, Guam."

"Pearl Harbor, Coral Sea, Guadalcanal, Saipan, Leyte Gulf, Luzon—30,000 Americans died there," my father says. "And then there's Okinawa, and don't forget Los Negros and Manus. That's where I was stationed during the war," my father reminds me, as if I could forget it.

2005

One day when I come to the nursing home to visit my father, an attendant stops me before I can go to my father's room. It's two weeks before my father's death.

"I wouldn't go in there," she says.

"Why not?" I ask.

"He's not himself," she says. And then she tells me that, after lunch, my father was talking to the veteran, the man my father calls "The Admiral," the one who is always studying maps from Pacific battles while he sits at the picnic table in the garden.

But, the attendant says, something The Admiral said must have upset my father because he got up abruptly, almost fell over, steadied himself, and trundled his walker back to his room.

When the attendant went to see what happened, she told me that she found my father lying in his bed. But what was so strange about it, the attendant said, is that my father had pulled the sheet up over his head as if he were trying to hide. When she went over to talk to him, she heard him saying something.

"Failure, failure, failure," my father is saying. "I'm nothing but a failure. I never did anything right."

And I think of the burden this man has carried. A chronically depressed wife. A daughter who killed herself, that daughter, my sister, born nine months after my father's return, whom my parents ignored and turned over to me to care for when I was barely able to care for myself; my sister, whom I now think of as another casualty of that war. Did he blame himself for not being able to fix them, make them right? And then there is me. The daughter who rejected him, who resisted him, who really didn't want him in her life, not until these past few years, and he must have known.

And the hell of it is that no matter how much I'd like to, I can't roll back time. I can't go back to that moment when I turned away from my father and make it right because of what I know now.

The attendant tries to tell my father that he's not a failure. He has a family who loves him. He's worked hard and made something of himself. He's a good singer. He tells wonderful stories. All the nurses and attendants love him.

"No," my father says. "I'm nothing but a failure. Go away. Leave me alone."

I decide that no matter what the consequences, I have to go to see my father, find out what this is about. I will remind him of all he's accomplished, of how he made our rundown house beautiful, of how hard he worked for so very long, of how he helped me raise my kids, of how his grandkids adore him.

Did his veteran friend say something to disparage him? I know this man saw action, and he's always reminding my father that he didn't—at least, not really.

"So," I ask my father after I pry the sheet away from his face. "Do you want to tell me what this is all about?"

My father won't look at me. He stares straight ahead. He tries not to cry.

"You know what this is about," my father says.

I don't. But then I remember something I'd overheard weeks before.

It is a sunny June day. My father is out in the garden, sitting across from The Admiral. They're arguing about the end of the war. Not about whether the United States should have dropped bombs on Hiroshima and Nagasaki, for the two of these old vets agree that it was a horrible necessity. By now I've heard my father talk about how many lives were saved (Japanese civilians' and soldiers' and Allied soldiers' lives) because the United States had intercepted communiqués stating that the Japanese were committed to fighting to the last person (man, woman, child) standing; about how, after Okinawa (where more than 77,000 Japanese and 14,000 Allied military men died and between 42,000 and 150,000 civilians were killed or committed suicide), the projected loss of life if the Allies continued to invade the Japanese home islands was half a million to a million American men and 7 million Japanese military men and civilians; about how the Japanese government had shown no concern for the loss of life of their people and, instead, continued to preach that victory or suicide was the only acceptable end to the war in the Pacific.

I know that there are other sides to the stories these old men tell themselves about the end of that war: that the use of the atomic bomb alone didn't end it; that the figures of lives saved have been disputed; that the Soviets' entry into the war surely helped; that the American decision to be lenient to Hirohito was important, too. But I've never challenged him.

No, they're not arguing about how the war ended. They're arguing about whether my father should have been one of the first men to return home. My father has often told me how angry he was that he was forced to stay on that island to "mop up," and how he'd gotten screwed because men without wives

and children got to go home before he did. He's told me about the complicated points system—so many points for having seen action; for combat
wounds; for rank; for how long you've been deployed; for previous service;
for being married; for having children—that was used to determine when
men were sent home. And he's told me, too, about the rumors circulating
through their base about how quickly MacArthur had managed to demobi-
lize the Japanese troops—all 7 million of them—in contrast to how long it
took for U.S. troops to get home.

"It wasn't fair," my father told me. "Lots of guys who were younger than
me and without families got sent home earlier than me. I was one of the last
men to be sent home. And to top it off, instead of flying to the West Coast,
I went by sea, and then by rail. Just like the Navy, they'll screw you every
which way they can."

"Hell, Lou," The Admiral says, "they deserved to go home first. After all,
you yourself said that all you did was fix airplanes." And here The Admiral
laughs. "All you did was fix airplanes so they could send another poor sucker
back up into the air to die."

And what The Admiral said about others deserving to go home was probably true. My father had enlisted for the duration of the war plus a year. A
month in service equaled a point; a month overseas equaled a point; a combat
award equaled five points; a dependent child under eighteen equaled twelve
points. So that surely there were men without children with more points than
my father who would be sent home first. Men who hadn't accumulated a
large number of points were required to stay back to assist with shutting
down the base.

And what The Admiral said, and my father admitted, about sending men
back up into the sky to die was also true. My father has already told me
about how, sometimes, pilots who were war-weary told my father there was
something wrong with their planes and that they couldn't fly a mission. And
then he tells me something about flow meters—how the pilots were always
telling him their flow meters weren't working. They used this complaint,
my father said, to try to stay behind because they knew it was an ordeal to
change one.

But my father said he figured out that nothing could go wrong with a flow
meter unless the ball was not calibrated for specific gravity. At least that's

what I remember him telling me—every time my father tried to teach me how something worked, I could never follow. Either that or they'd say something about an error in valve clearance. But my father had a crackerjack crew and it would take them only half an hour to either fix the valve problem or determine that nothing was wrong.

"Yeah," my father tells The Admiral, "that's all I did. Fixed airplanes so they could send pilots back into the air to die. That was my job. That's what I was supposed to do, you stupid fuck."

And so now I wonder whether The Admiral has brought back all my father's agony about all the pilots he knew who died or who didn't return during his first tour of duty and during the war, all those pilots whose planes he'd fixed or whose planes he'd determined had nothing wrong with them. (He'd once told me that pilots retired after flying twenty-five combat missions. But that most were dead after fourteen, either in battle, or because of equipment malfunction.)

Yes, my father's job was to fix airplanes to send men back into the skies. And I wonder whether he chastised himself for any pilot who came to harm in any airplane he'd worked on. Whether he bore, quietly and alone, a sense of responsibility for having, by error or lack of judgment or just plain bad luck, made a mistake that resulted in a pilot dying. I understand, now, that my father continues to carry this burden. And that for him, there is no possibility of redemption.

"You could never know," he once said, "whether something you did made a plane go down. And once a plane went down, unless we recovered it—and we almost never did—it was impossible to figure out what happened."

And then I realize that, when pilots' planes went down into the sea, their bodies couldn't be recovered. So that the people who'd worked with them, who'd bunked with them, who'd been their buddies, who'd loved them, couldn't mourn them in the traditional way. There was no body to prepare for burial; there was no body to bury; there was no body to indicate that the person was, in fact, even dead.

David Zellmer, a bomber pilot stationed, for a time, on the same island as my father, a man who survived the war, kept a diary that he published based upon the letters he sent home describing what happened while he served there. He speaks of the constant accounting pilots and everyone who worked with them made of all the pilots they'd known—the ones they'd served with; the ones they'd flown missions with; the ones whose planes they'd serviced.

Were they still alive and flying? Still alive but not flying for some reason? Retired from flying because they'd completed the requisite number of missions? Relieved of duty because they'd had a mental breakdown? Dead? Unaccounted for? Had anyone seen them shot down? Did anyone know if maybe they'd been picked up by a Japanese vessel and so weren't really dead? And so there were the men who were "really dead." And pilots who were "perhaps dead." And pilots who nobody could say were dead or alive.

He speaks of grounded pilots, crew chiefs, and mechanics, all staring "at the empty, darkening sky . . . for the sight of a returning plane; others, sitting on empty bomb crates, heads down, . . . listening for the sound of a [returning] B-24." And how those who stayed behind—pilots, crew chiefs, mechanics—felt "suffocated by a feeling of guilt, being here, safe on the ground, not out there, somewhere, with 'them,' sharing their fears and pain."

Not one plane returned to the base from the mission Zellmer describes. For the rest of the night, he "endured dreams of lost, pilotless airplanes circling in a black, empty sky; endlessly, silently circling."

And this was something like the dream my father told me he always had.

"I see a plane," he said. "Without a pilot. Circling. With nowhere to land. Sometimes it gets hit by a Jap. Sometimes it crashes into the sea. Sometimes it disappears into the ether. But sometimes it just keeps circling."

My father tells me about this dream during the time we spent together in his sunroom.

"This is the dream," my father says, "that always drives me crazy."

Ship's Model

1972

When my father is in his late fifties and recovering from his first heart attack, he orders a model of the battleship USS Missouri, and he spends well over a month building a replica of it. "It cost a fortune," my mother says, and she marvels that my father, a frugal, even penurious, man, has paid so much money for it.

I am married with two young boys, and when I visit my father in the hospital, he tells me he's decided he has to take good care of himself because of his grandsons (and not, I note, but don't say, because of his wife and daughters).

Building this model is a part of his plan. He's decided to try to slow down and take it easy. He figures if he spends part of each day sitting and working on the USS Missouri he won't be tempted to overdo it and jeopardize his recovery, which, his doctors warn, will take a very long time. As he convalesces, he is forbidden to work, lift anything heavy, get angry, or fight fires. He isn't even allowed to go down to the firehouse to visit his buddies if my mother drives him because his doctors know that if an alarm sounds while he's there he won't resist the impulse to climb onto the hook and ladder with the other men and race to the fire.

"I love my grandkids," he says, and I know that he does. "I want to see those guys grow into men." (And he does live long enough to see this happen, and even lives long enough to get to know his great-grandchildren.) When he is with my sons, I see the kind of affection I wished he'd shown me. But then again, I tell myself, they are boys, and he's a man's man, and the two of us have too much bad history between us.

When my father first sets out the pieces of his model, which take up the greater part of the dining room table, I think they are for a generic World War II battleship, an appropriate model for any ex–Navy man obsessed with that war to build.

But it isn't until after my father dies, and I am researching the battleships that played a part in the war in the Pacific, that I learn the USS Missouri wasn't just any battleship. It participated in the landmark battles of Iwo Jima and Okinawa and shelled the Japanese home islands. On its deck, Douglas MacArthur accepted signatures from the Japanese on the official instrument of surrender. So perhaps in building the USS Missouri my father is revisiting not only the carnage of that war but also U.S. victories and, perhaps most important, its ending.

Whenever I visit my parents' home to see him, he's sitting at the dining room table, working. My elder son climbs onto his lap and my father explains what he's doing. He shows my son a piece he was working on, shows him where it belongs according to the instructions, shows him where the actual part is on the illustration of the *Missouri* on the cover of the box.

My son is fascinated, and before long, he's learned the parts of the ship and he can point them out whenever my father asks. The hull. The catapult. The conning tower. The forward fire control tower. The nine 16-inch Mark 7 guns that fire 2,700-pound shells and could hit a target twenty miles away. The twenty Mark 12 guns mounted in twin turrets with a ten-mile range; the 80 anti-aircraft guns that defend the ship from enemy airstrikes. The forty-nine anti-aircraft cannons. The life rafts. The aircraft crane. The seaplanes. And each time my son's answer is correct, my father praises him, and he once tells me, without, I suspect, understanding the meaning of his remark, "He is one smart son of a bitch."

My son is especially intrigued by the guns, for ours is a household where toy guns are not permitted.

"When you build a model to scale," my father tells my son, "you have to assemble it in precisely the same order and in the same way that the ship was constructed. If you build a model of anything, you can learn how something was made."

My father likes this, I know, likes knowing how things are put together. He's spent the better part of his life as a skilled machinist, both in the war and after, and his job requires patience, dexterity, and a knowledge of how things work.

When I still live with my parents, I remember him taking something apart just so he can put it back together. He does this with every new appliance my parents buy so he can repair it when it's broken. My mother tells her friends that she wishes, for once in her life, she can have something brand new that stays brand new for a while without my father disassembling it and turning it into something that's used even before she has a change to try it out.

Each day when my father works on the *Missouri*, he takes a piece, cuts away the excess plastic with the blade of the blue penknife he always carries with him in his pocket (the one he's had since his first tour of duty, the one that always makes me nervous whenever he takes it out to pare his nails while he's watching the evening news).

He sands the piece, wipes it down with a solvent to clean it, paints it, and allows it to dry. Then he glues the piece into the place where it belongs and moves on to another. And another. And then another.

I witnessed, in those days, the kind of care my father took with every project—fixing a toaster, rotating the tires on his car, painting a room, sharpening the blades of a lawnmower, installing linoleum. Now, though, he doesn't become exasperated as he so often does when something doesn't work out the way he imagines it should, or when he makes a mistake.

Then he'd shout and swear until my mother begged him to stop working, to take a break until he cooled down. But he wouldn't stop, couldn't stop, until he got the job done, furious at the object, furious at himself, furious at anyone who came near him.

Did the doctors give him drugs after his heart attack to calm him down? Or does he finally realize that if he carries on the way he used to, he'll be a dead man before his time? Still, this calm during his recovery doesn't last, and before six months have elapsed, he's back to his old self.

When he finishes the scale model of the *USS Missouri*, my father makes a Plexiglas stand, mounts his ship's model upon it, and hangs it in the dining room above the sideboard. My mother makes no objection to his installing it in such a bizarre place in the household, or if she has, she hasn't dissuaded him from doing so.

Whether my father wants the battleship in our dining room to remind himself, or to remind us, of those deadly battles in the Pacific where he'd served during the war, or of the Japanese surrender, or both, he never says. But none of us tells him that we think this replica of perhaps the most famous killing machine of that war, whose big guns could hit a target twenty miles away, whose armaments could pulverize buildings on a distant shore, whose ammunition could—and did—kill women and children as well as enemy soldiers, isn't appropriate décor for a dining room.

So that whenever our family comes together for a meal at my parents' house, the *USS Missouri* trains its guns on us. My seat at the table is across from it. And the main battery of the 16-inch Mark 7 guns is always directly trained on me.

Mopping Up

1945

The days of waiting for the war in the Pacific to end were difficult, even agonizing, for those stationed on Manus Island. Most of those permanently stationed on the base had been there for at least seventeen months. They had followed the long and dreadful war in the Pacific as it routed its way westward, doing their part to keep the forward forces supplied and capable of fighting. They had taken part in the preparations for the Battle of Leyte Gulf. They had serviced aircraft that made reconnaissance and bombing runs to islands many hours of flight time away. My father knew that, compared with others in the military, compared with the pilots whose planes he serviced, he was comparatively safe. But he wanted hostilities to be over. He wanted American and Allied servicemen to stop dying. And he also knew that until the war was officially over, not even those who served on Manus were entirely safe.

Still, through all the time we talked about my father's tour of duty, he continues to maintain that he was never in grave danger. But I learn from reading *The Admiralties at War, 1944–1945* by Robert Manning Smalley, who was stationed on Manus Island, that on November 9, 1944, Japanese bombers attacked the airfield on Los Negros where my father and his crew worked. They sprayed gunfire on the airbase and sent ground crews running for cover. Eight men were injured; two aircraft were damaged. In late April 1945, two Japanese bombers flying from their base in Rabaul launched torpedoes to attack the floating dry dock I'd seen in my father's photos. No one was killed; thirty men suffered minor wounds. But, of course, compared with what other men experienced during that war, my father *was* safe. And it is the fact that he was safe, I have come to believe, that troubled him so very much.

Smalley was an announcer on the island's radio station, WVTD, which kept the men on the base up to date on the news, censored though it may have been. In early August 1945, he began to take notes about what was happening on the base when it appeared the Japanese were close to capitulation because he knew it was a momentous time.

On Tuesday, August 7, 1945, Joe Herbert, who transcribed the news transmitted from California to the radio station, delivered the news to Smalley to read over the air that a new kind of weapon, an atomic bomb, had been detonated on the Japanese mainland the day before. No one at the station believed him.

My father, like all the other men stationed on Manus, heard the news of the dropping of the atomic bomb by the end of the day, after he had finished his work, although rumors had circulated throughout the base before. Smalley wrote in his journal that the news was greeted with an enormous sense of relief among the men and women stationed there. Near the end of the war, everyone was estimating how many more Allied men would have to die to invade Japan, to defeat the Japanese, to force them to capitulate. And how many more Japanese would have to die? They all knew of the decree that every Japanese man, woman, and child was duty-bound to fight to the death, although they did not then know that the Japanese had been training women and children to fight with homemade weapons—sharpened bamboo sticks, shovels, axes, whatever was at hand.

After the war in the Pacific ends, before my father can come home, he has to spend a few more months on the island "mopping up." The servicemen who remain behind are ordered to destroy or disable the war equipment that has been stored there in preparation for the invasion of Japan that has never materialized because of Japan's capitulation after the United States drops atomic bombs on Hiroshima and Nagasaki.

They are also ordered to get rid of, or destroy, the base's supplies. Cots. Dishes. Knives. Forks. Spoons. Pots and pans. Trays. Stoves. Refrigerators. Tables. Chairs. Storage chests. Filing cabinets. Desks. Mosquito netting. Buckets.

Much of this, they dump into the sea. Some of the men begin to enjoy this spectacle of destruction. They hoot and holler as they toss things into the water. To my father, though, this is a grim and despicable business. He does it because he must. He does it so he can go home.

What the men can't dump into the lagoon, they are told to move to the acres of clearings the Allied forces have wrested from the bush after the invasion. A forest of cranes. Phalanxes of jeeps, buses, trucks, planes, tanks, amphibious vessels.

My father is a frugal man. He has always earned just enough money to meet his needs, but never enough money to be wasteful. He buys only what is absolutely necessary. He throws nothing away. He fixes what he breaks. He wears the few clothes he buys until they're in tatters. The thought of all this equipment being destroyed or thrown into the sea or left behind to rot sickens him. He knows that this island is not U.S. property.

My father tells me he imagines what it must have been like to be a native of these islands, a person who had never seen an airplane or an aircraft carrier before the Germans came, before the Japanese established their military base there. A person who had never before heard the sound of artillery fire. My father imagines what it must have been like to look out at the ocean past the coral reef beyond the lagoon, and see, not an outrigger canoe, but warships steaming their way, slowly, steadily, inexorably, toward your village, toward this lagoon where your home with its dome-thatched roof sits on stilts above a pristine sea, where you fish each day, where you teach your child, early, to swim and navigate the waterways in your village in a small canoe because the water is your home and your children must understand it. What must it have been like to hide in the water beneath your home in the lagoon as aircraft strafed your village, killed your people, what it must have been like to leave your home to seek cover in the mangrove swamps and deep into the bush where your people, being sea-dwellers, had never before ventured?

Not that you would not have known fear or warfare, because your village and others have engaged in it often, and you would have feared, too, the wrath of ghosts, and the repercussions of violating taboos, and you would have known how women were stolen during warfare and made into prostitutes and kept in the houses of the men, and how those who were the victors cooked and ate the bodies of those who had been vanquished in combat.

But you could never have imagined warfare on this scale. Could never have imagined machines of war this deadly. Could never have imagined machines that killed from the sea or from the sky.

When my father asks a superior officer why they're destroying so much of this expensive equipment that cost taxpayers a lot of money and why they're leaving so much of it to rot in a place that isn't U.S. territory, the officer replies, "It's orders." When my father counters that it's a terrible waste, and that some of the island people or poor people back home or people whose homes have been destroyed in other parts of the world could make good use of some of this stuff, my father is told that it's against orders to distribute goods to native or other populations, that it would cost too much to ship it all back to the United States, and besides, there aren't enough ships to bring it all back, and that even if they could bring it all back, it would have to be distributed, and that would take money and manpower. And besides, it would ruin the world market for new goods because there would be no demand for them if all this stuff were distributed, and so it would ruin the world's economy.

My father listens. But he doesn't understand. And then he does. What's behind all this, my father thinks, is that all this stuff will have to be remanufactured, and someone stands to make a good buck from it. He thinks, too, that the government wants to leave behind everything that has to do with the war, so that when the servicemen return home, they can forget the war, move on with their lives, for there will be no reminders in the United States that there has ever been a war.

For fifty years, a hundred years, or more, the island people will have to live with this gigantic mess. They won't be able to use any of it. But they'll have to look at it. They'll see it in the bottom of the lagoon when they set out their fishing nets, when they teach their children to swim. They'll see it in the bush when they gather plants. They'll see it on the shore when they travel in their canoes from one village to another. And every time they see it, they will have to think about the war. They will think about what happened to their island during the war.

In the weeks before my father comes home, he and his buddies try to figure out how they can get a jeep back into the United States. They've all been talking about how scuttling all this stuff is a waste, about how it's a goddamned shame that all this stuff is being left behind to rot and rust. They talk about how they would like to "liberate" something, take it home, make good use of it.

They are waiting for their orders. Waiting to begin the long journey home. Waiting to see their wives and girlfriends. Waiting to find out how their hometowns have changed. Waiting to see if their children will remember them.

Waiting, they find, is making them even crazier than listening to the night sky for Japanese aircraft, than searching the sea for Japanese ships, than staring at the lagoon for evidence that a Japanese midget submarine is making ready to torpedo an ammo ship.

So they decide they have to do something while they're waiting.

Hatching this plan to bring a jeep home gives them something to do in their spare time besides throwing hand grenades into the water to kill fish for a fish fry. Something to do besides rehashing war stories. Something to do besides asking one another whether someone they all knew lived or died. Something to do besides floating in the lagoon on their backs with a cigarette clenched between their teeth. Something to do besides lazing in a hammock under a palm tree, smacking mosquitos off your body.

One night, they play a few games of poker outside their Quonset hut under torchlight. They drink a few beers. Smoke a few cigarettes. Tonight, they're feeling fine.

It's good to be out at night. Good not to have to worry about showing a light, good not to have to worry about the war, although it will take many years, or it will take a lifetime, for them not to startle at the sound of a car backfiring, not to get jittery at a fireworks celebrations on the Fourth of July, not to want to duck and run for cover when they hear an airplane flying overhead.

One guy says, "Hey, let's break down a jeep. Take it home in pieces."

The men laugh.

The plan materializes.

They'll break down a jeep. Give a piece to each man. Keep a log of who gets what. Stateside, they'll have a reunion. Spend a weekend putting the jeep back together. Have an auction to decide who gets to keep it.

My father knows this is a cockamamie scheme. But he keeps his mouth shut. But a guy resting on his cot near the entrance to the hut overhears them talking. He walks outside, sits on his haunches.

"No can do," the man says. His name is Charlie. The men have taken to calling him "No Can Do Charlie."

"What the fuck are you talking about?" one of my father's buddies asks. "We've got a good plan here. Help us or keep your fucking mouth shut. All during this goddamned war, it's been, 'No can do this,' and 'No can do that.' If it were up to you, we would have sat around here with our thumbs up our asses waiting for the Japs to come and skin us alive. All during this war the rest of us have been busting ourselves doing what you said couldn't be done."

By now the man is angry, his voice strident. My father tenses. He's older than most of the men. He knows what can happen when servicemen have been waiting for something too long.

My father takes his buddy aside.

"Ease up," my father says.

No Can Do Charlie draws deeply on his cigarette. Exhales.

"Stealing government property," he says, "courts-martial, dishonorable discharge, no work, no GI loan. Go ahead and do it. See if I care, you stupid pricks."

No Can Do Charlie gets up. Saunters inside. Lies down on his bunk. Continues smoking.

One day, my father and other servicemen are given orders to set fire to a storage depot containing flammable paint and other supplies. My father doesn't like this at all. He knows that the fumes from burning paint can make a man pass out, addle his brain, even kill him. He remembers a kid who lived in North Bergen who set some paint on fire, sniffed the fumes, and never was the same again.

"He was screwed up," my father says, "and I mean permanently."

Again, my father resists. Again, he's told, "It's orders."

So he and other servicemen follow orders they don't want to follow and dig a deep trench from the storage depot to the beach, fill it with flammable paint, set the paint on fire. The trail of paint, my father knows, will burn slowly. So he waits until it's alight. Sticks a wet finger into the air to determine the prevailing wind, and hightails it up the beach.

My father is wiry and fast and sprints upwind of the fire that is making its way toward the depot.

"I ran like a bat out of hell," he says.

Other men don't run away. They are curious to a fault. The kind of men who move toward an explosion, a knife fight, a standoff between the police and some goons. Men too young to know they should take themselves out of harm's way. They wait around to see what happens. They're tense. They're excited. They call after my father, mock him, call him a coward for running away.

"Look at that pussy," one man says.

The snake of fire reaches the building. Ignites it. The depot starts burning. Soon there is smoke, acrid smoke. And explosions, bursts of colored fire.

My father fords a small rivulet, wades through a mangrove swamp. He makes a wide arc, and returns to his quarters on the base, far away from the fire. Still, he can smell the smoke in the air.

Many of the men who stayed behind are overcome by the fumes and pass out. Some wind up in sickbay.

The fire, my father says, lasts three days. Three days of dense smoke and foul air. No one has warned the islanders living downwind. Even my father didn't realize the fire would last that long. Until the day my father ships out, he can smell the stench from the fire in the air. Throughout this time, my father dons his gas mask often. But it's hot and annoying. He takes it off, cruises the beachfront trying to find some good air. The air is better by the sea. But not much. And not always.

On the second day of the fire, my father starts coughing.

"And I've never stopped coughing since," my father says.

And this, I tell myself, is one of the reasons my father becomes a volunteer fireman after he comes home. All these long years of his life, he's trying to put out a fire he didn't want to start.

Though my father and his pals abandon their plan for breaking down a jeep and taking it home, No Can Do Charlie's warning doesn't stop either my father or most of the other men on the island from trying to take something back from the war. They stow some booty in their sea bags as they are packing their gear to go home, even though they know it's against regulations and they can be punished if they get caught.

"Hell," my father tells himself, "I wanted to take something home from the war other than a bad case of jock rot, a lousy case of heartburn, a chronic cough, and a case of piles so bad they made taking a shit a torture."

My father justifies what he's doing by telling himself there's no harm in taking something home that would have been left out in the sun to rot anyway. Something that would have been set on fire, dumped into the sea, or shipped stateside only to be stored at some supply depot in Buttfuck, Arizona, never to be used again. And so he takes a set of binoculars, an 8 day clock, a couple of cotton blankets, the silk from a parachute.

Binoculars like these are hard to come by and cost a fortune. You can't get clocks like this outside the service. The blankets are very special. He's never seen anything like them before, never will again. "Perfect for spring, perfect for fall," my father tells me. And the silk from a parachute that he thinks it will be fun for me to play with.

(But when he pulls the parachute silk out of his sea bag on the day he comes home from the war and gives it to me, my mother stops smiling.

"Oh, Lou," she says, and nothing more. She walks away from him, goes to the sink, pretends to be washing dishes that aren't there.

And it has taken me until the moment that I write this to understand why.

My mother thinks my father is bringing the silk from a parachute that hasn't opened home from the war. My mother thinks my father is bringing the silk from a dead man's parachute that hasn't opened home from the war. My mother thinks my father is bringing the silk from a dead man's parachute that hasn't opened home from the war for me to play with.

And I do play with the silk from the parachute. I throw it over a card table to make a little house I can crawl into and hide inside. I wrap it round and round my body and pretend I'm in a cocoon. I sit on the linoleum floor of our kitchen and I throw it up into the air and let it float down over me so I can become invisible. I play with the silk from the dead man's parachute for years until it's tattered and torn and gray with age. One day, it disappears, I don't know how, but by now I've lost interest in it, and I don't ask my mother where it has gone.)

At sea, on the way home, my father is resting in his hammock below deck. It's nighttime. He's gone to bed early, but he can't sleep. He's filled with anticipation. But it's taking so very, very long for him to get home.

He thinks about how he can't wait to see my mother, can't wait to take her in his arms, how he can't wait to see me, can't wait to toss me high into the sky. He thinks about how he can't wait to sleep in a real bed. Can't wait to buy a car. Can't wait to take a ride into the country. Can't wait to have a plate of pasta instead of this slop they call food in the Navy. (Spam, he has vowed, he will never eat again as long as he lives. But he does, and without complaint, because my frugal mother buys it because it's cheaper than ham, bakes it, and serves it up with crushed pineapple and brown sugar glaze.)

Over the loudspeaker, my father hears some crackling. Then, an announcement. Which says that, in the morning, there will be a sea bag inspection.

"Holy shit," my father says. Much of what he's taken, he knows he'll have to get rid of. But he takes a chance and keeps the parachute silk and stuffs it deep into his sea bag, and he gets to keep it because there was no sea bag inspection after all, and all these years later, he tells me he regrets the loss of those special blankets.

In the middle of the night, under cover of darkness, hundreds of servicemen in their skivvies climb stairs and ladders to the pitching deck of the ship. They clutch their booty to their chests and pretend they're surfacing because it's too hot down below and they need a little fresh air, or because they can't sleep and need a smoke to calm them down.

And on that clear night, a few months after the war in the Pacific is over, hundreds of men who have survived the war, and who are on their long voyage back home to those who love them and miss them, lean way out over the deck's railing.

They throw hundreds of binoculars, 8 day clocks, altimeters, collapsible shovels, and other war-scarred objects, each of which bears some special meaning for the man who has risked packing it deep into his sea bag, down into the sea, that final resting place of so many men they've known, and so many men they haven't.

Then hundreds of men grab hundreds of cotton blankets by one corner, and wave them into the moon-drenched air like so many giant handkerchiefs, in a grand ceremony of farewell, of yearning, of mourning, or of welcome, who can say. And then, before their commanding officers have a chance to come up on deck to see what is transpiring, they release them.

The blankets flutter down to the sea. They look like so many phantom parachutes dropping behind enemy lines. No, they look like the kites they will fly with their children on a sandy beach on a windy day in summer when they are, at long last, home.

Cargo Cult

1975

I attend a seminar given by Margaret Mead when I'm a graduate student at New York University. To prepare for the occasion, we are given assigned readings. I read about Mead's anthropological work on an island called Manus. The name seems familiar, but I can't quite place it.

2004

When my father and I talk about his stay on Manus Island, I go back and reread Mead's account of the Manus people in the late 1920s and after the war in the 1950s, the one I read for Mead's seminar that I'd attended, and I read, too, what happened to the Manus during and after the war. And I tell my father about what I learn.

Mead reported that when the Americans invaded, the Manus were a warring, headhunting, cannibalistic, Stone Age culture, although there had been some contact between some of the islanders and the plantations and scattered missionary settlements there. And she stated that the culture changed quickly and dramatically after the war for the better, although other anthropologists and ethnographers have challenged this conclusion. Still, Lola Romanucci-Ross, who studied the Manus after Mead, concluded that the Manus loved the Americans despite the war, the loss of lives, and the destruction of their villages. After the Japanese arrived, they thought everything was turned upside down and the Manus believed that the Americans had come to their island to make right what had gone wrong under the Japanese occupation.

According to Mead, the Manus were dazzled by the sight of Americans using huge machines to level mountains, blast waterways, level the land for airstrips, clear miles of bush. The Manus concluded that Americans revered life because they used machines for backbreaking toil, rather than human effort. After the war, they incorporated this value into their culture, which, formerly, had not respected human well-being.

My father tells me he did not know that the harbor where hundreds of ships were anchored had once been a prime fishing area for the Manus. That the islanders had acted as scouts during the initial American assault. That, during the invasion, American planes machine gunned natives but that the islanders didn't blame the Americans for killing their people and destroying their settlements, they blamed the Japanese. That the land where Seabees built Quonset huts and barracks to house the Allied forces had been cleared of native habitations. That the islanders themselves helped clear land and build the structures on their land. That island women were moved far offshore to small islands during the Allied occupation to protect their virtue.

When I told my father these things, he said, "What do you expect? During wartime, the innocent always suffer. That's the way it goes."

POST-1945

After the Allies leave Manus, some of the island people, too, begin to throw their possessions into the sea. They throw strands of dog teeth, the skulls of their ancestors, the rib bones of the dead worn in mourning, the braided hair of the dead worn as amulets, spears, baskets, gongs, grass skirts, pottery, bodily ornaments, and many other things signifying the old ways they want to let go. They throw these things into the sea because a prophet has told them that if they do, ships will appear on the horizon carrying a cargo of foreign goods and money and ships and planes and machines and food and everything else they will need to lead an easeful life.

The ship will dock, and all they will have to do to claim the cargo is board the ship and unload it. But the only way the ancestors or a deity will allow these ships to come is if everyone throws away all the old things into the sea so that all the island lagoons are filled with objects.

After the Manus throw their goods into the sea, they watch the horizon and wait for the cargo to appear. Behind them, there are rusting Quonset huts and rotting aircraft. In the lagoon, there are the skeletons of landing craft and jeeps and all kinds of other things they cannot reach and cannot use.

As the Manus await their cargo, the children on the beach play with airplanes they have made from scraps of bark and pieces of metal they have found. They fashion them so that they resemble the planes that have come to their island during the war. But their little airplanes do not fly by themselves, they cannot fly. And so the children run up and down the beach and make whirring noises, hoping the wind will catch their planes and send them high into the sky. They play this game whenever they can. They play this game again and again.

When the cargo doesn't appear, their elders, who are waiting for the cargo, conclude either that the prophet is wrong, or that they haven't thrown their goods away in the proper manner, or that their cargo has gone, by mistake, to another village.

FIVE

Coming Home

2004–2014

Although it takes me years to write about how my father left for the war, the first words I write for this book are the ones about my father coming home from the war. And it's only when I revisit all the work I've written that I find I've penned at least seven versions of this moment in my father's life. So that I must conclude that the story of how my father came home from the war is the one that I needed to tell myself over and over again. That I needed to tell myself this story because the loss of my father both during the war and after he came home was so very great. But what I find curious about all these versions is that I tell them not from my point of view but from my father's. It's as if I need to imagine what it must have been like for him to come home because, if I can figure this out, then I can figure out what went wrong between us.

Once, I ask him. It's a few weeks before he destroys the house he's sharing with his second wife. He isn't well. But he isn't, yet, crazy.

"What was it like to come home from the war?" I ask. I hope he'll tell me something helpful, something that'll help me understand him, something I can use for the book I'm writing about him.

His eyes are blank. He stares down at his stained trousers. Looks outside the window at the leaves on the ground that he can no longer clear away.

"What war are you talking about?" he says.

And when I tell him it's World War II I'm talking about, and tease him that he isn't old enough to have come home from the Great War, or young enough to have come home from the Korean War or the Vietnam War or Desert Storm or the invasion of Iraq, he sighs and says, "Oh, of course, World War II. Your father is getting to be a very old man."

This is the first time my father can't remember when something happened. The next time I ask my father about what it was like to come home, he tells me about what happened on the island where he was stationed after the war was over, about how pissed off he was that he had to wait four months after Japan surrendered to come home, about how he came home by ship and railroad, about the presents he brought home for me. But he doesn't tell me what I want to learn: what it felt like for him to come home.

So, then, this is what I write. This is how I imagine my father coming home from the war, for if I want to know what it was like for him to come home from the war in the Pacific, I must imagine it, piece the scene together from the bits and pieces of the stories my father has told me, from the details I've remembered, even from those I've misremembered, and then fill in the blanks with the details of my own invention based upon what I know.

1945/2004–2014

The Navy man with the duffel bag gets off the bus at the corner of Washington Street and Fourth in Hoboken, New Jersey. It's winter, it's nighttime, and he's been traveling all day. He's been toting his duffel for weeks on his long journey home from the Admiralty Islands in the Pacific, all the way back home to his wife and little girl. He's been stowing it under his bunk on a ship, up on a luggage rack on a train, behind his legs on one subway and then another, on the seat next to him on a bus, between his legs on a ferry, and finally, up on the luggage rack of this bus, too. Never let the duffel out of his sight. Used it as a pillow, as a hassock, as a bench.

Force of habit, never letting it out of his sight. Because one of the first rules you learn when you go to war is: Make sure you have the right gear; never let your gear out of your sight; never leave your gear behind even if you think leaving it behind will save your life; lug your gear everywhere because without it you're a dead man.

"War's over now," he tells himself. "It's peacetime."

He's sick and tired of his duffel, so when the driver asks if he needs help
to wrestle his gear down the steps, he accepts, making an exception to his
general rule of never accepting someone's help because there are always strings
attached. Not that the duffel's heavy. Not that there's much inside—he's jet-
tisoned some contraband overboard somewhere in the Pacific, so all that's left
is some underwear, a cowrie shell bracelet for his daughter, a pair of stockings
for his wife, the silk from a parachute.

It's not that he can't handle his duffel himself. But he's come a long way,
and he's tired, and he's glad the bus driver has offered to help him even
though he's not a man who asks for help because he believes that if you want
something done right, you have to do it yourself; not a man who asks for help
because he's never gotten any help, not from his father because he wouldn't
help, not from his mother because she couldn't help, and not from any of his
sisters because they were all running fast just to stay behind.

It won't be long now, just a few blocks' walk down Fourth, and then
around the corner to Adams, and up the stairs to their apartment, until he
sees his wife and daughter. And although his wife has sent him pictures of
them both, lots of pictures—in Sunday dresses, in bathrobes, in bathing
suits—tucked into the long letters she's written almost every day during the
war, he hasn't been able to draw the information he needs from the smiles in
these pictures. Are they really as well as his wife says? Is his little girl thriving?
Will his wife slip into a place where he can't reach her?

He's been gone a long time. It's been more than two-and-a-half years since
he's seen his wife and daughter, his little girl with the dark mop of curls, so
small she could barely stagger around the room when he shipped out. His
little girl whose chubby hands grasped at his trousers as he tried to slip out the
door and moved out of her life and out of his wife's life and into the life of a
sailor serving his country at war. And this image of his daughter clutching at
him, then clutching at the air, has seared his memory each day he's been away.

He stands on the corner, his duffel beside him, inhaling the cold night air,
trying to get his bearings, looking up and down the streets of Hoboken that
had once been so familiar to him but that now look like the streets of a foreign
country.

The home my father is returning to is a home that he's never lived in,
never seen, except in the photographs my mother encloses in her letters to

him. The home my father is returning to is not the apartment on Fourteenth Street where we lived before he went away to war, the place that he and my mother worked hard to turn into a home, the place he still thinks of as home, the place where he hoped he could live with my mother and me throughout the war if he were lucky enough to stay behind. So though he is coming home, he is coming home to a home that wasn't ever his, that isn't his yet.

She has told him that she's tried hard to make the parlor, the bedroom, and the kitchen look like the ones in the Fourteenth Street apartment, not only so she didn't have to spend money on new furnishings, but also because she wants my father to come home to a place that seems familiar. The furniture in the parlor is almost the same, although my mother has sold the Chinoiserie side table that didn't fit into this smaller room. The curtains are the same, too, although they've been refashioned for windows with different dimensions. The carpet is the same, but it's been ripped up from the floor, cut, and bound as an area rug. The bedroom furniture is the same, but in this smaller space, the chifforobe looms over the bed, and, instead of the crib that was in the corner of their bedroom, there is now my cot jammed into the space on one side of their bed.

But the door into the apartment is in a different place, and the arrangement of the furniture is different, and so, from when my father first walks into it, the apartment on Adams Street doesn't feel like home. It's unsettling for him to see all the familiar and cherished furniture that my mother and he had carefully chosen for Fourteenth Street arranged differently. And there are no doors separating the parlor from the bedroom, the bedroom from the kitchen, so there is no private space for him and his wife to sit and share confidences after I have been put to bed.

My father feels like he's walked into a stage set that resembles the home he loved and missed and yearned for through all the years he was away. No, it feels as if someone has burgled their old apartment when no one was home, stolen the furniture, and used it to outfit a different place. Through the years we live on Adams Street, until we move to Ridgefield, my father will continue to yearn for the apartment on Fourteenth Street, the life he lived there, no matter how difficult it sometimes was, and the woman and child he left behind.

Still, he's sure of his wife's love, and he knows she's been faithful to him, and he wouldn't have married her unless she was steadfast and true, and she has signed the hundreds of letters she's written him during the war, "Faithfully yours." She's not like the wives of some of his buddies, women who floozed around, who even wrote their combat-worn and battle-weary husbands of their infidelities, sometimes describing in graphic detail what they did with other men. One of his buddies was so undone by his wife's infidelity that he poured gasoline over himself, set himself on fire, and killed himself.

But whether his daughter loves him, or even remembers him, he doesn't know and can't say. And only time will tell. But, my father tells himself, once he's home, he'll get to know his daughter again, know the little girl she's become. A strong-willed little girl is how his wife describes her. A girl who won't take no for an answer. A girl who knows what she wants. You could see that when she was only a year old and crawling at high speed across the linoleum over any barrier that got in the way of what she wanted. A girl, he tells himself, very much like the man he is.

And he'll make up for all the times they've missed. He'll take her to the park, and to the beach, and on Sunday drives into the country so she can breathe some fresh air. He'll toss her high into the air because his girl likes being tossed high into the air, and he won't stop even though his wife tells him to, because the two of them are having such a good time together.

Now that the war is over, my father thinks, life can get back to normal. This is what he and his wife have written about in their letters as he awaited his orders for returning home. Now that the war is over, they can pick up their life where they left it off. This is what his buddies say, too. "We'll pick up where we left off." They'll live their lives as if the war never happened. They believe that because they were strong enough to have survived the war, they are strong enough to forget it.

My father has told himself that he will not think of the war once he's home. Not if he can help it. But when he's in his nineties and we talk about the war, and how he came home from the war, and what happened to us after he came home, and how filled with rage he was, and how he took it out on me, my father tells me that, throughout his life, even when the United States moved into a profound forgetting of that war, even when he did not speak of it to his wife or to me or to any of his friends, really, he thought about the war, read about the war, dreamed about the war, relived the war, and tried to forget about the war, but could not forget, and was angry at himself for not being able to forget.

What my father is returning to is the idea of home. A place where the war can be forgotten. A place where he can pick up his life where he left it off. A place that will soothe and comfort him and heal all the pain he's lived through and witnessed but is not yet willing to—and might never—discuss.

Still, how can that happen for my father? His wife has told him that she moved to the apartment on Adams Street to be close to her father and step-mother during the war. But he thinks we've moved here, not because my mother has chosen to, but because something terrible happened to her on Fourteenth Street, something far worse than what she wrote him about some soldiers thinking their apartment was a whorehouse. For why else would she leave an apartment she cherished, a place they'd both worked on with such loving care, why would she leave their home to move next to her stepmother whom she can't abide?

When my father returns from war, he feels like the doppelgänger of the man who has gone away. He looks the same, though he is thinner and stronger and darker. But he knows from the moment he walks into our apartment, puts down his duffel bag, and embraces my mother, and kisses me, that he is not the same.

Years later, he tells me he felt like a man pretending to be the man who had gone away. But he knew he was no longer that man, though he did not yet know the man he had become. When he came home to an apartment he'd never lived in, to a wife and daughter he hadn't seen in years, and looked around at all the furniture my mother had arranged, and the bedroom with my cot in it, and the cupboards with their dishes and glassware, he did not feel as if he belonged there, in that civilized place, and that he had left his true self, the man he had become, back there on that Pacific island.

(When my mother talked about my father's return from the war, she said he came back a changed man. When pressed about how he'd changed, she'd always utter just a single word. "Angrier.")

The time they've lost can never be reclaimed. He carries a burden he can never share with her. She's changed; she, too, must bear what she's experienced alone; she's not the shy, smiling girl he fell in love with, and whatever playfulness she sometimes had has vanished. And his daughter, too, has changed, for she treats him as if he is an intruder in her life. Still, he vows that there will be good times aplenty. Swims in the ocean. Sunday walks to the parapet on the Heights to look at the Hudson River. Games of pinochle with his male relatives. Celebratory family meals.

He tries to splice his new life with us into the life he left behind. But at least right now, there is no continuity, and nothing seems to make much sense. And the worst of it is that my father feels as if he has invaded my and my mother's home and that he doesn't belong there. He feels as if he has to adapt himself to our routines. He tells everyone that if anyone rules the roost, I do. For since we have moved to Adams Street, I have been pampered and spoiled and doted on by my grandparents, and my father thinks I've become a willful child, used to being the center of attention and greatly in need of discipline.

Still, it's not as if the war hasn't given him something for all the things it's taken away. If my father has learned anything during the war, he's learned not to think about the future, because you may not have one. He's learned that you must create your own good times right here, right now, because there's no telling when your life will be over. And perhaps this is why, in so many of the photos of my father from the war, he's the only man smiling. A good life isn't something that will happen next year. It's not something that's handed to you on a silver platter. It's not something you're entitled to. Knowing that your life can be over in a moment hasn't stopped my father from living his life. As he's learned in the war, and as he tells his daughter at the end of their life together, "You can't sit still and play possum. You gotta present a moving target."

And so he's found that curiosity, at all times, and in every situation, above all else, breeds pleasure. He will find it after the war, no matter what else goes on in our family, in reading a good book, in learning all he can about the war so he can understand it, in fixing something that's broken, in standing with his face to the wind at the edge of the sea, in watching the moon crest the trees, in climbing to the top of the next hill to see what's on the other side, in listening to the thrum of a well-tuned engine, in making something with your own hands. And he's learned, too, that you must take pleasure in the small and quiet moments of life—a good strong cup of coffee, the smell of the earth after a summer rain, the bite of a Scotch and water at the end of a hard day, a bracing swim in the ocean, standing back and admiring a desk you've made for your daughter. And you must do this even during life's catastrophes, tragedies, griefs, and disappointments, because you will never be free of them.

What my father wants, most of all, when the war is over, is for his family to be happy and for him to earn enough money so that he can be secure. Beyond that, his desires are few. A car, maybe. A road trip to take with his family once a year during his week-long vacation.

But he and his wife have exchanged letters about how, someday, maybe, they can move to a nicer neighborhood or even out of Hoboken. Before the war, my father never imagined that a working man like him could own a home. Before the war, the only people who owned their own homes were rich. Before the war, and during the war, even finding an apartment to rent unless you knew someone was almost impossible.

Now, though, there are articles in magazines, my mother has written, about how every serviceman can own his own home after the war. Payback for service to the nation, for hardships endured, for putting your life on hold. And she tells him that thinking about how they will start a new life and live happily together in that home—she'll bake the pies he loves, she'll garden, she'll make curtains for the windows—is helping her "buck up" the way he wants her to, helping her to carry on. And, yes, in three years' time, my parents will move out of Hoboken, they will move to Ridgefield, they will own their own home.

What my father didn't know then was that no matter where he moved—and veterans and their families moved, in the years after the war, in enormous numbers, from small apartments to larger ones or into single-family dwellings constructed at a furious rate to house homecoming GIs—the men they had become during the war could not be left behind on the curb with whatever they had chosen not to take with them into their new lives. The men they had become during the war were the very ones moving into these new spaces that promised much and delivered little of what these men needed: a life that could erase the war; a life that could recover the men they'd left behind; a life where those who died could be resurrected.

For my father, and countless others, and for their families, there will be no normalcy, although there would be its pretense. Lawns mowed and watered. Gardens planted and fertilized. Bushes pruned. Houses painted and decorated. Fires in coal-burning furnaces stoked and banked. Thanksgivings celebrated. Vacations taken. Christmas trees decorated, presents given. Graduations attended. Veterans Day parades marched in.

When my father sees the house in Ridgefield, he's filled with hope that, here, they will have a better life, a life that will erase the pain of war, that will obliterate his wife's sorrow. Here, his wife and her stepmother—who will move in with them after her husband's death—won't get on one another's nerves, for there will be bedrooms for them to retreat into. Here, his daughters will be able to play outside and grow robust and strong. Here, he will come home at the end of the day, settle into a comfortable chair in front of a fire in winter, or in a lounge chair on the porch looking at the sunset in summer, and put his troubles behind him.

But my father cannot predict the future. No, my father does not yet know what will happen in this wreck of a house that his and his wife's hard labor will turn into something beautiful. And so, he thinks, "This is a nice place. We'll fix it up. And we'll be very happy here."

Throughout his life, my father flies the American flag outside a window of his apartment, outside a window of his house, outside the door of his second wife's house, "for respect," he tells me. He flies the flag until he's in his nineties, even though it's risky for him to climb a ladder. He flies the flag every Memorial Day, Fourth of July, Veterans Day, and Labor Day. He flies it on the anniversary of the bombing of Pearl Harbor, on the anniversary of the Allied assault on the beaches of Normandy, from which, he will instruct me, when I visit there, to bring him home one stone for each of his friends who died there (I bring him five). He flies the flag on VE Day, on VJ day.

And he flies the flag, too, on November 10, takes it down at the end of the day because it's disrespectful to fly a flag after sunset, and then flies it again the next day, Veterans Day, and for years, I don't understand why, but now I know. For November 10 is the day the USS Mount Hood exploded; November 10 is the day my father stopped his work and stood on the shore of Seeadler Harbor in the Admiralty Islands and watched, helplessly, as so very men died.

The Evening News

1957

After supper, my father goes into the TV room to watch the news while my mother cleans the kitchen. I go upstairs to do my homework, and my sister goes into our bedroom to do hers. From my perch at my desk at the top of the stairs, I can hear the hum of Chet Huntley's and David Brinkley's voices and the thrum, thuds, explosions, and retorts from the footage they're showing.

Somewhere, elsewhere, there's a war. Somewhere, elsewhere, there's always a war, and there'll always be a war, my father says.

No one interrupts my father during the evening news and I know enough to stay away. It's quiet time I can count on, if you can call the sound of a battle raging somewhere in the world quiet. Sometimes, though, my curiosity overwhelms me and I sneak down the stairs, pretending to get a snack even though my father has declared that the kitchen is closed, as it always is after supper, so I can peek into the TV room and see what's happening.

My father stares at the television with fierce concentration, his fists balled tight, his lips tensed. He would turn on me with fire in his eyes if I bothered him, so I make sure to stay out of sight.

My mother wishes he wouldn't watch the news every night, says it's no way to end the day, it upsets him, it makes him crazy.

He tells her it's a citizen's duty to be informed. He says he wants to know what's going on; he wants to know the story behind the story even though he says you'll never know what's really going on because the "powers that be" never let you know. So why does he watch, I wonder, but then think he'd rather be over there in the middle of the action than here with us. He'd rather be anywhere, even in a place where you might get killed, than here with us.

After my mother finishes the dishes, she brings my father another cup of coffee and settles into her rocking chair in the farthest corner of the room from the TV. She wants to be with him even though he's not with her. She embroiders, darns a sock, or leafs through a magazine. She tries to keep her eyes off the screen but can't. Every so often, she glances at what's happening, purses her lips, and turns back to what she's doing.

Sometimes she interrupts him to say, "Lou, haven't you had enough of this by now?" Sometimes he glares at her before resuming his viewing; sometimes he ignores her. But he never answers her. We all know he hasn't had enough of this by now, and that he'll never have enough of this.

One time, when my father gets up from the supper table as usual and tells my mother he's going to watch the evening news, she asks him why he bothers.

"You can't do anything about it," she says. "Nothing ever changes. Every day, it's the same old thing. You did your duty. You served your time."

My father slams his fist on the table. The dirty dishes rattle.

"It's *not* the same old thing, goddamn it," my father says. His voice is loud, his body tense. I wonder whether I'll have to run for cover.

"Every battle, every day of every battle, every minute of every battle is different. Just ask the poor bastards who are there."

For the past six months, my father's been following the news about Israel's invasion of Sinai and Gaza. While he watches, my father says nothing. Sometimes he shakes his head. Sometimes he gets up from his chair, turns up the volume; sometimes he gets up and turns the volume down. From watching him, I can't tell whose side he's on.

After the news, my father picks up a history book and reads. That's what he always does after he watches the evening news. Now he's reading *Breaking the Bismarcks Barrier* by Samuel Eliot Morison, and it will take him several months to finish because he reads so slowly, mouthing the words, moving his index finger under the line of print, like a kid in grammar school.

One day, when he's at work, I peek at the table of contents and learn that it's another book about World War II. At the back of the volume is a foldout map of the Pacific Ocean. My father—I'm pretty sure he's the one who's done it—has circled the Admiralties with a sharp red pen that's cut through the paper. They're in the Bismarck Archipelago, a few black dots in the vastness of that ocean, so very far away from the western coast of the United States and from the Hawaiian Islands, and closer to New Guinea, Australia, the Philippines, and Japan.

The Admiralties, I know, is where my father was stationed during the war and I see how very far away he was from my mother and me.

At the back of the book is a chapter my father has dog-eared, Chapter XXVI, "The Admiralties Annexed." I don't yet know anything about what happened on the Admiralties; I haven't yet learned about the battle that wrested this place from the Japanese. I don't yet know anything about World War II, and I won't learn anything until I'm in college because my high school American History teacher never gets to World War II—it's the Great War that fascinates him. Although I'm curious and want to read what my father has read, I put the book down. I'm afraid that he'll find out I've looked at it, and I know he'll consider this a serious offense.

Two years later, when I'm a senior in high school, my father asks me if we're studying the war in the Pacific in history. I tell him we're still learning about trench warfare. It's late May, and when my father figures out that at the rate my teacher is covering the material, we'll never get to World War II, he calls him an ignoramus.

"What could be more important than you kids learning about the war your fathers fought?" he asks.

He rarely asks me about school, rarely knows what's going on, although he insists that I do my homework and is happy when I do well. But when he hears this, my father decides he'll set up a meeting with my teacher to give him a piece of his mind. But the meeting never happens.

Maybe my father doesn't get around to it because he feels uncomfortable around anyone who's gone to college. Or maybe it's because he can't take a day off from work. I'm grateful he never does because I could never face my teacher again if my father had treated him to one of his harangues.

When I'm in college, every now and then my father asks, "Have you learned anything about World War II yet?" And maybe because of my father's questions, or because of my wanting to know what he's lived through, I do begin learning about that war, and when I tell him that I have, he says, "Good, about time," and nothing more.

During those months when my father watches the news about Israel's invasion of Sinai and Gaza, I'll still be working on my homework at ten o'clock when my parents go to bed. If I've finished my homework, I'll pretend I have even more work that I tell them I absolutely have to finish.

I'm always the last person in the house to go to bed, the last person to go to sleep. My parents think it's because I have all this homework and my mother wonders why they give so much to kids in high school. But I stay up and don't go to bed yet because I know I won't sleep until I hear my father snoring.

The Last Time My Father Almost Died

2004

The last time my father almost died, I held his hand and told him he was the best father in the world. I told him he was a terrific grandfather, that my kids adored him. I told him he'd done a great job raising me. I thanked him for everything he'd done for me, told him I loved him, told him I'd always love him, that I'd never forget him. I told him that we'd miss him. But that if he wanted to, he could go, that he didn't have to stick around for me, that I was fine, that my husband and children were fine.

He was suffering, had been suffering for some time. His heart was failing and there wasn't anything anyone could do about it, they told me at the nursing home. I wanted to trust that they knew what they were talking about. But it was a piss-smelling nursing home, one that I'd tried to move my father out of, but that I couldn't, at least not right away, because there were no empty beds anywhere else.

On the day when I told my father he could go if he wanted to, he'd slipped into a coma in the middle of the night and the nursing home had called me to come see him.

"It won't be long," the counselor said. My husband disagreed. We'd been through this before. My father seeming to be dying. Rebounding. Getting somewhat better. Getting much better. Getting worse again. Then rallying against all expectations.

"He won't go easily," my husband said. "Not your father. He'll stick around a little while longer to torment you." Despite everything, my husband loved my father. Most people did. He helped my husband fix things. Played with our kids. Never lost his temper with them even though he swore a lot. Still, all these years of our marriage, except for the time when my father was in the hospital or the nursing home, my husband still never left me alone with him. He knew better than that.

The last time I'd come to the nursing home, my father was very much alive, and as pissed off as ever.

"When you see my wife," he'd said, "tell her to haul her ass up here to see me. No one ever comes to see me. Not her. Not you."

I'd been there the day before, but there was no use reminding him. Either he'd forgotten, or pretended I hadn't come so he could yell at me. He didn't say hello. Didn't thank me for coming. Didn't say he was glad to see me. He never did.

I didn't want to go through it all again. How her daughters wouldn't drive her to see him because they didn't want her near him.

"The next time I see her," I said, "I'll tell her to come and see you."

He'd wanted to come and live with me. I'd considered it. My husband, though, said no way, absolutely not, under no circumstances.

"If he comes," my husband said, "I go." I knew he wasn't being heartless. I knew he wanted to protect me.

Before we took my father to the nursing home, I'd bought him a new wardrobe when I realized he didn't have any clothes that weren't completely worn out or so encrusted with filth they were impossible to clean. Why I hadn't noticed this, I can't say. Maybe I was too wrapped up in his stories. I'd seen him several times a week for the past few years. We'd sit in the sunroom and talk. The sicker he got, the nicer he was to me. Not always. But often enough to make me think he'd changed.

I'd bought him his new wardrobe from TravelSmith. I knew all his sizes so it was easy. I even had fun doing it. I called the 1–800 number. Told the person on the other end of the line the items I wanted. It was better than going to the mall. I'd made a list and set him up with clothing he could have worn on an Elderhostel cruise. A few pairs of khakis. A few pairs of blue and black trousers. Several plaid shirts. (All nonwrinkle; all machine washable.) A few sweaters. Underwear, undershirts, handkerchiefs. A black belt, a brown belt. A windbreaker and winter jacket and hat. I thought he'd like his new clothes. I thought maybe he'd thank me.

"Where the hell do you think I'm going?" he asked. "What'd you buy all this stuff for? I'm on a long, slow road to hell and there's no way out and no way back."

I knew he didn't want to go to the nursing home, but there wasn't anything I could do about it. Still, I wanted him to look nice while he was there. But maybe I was trying to assuage my guilt. Because I still thought that, no matter what, it was my duty to take him home and care for him.

The only thing I couldn't buy from TravelSmith were new sneakers. He'd ruined the only pair of sneakers he had when he shit all over himself. I'd tried to throw them away; he'd taken them out of the trash and cleaned them the best he could and refused to part with them. The new ones were hard to find. I had to trace the outline of his old sneakers on a piece of paper and take it to a bunch of stores because he couldn't come with me. The kids who worked in these stores (hip, tattooed, spiked hair, very cool) had no idea why I insisted on Velcro. None of them sold sneakers with Velcro.

"He can't lace his shoes," I told one, then another. "He needs Velcro, not laces."

"Oh," they'd say, and then bring me more sneakers with laces. I finally found what I needed in a store for nurses.

"You came to the right place," the salesman said. "Nurses like Velcro, even male nurses." I wanted to tell him these sneakers weren't for a male nurse, but I didn't bother.

The morning when my father was in a coma, before I went up to his room, I stopped in to see the counselor who managed his care.

"It won't be long," she said, and gave me a pamphlet about how to talk to loved ones when they're dying. She was all business, no condolences, she went through this all the time. That's why I told my father all the things I did, about how he was a good father, and how I loved him.

Still, I wanted my father to die. It was time for him to die. But I didn't want him to die. Not for his sake, but for my own. During these last long years of his illness, I had come to count on the stories about his life. He never told me he loved me. But he gave me these stories. Maybe he knew he didn't have long to live. Maybe he wanted me to understand who he was and what had happened to him.

I'd listened to him. Asked questions. Wrote things down as soon as I got home. I thought it was unusual that my father was talking to me like this. We had never been that close. I'd never wanted to spend much time with him. As I was growing up, he didn't talk much about life or about his time in the Navy, elliptical comments every now and then, stories that were started but never finished, although the war was always there between us. I was interested in what he had to say, and wasn't. I wanted to know why he was the man he'd become, and I suspected that what had happened to him when he was in the Navy would tell me what I needed to hear. I wanted to forgive him for being such a bastard and I figured that if I understood him I could.

But I also didn't want to know, didn't want to forgive him. After all this time, I still didn't want to understand him. Hating him (or pretending that I hated him) was easier than understanding him, easier than loving him. Understanding him would lead to love, I knew, and that, I feared, would be way too hard. I loved him, sure, I had to; he was my father. But I was afraid that his stories would mire me in a different kind of love, a caring kind of love rather than a doing-my-duty-by-my-parent kind of love. But of course the caring kind of love was the kind of love I wanted to have for him, had wanted to have for him, but couldn't, for ever so long.

"What you should say to a loved one near death," the pamphlet read, "is this: If you want to go, you can go. I love you. I'll be fine." If you say this, your loved one won't fight death. Your loved one will know there's no unfinished business between you, and he or she can slip away peacefully.

When I told my father he was the best father in the world, that he did a great job raising me, I wasn't saying what I believed. But I thought it needed saying, even if I didn't believe it. I owed him that much, at least. I thought it was okay to pretend.

"Look," my father had once said to me. "It's only the two of us now. We'd better learn to get along." Which meant that I had to be nice to him while he still could be mean to me. My sister was dead: a suicide. She was thirty-six when she died; I was forty; it was a long time ago; I rarely thought about her. My mother was dead: a slow suicide—she'd stopped taking the pills that were keeping her alive without telling anybody; she'd never been the same after my sister's death. My father blamed me for my sister's death, blamed me for my mother's depression, blamed me for his rages, blamed me for almost everything.

"If only you were nicer," he once said, "if only you weren't so cold-hearted and selfish, they'd both be alive." I couldn't argue with my father about that. I was cold-hearted. I had to be. And I knew if I wasn't selfish, if I didn't take care of myself, if I didn't put up a wall between me and them, my fingers would slip off the gunwale of my life raft and I'd drown.

I was the next-of-kin, responsible for my father's medical care. My husband had made my father sign the legal documents. I could order the nursing home to call an ambulance; order them to take my father to the hospital; order the hospital to see what, if anything, could be done to save my father's life. But that would be risky, the counselor said. He might live on in a chronic vegetative state, and I wouldn't want that.

"I wouldn't do that," she'd said. "He's suffered enough. Let him go."

I didn't like being the one to decide whether my father lived or died. I wanted him to go. But I wanted him to stay, too. I wanted nature to take its course. But I couldn't figure out if he was dying or if this piss-smelling nursing home was killing him.

For hours, I sat there, holding my father's hand, telling him he could go if he wanted to, and not meaning it. He didn't open his eyes, though his eyelids fluttered. He didn't utter a comprehensible sound, though once in a while he moaned.

I looked out the window at the water meadow behind the nursing home. I was glad that my father had had this nice view to look at. There were geese on the water. A flock of them. They took off. They landed. They took off again. It was my father who had told me that geese mate for life and that when their mates died, they mourned.

I listen for my father's last breath, listen for that last long, slow expulsion of air. It's a beautiful day outside, I think, far too beautiful a day for my father to die.

One hour passes. Then two. Then six. And still, he lingers. Still he isn't gone.

* * *

Late that afternoon, after work, my husband comes to the nursing home.

"He's hanging on," my husband says. "He won't let go."

I'm tired of sitting, tired of waiting, tired of holding my father's hand.

"Jesus," I say. "Let's get him the hell out of here. Let's call an ambulance, take him to the hospital, let's see if they can bring him back."

"Are you sure?" my husband asks.

I am sure. I'm not ready, even if my father is. I think maybe, if he gets just a little bit better, we can have some time to make things right. Or at least, righter than they are.

"Yes, I'm sure," I tell my husband. "I still need a little more time."

EPILOGUE

Wearing My Father's Bones

2008

"Do you believe you'll see your beloved parent in Heaven?"

It's three years after my father's death. My husband and I are attending the funeral of my daughter-in-law's grandmother, who died just weeks short of her hundredth birthday. The priest is standing behind the lectern, it's the end of his sermon, and he's asking her children this question.

Like my father, this old woman had been shoveling snow, cleaning gutters, mowing her lawn, trimming bushes, and driving her very old and very large car too fast and not quite on the right side of the road until she moved into a nursing home at the very end of her life. She was what my father would have called an "ornery bastard"—unforgiving, critical, obstinate, sharp-tongued. But, like him, too, she was also hardworking, independent, active, intelligent, and passionate about life.

So here I am, sitting in a Roman Catholic church for the first time since my father's funeral a few years before, just behind the members of the grand-mother's immediate family, who haven't yet answered the priest's question. I'm thinking about how much I'd loved going to Sunday mass as a girl because the church was beautiful and flower-bedecked and comforting, with the priest intoning the Latin mass, the altar boys responding, the organ playing, and the choir singing, and also because it was a place your parents couldn't talk to you, a place where you couldn't be yelled at, and a place where, for one blessed hour every week, you could have some peace.

"Do you believe that you will see your beloved parent in Heaven?" The portly priest, in his floor-length gold-embroidered cream vestment, comes down from the altar and now stands facing the deceased's children. His sermon has dwelled upon the message that, although death seems terrible to the living, it isn't so for the dead because they are now with God, and it's only our own selfishness that prevents us from celebrating their death rather than mourning it.

But now he wants an answer to his question so he can get on with his prepared remarks, which will, no doubt, be about how all the souls of the saved will be reunited in heaven.

There is another long pause. The rustle of clothing. A few coughs. A squawk of irritation from a great-great-grandchild followed by the hushed and comforting words of the baby's mother.

"Do you believe that you will see your beloved parent in Heaven?" he repeats, now looking directly at one of the daughters, the woman most responsible for her mother's care throughout her last difficult months.

And as I await the inevitable answer, "Yes, I do believe I will be reunited with her in Heaven," for no one, I think, would have the courage to defile this sacred ritual, I myself respond to his question in what I think is a hushed whisper. But it turns out that what I say is loud enough for the congregation to hear.

"I hope to hell not."

2005

When I answer the call that comes in the middle of the night to tell me that my father has died, I say to myself, "I'm glad it's over," although of course it isn't, because, in a way, it has just begun.

We've had that time together, those moments of closeness I'd craved for years. But then there was that day when the violence in him that had been submerged for close to two years resurfaced, and he destroyed everything he could get his hands on in the house he shared with his second wife, and he tried to get his hands on me. In the months before he died, we reverted to the worst of the life we'd shared before.

After I learn my father is dead, I struggle back to sleep, and into a dream. In the dream, my father is in the nursing home in the bed where he died. His body is covered with a shroud and he has a hood over his head and wrappings around his face.

I stand at the foot of the bed, watching. I don't want to stay, but I can't leave. So I say to the body in the bed, "Can I go now? Are you really, really dead?"

My father pulls his hands free of the shroud, pushes the hood off his head, unwraps the swaddling from his face, sits up, looks at me, and says, "Not yet." Then he lies back on the bed, pulls the shroud back over him, and leaves me standing there knowing that it will start all over again, our life together, one I don't want, but one I'm bound to.

During the last weeks of my father's life, he barely speaks to me. He insists I've captured him and incarcerated him in a motel. I decide, one day, to bring a few art books and show him some of his favorite works. If he doesn't talk to me, fine. But maybe he will. A nurse who cares for him thinks the paintings are a good idea.

"Sometimes," she says, "angry men like your father find their sweeter side before they die."

She knows the story of how my father wound up here. Knows that he became enraged at his wife one day because she wouldn't stop asking him questions he'd answered many times before. Knows he became abusive to me when I tried to calm him down. Knows he went through their home smashing everything breakable he could get his hands on. Knows he went through drawers and closets and tossed all their clothing onto the floor. Knows he tore books and papers into very small pieces, flinging his madman's confetti into the air. Knows the destruction went on for two days. Knows that nothing could stop him, not even the police who were called, knows that he finally fell down exhausted, hit his head against the floor, gave himself a subdural hemorrhage, got himself taken to the hospital in an ambulance, spent some time in the locked psychiatric ward, and, after a while, got taken to the nursing home because he was weak and because his wife's family wouldn't let him go back home because they thought he was too dangerous.

Though he'd never visited a museum, my father loved art, especially the paintings of Leonardo da Vinci, Michelangelo, and Raphael, whose works he studied in the Time-Life books he'd bought in middle age. Often, after a long day's work, and supper, and after he'd looked at the evening news, he would sit and leaf through a volume.

During the last weeks of his life, I bring him a reproduction of Michelangelo's *Last Judgment*, and it captures his attention.

What can it have been like for him, so close to death, to look at Michelangelo's work, to see the hand of Christ committing sinners to hell? To see the names engraved in the book of sinners? To witness the decaying flesh of the newly buried? The skeletons of the dead? The devils massed under a fiery sky? Charon's boat ferrying the damned to Hell?

My father points to an old, gray-haired, flaccid-breasted sinner, his body encircled by a snake, the snake's mouth clamped around the man's genitals.

"Death's got him by the balls," my father says. These are the first words my father says to me in days.

And death will have you by the balls soon enough, old man, I think, but don't say.

My father never tells me whether he believes in Heaven and Hell, or whether he believes that after death he'll be reunited with my mother, his one, his only true love. He never tells me he's afraid of dying, never tells me what he thinks will become of him after his death, never discusses how to arrange his funeral.

Whenever I'd asked him if he'd been afraid of dying during the war, he'd said no, he never thought about it, he just kept his head down, did his job, never volunteered, tried to present a moving target, and tried to get through the war in one piece so he could come home.

Now, a few days before his death, with Michelangelo's representation of the battle for the souls of the dead before him, my father runs his coarse, working man's fingers over the bare flesh of angels, sinners, and the saved, to touch life one last time.

The morning after my father dies, I tell my husband my mid-night dream and how my father says he's not dead yet.

"Sounds like something your father would say," my husband remarks. I tell my husband it isn't funny, that I'm afraid my dream is telling me I'll never be free of him.

What I don't tell my husband is that I dream, too, that my father tells me how he wants me to arrange his funeral. He wants a simple coffin, and not too many flowers. But he wants an honor guard of firemen, a cortege accompanied by fire engines and motorcycle policemen, and a military honor guard. "The whole shebang," he says.

"What's with you and all this hoopla?" I ask. "I thought you were a simple man."

"Don't argue with me," he says. "Just do as you're told."

He tells me he wants his wife to ride in the first limousine with her family.

"But I've taken care of you all these months," I say, "and she only came to visit you a few times."

"What's right is right," my father says. "She's my wife. You're just my daughter."

The day after my father dies, I arrange my father's funeral just like he tells me in my dream. I make sure the fire engines will sound their sirens and the motorcycles will rev their engines as they speed along beside the hearse. I make sure that police cars will clear the route to the cemetery. I make sure the hearse will pass by the house where my father lived with my mother, my sister, and me; the house where he lived with his second wife; and the firehouse where he spent so much time.

At the graveside ceremony, his coffin will be covered with the United States flag and he will be given a military burial befitting a veteran of that war. The honor guard of firemen will take off their white gloves and throw them atop the coffin before it is lowered into the ground. There will be a sailor in full dress regalia playing "Taps" as my father's coffin disappears into the earth. The sailor will fold the flag ceremoniously and present it to his wife. And then there will be a lavish dinner for the mourners at his favorite restaurant.

"Take me to the ocean, set me on fire."

It's the last week of my father's life. He's on morphine, in pain, hallucinating. He's thrashing. His eyes are open. He seems conscious. Yet he's making no sense.

Is he telling me he wants his body cremated? That he doesn't want to be buried in the family plot with my mother, my sister, and my mother's parents?

And then I remember.

A few months ago, just before he became violent, before he went to the hospital and then the nursing home, my father and I sit together in his sunroom, talking about the war one last time, and my father takes a book down from his shelf.

"You're interested in anthropology," my father says. "Didn't you take a course in it when you were in college? You might be interested in this."

I'm stunned that my father remembers. Until now, I myself have forgotten.

My father hands me a book about the customs of the Manus people of the Admiralty Islands. Is it the book I've read and brought to him and left there? In it, there's a description of a warrior's funeral, and a series of photographs of artifacts used in the ceremony.

My father tells me he'd witnessed a part of that ceremony when he was stationed there. The body of the deceased man was placed on a canoe carved with birds and bedecked with palm fronds, just like in the photo. The body was taken from the canoe, placed on the sand, together with the dead man's bed that was turned upside down atop his body. The bed was set afire, and after, the remains of the charred body were left until birds picked the bones clean.

I read how family members took the deceased's bones and cleansed them in salt water. How, with tools of obsidian, they crosshatched images upon the dead man's bones. How they painted their own bodies black and bound their arms with plaited bands. How they took the bones of their ancestor, wrapped them in leaves, and wore them on their bodies for a month of mourning. How, after a month, they cleansed their own bodies in the sea, and threw the dead man's bones into the deep.

I imagine how it would be to give my father that kind of burial, how it would be to crosshatch my grief upon my father's bones, to wrap them in leaves, to wear them on my body for a month. I imagine how it would be to wash away my grief in the sea and throw my father's bones into the deep, where they would mingle with the corals and the remains of sea creatures and all his lost comrades.

2010

It's the fifth anniversary of my father's death. My elder son calls me. He's upset and angry.

He's visited the cemetery where my father is buried. He's found the gravesite. The grass hasn't been tended. The gravestone is sinking. The date of my father's death hasn't been engraved on the tombstone.

"Have you ever even visited?" my son asks. "Your father went there once a week. He kept the grave meticulous, washed the tombstone, planted flowers."

My son visits the grave of his ancestors once every few months. I haven't been there since my father's burial. I've been too busy writing my book about him. On this day, I've been looking at pictures of my father taken during the war. Photographs of that young, beautiful, bare-chested, dog-tagged man, crouching in front of his Quonset hut. Photographs of that young man with aviator glasses standing in front of a tree clutched by vines. That man, wearing his flight jacket with his sailor hat tilted rakishly back on his head. That smiling man, crouching with his buddies in front of palm trees and grass huts with a can of beer in his hands. That man with ear protectors, sitting in the cockpit of an airplane, and another of him standing on its wing. That man, taking his ration of water from a drum suspended from a tree. That man sitting at the wheel of the jeep he and his buddies tried to figure out how to take back home. That man who left me when I was fourteen months old and who never came back.

My son tells me he went to the cemetery office and complained about the neglect. He told them our family paid for perpetual care of the gravesite. He wants the gravestone to be righted, wants the date of my father's death carved on the stone.

"His next of kin has to arrange that," the manager answers. And then he gives my son the number of a stonecutter to call.

I take down the information, and thank my son for it. I file it away. My father's relationship with both my sons has been everything a grandson could desire. They've played games together; cooked together; watched funny movies together; gone out to lunch together; gone down the Jersey shore together. It's no wonder my son visits his grave.

I'll get around to doing it, I tell myself, when I've finished this book, when I'm not so busy.

A year goes by. Then two. Then four.

My son visits the cemetery, calls me, tells me the stone's been righted; the lawn's been mowed.

"But what about the date of death on the gravestone?" he asks. "Have you called the stonecutter?"

I haven't. And I tell him I'm not going to call the stonecutter until I finish writing this book.

"But if someone your family knows visits the gravesite," my son says, "they won't realize he's dead. They'll think he's still alive."

"Maybe that's the whole point," I reply.

Maybe I don't want to admit that my father's really dead and that's why I haven't had the date of his death carved onto his tombstone. Maybe it's taking me so long to write this book because by holding on to it, I'm holding on to my father, I'm trying to undo the moment when he went to war. Maybe I don't want my father to leave me; maybe I don't want to leave my father. Still, I know that I have to finish this book. I know that I have to acknowledge my loss of him, back then, and now, by finishing.

I know the greatest challenge for me lies ahead. To let go of this book. To let go of my father and move on. To call the stonecutter and tell him, after all these years, to carve my father's name, the date of his death, and the words "Beloved husband and father, and a veteran of World War II" onto his tombstone.

2014

I awaken in the middle of the night with another dream about my father. I'm close to finishing this book, I think. Finally. I'll be finished in a week, two at most, I tell myself. Still, there are so many files I want to review for a detail I might have missed, and I tell myself there's no reason to rush this. So maybe not a week or two. Maybe I'll be finished in a few months. Maybe by Christmas.

"So," my father says in the dream, "it's time for you to put a stop to this. You've dragged this book on far too long. Don't you realize you're torturing me? Don't you know you're making me live through all those years all over again? Some of them were hard enough to live through once. But again and again and again? Look, I've worked long and hard in my life and now I deserve a rest."

"You're kidding me," I say back to my father in the dream. I want to say that writing about him has been no walk in the park. As always, I'm ready for a battle. "Torturing you by writing about you? How do you even know what I'm writing? Where are you, anyway?"

"Not where I want to be," my father says. "As I said, I want to be resting. I lived a long life; worked hard; I deserve a rest."

In the dream, my father suddenly materializes in my study. My desk is cluttered with a stack of folders I want to review. The pages of the manuscript of this book that might be so near completion are in a neat pile on the table under the window. My father isn't standing behind me, looking over my shoulder, trying to read what I'm writing. He's standing in front of my desk, not looking at me, but looking around the room at the shelves of books about the war, at the open filing cabinet stuffed with information, at the manuscript. I'm afraid that he's going to ask me if he can read this book. But he doesn't ask me; he doesn't move; he just stands there and watches me.

"A helluva life," he says. "Is this what you do all day, sit at your desk and write? If I had to do what you do, it would drive me batshit."

I don't want to laugh. But I have to.

"Look," my father says. "I know I knocked you around. But I'll make you a deal. If you finish this frigging book and stop torturing me for what I did to you and let me rest, and we go our separate ways, I promise you that you'll be fine, that nothing bad will happen to you. You're a chip off the old block, after all. You can take care of yourself."

I don't answer him at first. I don't want to think about what it will be like to sit at this desk without writing this story, his story, our story. I don't want to think about what it will be like not to write about my father day after day after day.

"So," I say to him, "what will you do if I don't stop writing about you?"

"That's easy," my father says. "I'll start writing about *you*."

And now we're both laughing. We're both laughing hard because we know this is an empty threat, this will never happen. We both know that writing is the last thing in the world my father would want to do. We both know that if he wrote about me, then he'd be torturing himself, he wouldn't be torturing me.

"Okay, okay," I say. "It's a deal."

I look at my father. My father looks at me. I don't want another parting. I don't want to say goodbye.

"Don't look so sad," my father says. And then he reaches down into the pocket of his jeans, the old stained and tattered ones that he wore every day in that sweetest of times, those last months we spent together while he told me about his life, about his first tour of duty in the Navy, about how he'd met and married my mother, about how he took care of me after I was born, about how he had to go to the Pacific but didn't want to, about how hard it was for him after he came home. He reaches deep into the pocket of his jeans, pulls out a crumpled twenty-dollar bill, straightens it out, and puts in on my desk.

"Here's a twenty," my father says. "Go out and buy yourself something nice. You've been working hard. You deserve it."

ACKNOWLEDGMENTS

Thanks, first, and always, to my husband, Ernest J. DeSalvo, who has lived with this book for far too long, who has read it and helped edit it, who did not flinch when I told him I was beginning the book, and transforming it, yet again. And thanks, too, to my sons, Jason and Justin, who reported stories my father told them, and to my daughters-in-law, Deborah and Lynn, who are such important presences in my life, and to my grandchildren, Steven and Julia, who bring such joy at the end of a day's work.

I thank President Jennifer J. Raab; Cristina Alfar, past chair of the Department of English; Sarah Chinn, current chair of the Department of English, and Hunter College for granting me two sabbaticals, during which much of this book was written. Thanks, too, to Amy Jo Burns and Lia Ottaviano, for research help through many long years.

This book took on a new life, and new possibilities for it emerged, when I read portions of it to Christina Baker Kline and Pamela Redmond Satran many years ago, and I'm grateful to Christina Baker Kline for her careful reading of an early manuscript. Jan Heller Levi urged me on, also, and her reading of early sections of the work was extremely useful. Edvige Giunta, my writing partner, helped enormously through the years by reminding me how long this book might take, by cheering me on when I was despondent, by listening to my challenges and offering me concrete solutions, and for insisting that I finish. And without Audrey Goldrich's help through the years and critical advice about how I might finish, I might still be mired in yet another rewriting.

My thanks to Fredric Nachbaur, director of Fordham University Press, for his encouragement through the years and for seeing this book through to publication. I thank Will Cerbone, assistant to the director, for his help. I am grateful for the suggestions made by four anonymous reviewers and to G. Kurt Piehler, series editor of "World War II: The Global, Human, and Ethical Dimension," for his careful reading of the manuscript and for his important suggestions. Thanks, also, to Eric Newman, managing editor, for his and his staff's help during the final stages of publication; to Susan Zucker, who designed the cover; to Ann-Christine Racette, production manager, who created the text design; and to Kate O'Brien-Nicholson and Kathleen A. Sweeney for all they've done to help market this book.

Sources Consulted

A note to the reader: This memoir is based upon the stories my father told me. After he described an event—say, the explosion of the *USS Mount Hood*—and as I was writing, I located and checked sources relating to that event to describe it more fully in the narrative, or to check my father's recollection against other sources. I read, too, background material to deepen my understanding of my father's story. Still, this is a work of memoir, not a purely historical accounting of the events I describe.

In addition to the sources listed here, I perused issues of *The New York Times* from 1935 to 1945 to establish a timeline against which to read my father's and my parents' experiences.

"Admiralty Islands Campaign," From Wikipedia, http://en.wikipedia.org/wiki /Admiralty_Islands_campaign.

"Admiralty Islands: 15 February 1944–4 April 1944," http://ussjpkennedyjr.org /swanson443/swanad.html.

Ambrose, Hugh. *The Pacific: Hell Was an Ocean Away* (New York: New American Library, 2010).

Anders, Tex. "Oral History of the Bombing of the *USS Panay*," http://archive.org /details/1937-12-12_Bombing_of_USS_Panay.

Anonymous. *A Woman in Berlin: Eight Weeks in a Conquered City, a Diary* (New York: Henry Holt and Company, 2000).

Atkinson, Rick. *The Day of Battle: The War in Sicily and Italy, 1943–1944*, Volume Two of The Liberation Trilogy (New York: Henry Holt and Company, 2007).

"Aviation Machinist's Mate," http://www.tpubcom/content/administration/14214 /css/14214_46.htm.

Baker, Nicholson. *Human Smoke: The Beginning of World War II, the End of Civilization* (New York: Simon & Schuster, 2008).

Baldwin, Hanson W. "Solomons Action Develops into Battle for South Pacific," *The New York Times*, September 27, 1942, p. 1.

"The Battle for Los Negros Beachhead," http://www.history.army.mil/books/wwii/admiralties/admiralties-ch 2-losnegros.htm.

"Bella, Italy: Bella guide, city of Bella, Basilicata Italy," http://www.initalytoday.com/basilicata/bella/index.htm.

Berger, Meyer. "The Making of a Bluejacket," *The New York Times Magazine*, July 6, 1941, p. SM8.

Bettina, Elizabeth. *It Happened in Italy: Untold Stories of How the People of Italy Defied the Horrors of the Holocaust* (Nashville: Thomas Nelson, 2009).

Bissell, Tom. *The Father of All Things: A Marine, His Son, and the Legacy of Vietnam* (New York: Vintage Books, 2007).

"Black Cat Rescue Missions," http://www.daveswarbirds.com/blackcat/historyq.htm.

"Black Cats: US Navy PBY Catalinas," http://www.daveswarbirds.com/blackcat.

"Block in Hoboken Swept by Flames," *The New York Times*, January 2, 1940, p. I.30.

The Bluejackets' Manual, United States Navy (Annapolis, Md.: U.S. Naval Institute, 1940).

Brown, Eva Metzger, Ph.D. "The Transmission of Trauma Through Caretaking Patterns of Behavior in Holocaust Families: Re-Enactments in a Facilitated Long-Term Second-Generation Group," *Smith College Studies in Social Work* 68:3, June 1998, http://www.tamach.org/fileadmin/dateien/pdf/caretaking_patterns.pdf.

"Building the Navy's Bases in World War II: History of the Bureau of Yards and Docks and the Civil Engineering Corps, 1940–1946," Chapter XXVI: Bases in the Southwest Pacific, Department of the Navy Bureau of Yards and Docks, http://ibiblio.org/hyperwar/USN/Building-Bases/bases_26.html.

"Cargo Cult," http://www.bookrags.com/dandf/cargo-cult-tf.

Carnavale, Nancy C. *A New Language, A New World: Italians in the United States, 1890–1945* (Champaign: University of Illinois Press, 2009).

Carroll, James. *An American Requiem: God, My Father, and the War That Came Between Us* (New York: Houghton Mifflin, 1996).

Childers, Thomas. *Soldier from the War Returning* (New York: Houghton Mifflin, 2009).

Collins, Julia. *My Father's War* (New York: Four Walls Eight Windows, 2002).

Colrick, Patricia Florio. *Images of America: Hoboken* (Charleston, S.C.: Arcadia Publishing, 1999).

"Court of Inquiry Findings Related to 'Panay Incident,'" Official Press Release from Friday, December 24, 1937, http://www.uspanay.org/court.pdf.

Cressman, Robert J. *USS Ranger: The Navy's First Flattop from Keel to Mast, 1934–1936* (Washington: Potomac Books, 2003).

"Curtiss BF2C Goshawk," From Wikipedia, http://en.wikipedia.org/wiki/Curtiss _BF2C_Goshawk.

Czachowski, Joe. *Historic Photos of Hoboken* (Nashville: Turner Publishing Company, 2008).

Davis, Stuart. "The Hoboken Series," February 4–March 4, 1978 (New York: Hirschl & Adler Galleries, 1978).

Diehl, Lorraine B. *Over Here!: New York City During World War II* (HarperCollins e-book, n.d.).

DiStasi, Lawrence, ed. *Una Storia Segreta: The Secret History of Italian American Evacuation and Internment during World War II* (Berkeley, Calif.: Heyday Books, 2001).

Doherty, Joan F. *Hudson County: The Left Bank* (Chatsworth, Calif.: Windsor Publications, 1986).

Eisenberg, Nora. *The War at Home: A Memoir-Novel* (Wellfleet, Mass.: Leapfrog Press, 2002).

Ellis, Jacqueline. "Revolutionary Spaces: Photographs of Working-class Women by Esther Bubley, 1940–1943, *Feminist Review*, No. 53 (Summer 1996), pp. 74–94.

Fagelson, William Friedman. "Fighting Films: The Everyday Tactics of World War II Soldiers," *Cinema Journal* 40, No. 3 (Spring 2001), pp. 94–112.

"Fleet problem," From Wikipedia, http://wn.wikipedia.org/wiki/Fleet_problem.

Franks, Lucinda. *My Father's Secret War: A Memoir* (New York: Hyperion, 2007).

Gamba, Claudio. *Michelangelo* (New York: Rizzoli, 2004).

Garnett, David. *War in the Air, September 1939–May 1941* (New York: Doubleday, Doran & Company, 1941).

Gates, Thomas F. *Fighter Squadron Fourteen "Tophatters"* (Carrollton, Tex.: Squadron/ Signal Publications, 1993).

Gawne, Jonathan. *Finding Your Father's War: A Practical Guide to Researching and Understanding Service in World War II US Army* (Drexel Hill, Pa.: Casemate, 2006).

Gorham, Ethel. *So Your Husband's Gone to War!* (Garden City, N.Y.: Doubleday, Doran & Company, 1942).

Goytisolo, Juan. *Landscapes of War: From Sarajevo to Chechnya*, translated from the Spanish by Peter Bush (San Francisco: City Light Books, 2000).

"Great Vintage Films of WWII," 5 discs, Quality Information Publishers, 2007, www.qualityinformationpublishers.com.

Groom, Winston. *1942: The Year That Tried Men's Souls* (New York: Grove Press, 2005).

"Grumman F2F," From Wikipedia, http://en.wikipedia.org/wiki/Grumman_F2F.

"Grumman F4F Wildcat," From Wikipedia, http://en.wikipedia.org/wiki/Grumman
_F4F_Wildcat.

Hastings, Max. *Retribution: The Battle for Japan, 1944–1945* (New York: Alfred A.
Knopf, 2008).

Heaney, John J. *The Bicentennial Comes to Hoboken* (n.p.: n.d.).

"Hoboken: A Guide to the City" (Hoboken, N.J.: Hoboken Community Develop-
ment Agency, 1987).

"Hoboken: A Walking Tour and Street Map," The Hoboken Historical Museum
(Hoboken, N.J.: The Hoboken Historical Museum, n.d.), www.hoboken
museum.org.

Hogan, Michael J., ed. *Hiroshima in History and Memory* (New York: Cambridge University Press, 1996).

Howarth, Stephen. *To Shining Sea: A History of the United States Navy, 1775–1991* (New
York: Random House, 1991).

Huffman, Fon B. "Oral History of the Bombing of the USS Panay," www.archive
.org/details/1937-12-12_Bombing_of_USS_Panay. (Note that in the official
court inquiry, his name appears as Hoffman.)

Hynes, Samuel. *Flights of Passage: Recollections of a World War II Aviator* (New York: Penguin Books, 1988).

"John McCain," World War II Database, http://www.2db.com/person_bio.php
?person_id=511.

Kaima, Sam T. "The evolution of cargo cults and the emergence of political parties
in Melanesia," *Journal de la Societe des oceanistes*, 92–23, 1991–1–2, pp. 173–80.

Keegan, John. *The Second World War* (New York: Penguin Books, 1989).

Kennedy, David M. *Freedom from Fear: The American People in Depression and War, 1929–1945*
(New York: Oxford University Press, 1999).

Krepinevich, Andrew. "Transforming to Victory: The U.S. Navy, Carrier Aviation,
and Preparing for War in the Pacific," The Olin Institute, http://www.csba
online.org/4Publications/PubLibrary/A.20000000.Transforming_to
_Vi/A.20000000.Transforming_to_Vi.php.

"List of sunken aircraft carriers," From Wikipedia, http://en.wikipedia.org/wiki
/List_of_sunken_aircraft_carriers.

MacDonald, Scot. "Evolution of Aircraft Carriers: Flattops in the War Games,"
Naval Aviation News, August 1962, pp. 28–33, http://fas.org/man/dod-101/
sys/ship/docs/car-evo/car-5.pdf.

————. "Evolution of Aircraft Carriers: Last of the Fleet Problems," *Naval Aviation News*, September 1962, pp. 34–38, http://www.history.navy.mil/content/dam/ nhhc/research/histories/naval-aviation/evolution-of-aircraft-carriers/car-6.pdf.

Manchester, William. *American Caesar: Douglas MacArthur, 1880–1964* (New York: Little, Brown and Company, 1978).

————. *Goodbye, Darkness: A Memoir of the Pacific War* (New York: Little, Brown and Company, 1979).

"Manus Island," http://www.manusisland.com.

"Marines at Tarawa (1945)," Documentary short film, Synergy Entertainment, 2000, www.synergyent.com.

Mathews, Tom. *Our Fathers' War: Growing Up in the Shadow of the Greatest Generation* (New York: Broadway Books, 2005).

Mead, Margaret. *Cultural Transformation in Manus, 1928–1953, New Lives for Old* (New York: William Morrow and Company, 1956).

————. *Growing Up in New Guinea: A Comparative Study of Primitive Education* (New York: William Morrow and Company, 1930).

"Missing Air Crew: The Search for the Coleman B–24 Crew," http://www.missing aircrew.com/307/losnegros.htm.

Morison, Samuel Eliot. *History of United States Naval Operations in World War II, Volume Six: Breaking the Bismarcks Barrier, 22 July 1942–1 May 1944* (New York: Little, Brown and Company, 1950).

Murphy, Audie. *To Hell and Back: The Classic Memoir of World War II by America's Most Decorated Soldier* (New York: Henry Holt and Company, 1949).

"Nautical Terms and Phrases: Their Meaning and Origin," http://www.history .navy.mil/trivia/trivia03.htm.

"Navy Lists 5 Ships as Pacific Losses," *The New York Times*, December 6, 1944, p. 13.

"News Blanket," *Time*, December 27, 1937, p. 7.

"Norman Alley's Bombing of the *USS Panay*: The First Pictures of the Bombing of the *USS Panay*," A Universal Special Feature, www.archive.org/details/1937 -12-12_Bombing_of_USS_Panay.

Ohnemus, Sylvia. *An Ethnology of the Admiralty Islanders* (Honolulu: University of Hawai'i Press, 1998).

Origo, Iris. *Images and Shadows: Part of a Life* (Boston: David R. Godine, Publisher, 1999).

————. *War in the Val D'Orcia, 1943–1944: A Diary* (Boston: David R. Godine, Publisher, 1948).

"Paliau Maloat," *The Concise Oxford Dictionary of World Religions*, http://www.encyclo
    pedia.com/doc/1O101-PaliauMaloat.html.
"Panay Pandemonium," *Time: The Weekly News Magazine*, XXX:26, December 27, 1937,
    pp. 7–8.
Plakke, David. *Portraits of a Mile Square City: Stories from Hoboken* (Hoboken, N.J.: Art
    Ink Press, 1991).
"Presidential Thanksgiving Proclamations 1940–1949: Franklin D. Roosevelt,
    Harry S. Truman," Pilgrim Hall Museum, http://www.pilgrimhall.org
    /ThankxProc1940.htm.
"Prisoners Among Us: Italian-American Identity & World War II," Michaelangelo
    Productions, 2003, www.prisonersamongus.com.
Procter, Mary, and Bill Matuszeski. *Gritty Cities: A Second Look . . .* (Philadelphia:
    Temple University Press, 1978).
"R-1340 Wasp," http://www.pratt-whitney.com/About+Us/Classic+Engines/R
    -1340+Wasp.
"R-1535 Twin Wasp Jr.," http://www.pratt-whitney.com/About+Us/Classic+
    Engines/R-1535+Twin+Wasp+Jr.
"R-1690 Hornet," http://www.pratt-whitney.com/About+Us/Classic+Engines
    /R-1690+Hornet.
Raithel, Captain Albert L., Jr., USN (Ret.). "Naval Aviation in WW II," Part 2,
    http://www.vpnavy.org/adobe/patrol_aviation_part_2_25may2003.pdf.
Romanucci-Ross, Lola. *Mead's Other Manus: Phenomenology of the Encounter* (Santa Bar-
    bara, Calif.: Bergin & Garvey Publishers, Inc., 1985).
Roosevelt, Franklin Delano. *The Roosevelt Reader: Selected Speeches, Messages, Press Confer-
    ences, and Letters of Franklin D. Roosevelt* (New York: Holt, Rinehart and Winston
    1957).
Rottman, Gordon L. *World War II: Pacific Island Guide, A Geo-Military Study* (Westport,
    Conn.: Greenwood Press, 2002).
Scarborough, Capt. William E., USN (Ret.). "To Keep Us Out of World War II?"
    Part 1 of 2, *Naval Aviation News*, March–April 1990, pp. 18–23.
Scull, Theodore W. *Hoboken's Lackawanna Terminal* (New York: Quadrant Press, 1987).
"Selective documents relating to the loss of USS Mount Hood," http://www
    .ibiblio.org/hyperwar/USN/ships/logs/AE/ae11-Loss.html.
"Selective Service and Training Act of 1940," http://findarticles.com/p/articles
    /mi_g1cpc/is/tor/ai_2419100363.
"Sending Them Off to War: Pre-Induction Information Programs," http://www
    .sos.state.or.us/archives/exhibits/ww2/services/induct.htm.

Shay, Jonathan. *Achilles in Vietnam: Combat Trauma and the Undoing of Character* (New York: Scribner, 1994).

————. *Odysseus in America: Combat Trauma and the Trials of Homecoming* (New York: Scribner, 2003).

Sledge, E. B. *With the Old Breed at Peleliu and Okinawa* (New York: Ballantine Books, 1981).

Smalley, Robert Manning. *The Admiralties at War: 1944–1945* (Victoria, B.C.: Trafford, 2002).

"The Sorry Saga of the Brewster Buffalo," http://www.warbirdforum.com/saga.htm.

Spark, Nick T. "Suddenly and Deliberately Attacked! The Story of the Panay Incident," http://www.usspanay.org.

Spector, Ronald H. *Eagle Against the Sun: The American War with Japan* (New York: Vintage Books, 1985).

Terkel, Studs. *"The Good War": An Oral History of World War II* (New York: The New Press, 1984).

"Text of the Selective Service Measure as It Was Finally Passed by Congress Yesterday," *The New York Times*, September 15, 1940, p. 30.

Toffey, John J., IV. *Jack Toffey's War: A Son's Memoir* (New York: Fordham University Press, 2008).

Tregaskis, Richard. *Guadalcanal Diary* (New York: Random House, 1943).

Tuttle, William M., Jr. *"Daddy's Gone to War": The Second World War in the Lives of America's Children* (New York: Oxford University Press, 1993).

"The United States Army Air Forces in World War II: Combat Chronology of the US Army Air Forces," http://www.usaaf.net/chron/43/sep43.htm.

"United States Naval Aviation 1910–1995," http://www.history.navy.mil/branches/usna1910.htm.

"USS Enterprise CV-6: The Most Decorated Ship of the Second World War: All Hands—Rates, Divisions & Pay Scales," http://cv6.org/company/muster/organization.htm.

"USS Ranger (CV-4): US Navy Aircraft Carrier of World War Two," http://www.acepilots.com/ships/ranger.html.

Vento, Carol Schultz. *The Hidden Legacy of World War II: A Daughter's Journey of Discovery* (Mechanicsburg, Pa.: Sunbury Press, 2011).

Veterans of Foreign Wars. *Pictorial History of World War II, Volume 2, The War in the Pacific* (Veterans' Historical Book Service, 1951).

"Victory at Sea: The Legendary World War II Documentary," 4 volumes, The History Channel, National Broadcasting Company, Inc., 2003.

"A Walk Through Hoboken," with David Hartman and Barry Lewis, http://www
.thirteen.org/hoboken/history.html.

Waller, Willard. *Veteran Comes Back* (New York: Dryden Press, 1944).

"The War: A Ken Burns Film, 1941–1945," 7 discs, The American Lives Film Project,
2006.

"War in China: 'A Great Mistake,'" *Time*, December 26, 1937, p. 15.

"War in China: 'Regrets,'" *Time*, December 27, 1937, p. 13.

"War in China: 'Victory Bomb, Invasion,'" *Time*, December 13, 1937, p. 18.

Warren, Mame. "Focal Point of the Fleet: U.S. Navy Photographic Activities in
World War II," *The Journal of Military History* 69 (October 2005): 1045–80.

Wildenberg, Thomas. "Midway: Sheer Luck or Better Doctrine?" Navy Department Library, Department of the Navy, Naval Historical Center, http://
www.history.navy.mil/library/online/sheerluck_midway.htm.

"Wing-Folding Mechanism of the Grumman Wildcat," http://files.asme.org
/asmeorg/Communities/History/Landmarks/10382.pdf.

Woods, Katherine. "A Realistic Picture of the Islands of the South Seas: Felix
Keesing Surveys Their Place and Problems in the Modern World," review of
The South Seas in the Modern World by Felix M. Keesing (New York: The John
Day Company, 1941), *The New York Times*, July 13, 1941, p. BR3.

"The World at War," 11 discs, Thames Television LTD, 1973, A&E Television Net-
works, 2004.

"World War One: Total Casualties," http://www.historylearningsite.co.uk/FWW
casualties.htm.

"World War II Casualties," http://valourandhorror.com/DB/BACK/Casualties
.htm.

"World War II Rationing," http://www.ameshistoricalsociety.org/exhibits/events
/rationing2.htm.

"World War II—Part 3, 1943–1944: Salerno Naples Garigliano Abruzzi Advance to
Perugia," http://www.qdg.org.uk/maintext/worldwar2pages.htm.

"Wright R-1820," From Wikipedia, http://en.wikipedia.org/wiki/Wright_R–1820.

Zellmer, David. *The Spectator: A World War II Bomber Pilot's Journal of the Artist as Warrior*
(Westport, Conn.: Praeger, 1999).

WORLD WAR II: THE GLOBAL, HUMAN, AND ETHICAL DIMENSION

G. Kurt Piehler, *series editor*

Lawrence Cane, David E. Cane, Judy Barrett Litoff, and David C. Smith, eds.,
Fighting Fascism in Europe: The World War II Letters of an American Veteran of the Spanish Civil War

Angelo M. Spinelli and Lewis H. Carlson, *Life behind Barbed Wire:
The Secret World War II Photographs of Prisoner of War Angelo M. Spinelli*

Don Whitehead and John B. Romeiser, *"Beachhead Don":
Reporting the War from the European Theater, 1942–1945*

Scott H. Bennett, ed., *Army GI, Pacifist CO: The World War II Letters of Frank and Albert Dietrich*

Alexander Jefferson with Lewis H. Carlson, *Red Tail Captured, Red Tail Free:
Memoirs of a Tuskegee Airman and POW*

Jonathan G. Utley, *Going to War with Japan, 1937–1941*

Grant K. Goodman, *America's Japan: The First Year, 1945–1946*

Patricia Kollander with John O'Sullivan, *"I Must Be a Part of This War":
One Man's Fight against Hitler and Nazism*

Judy Barrett Litoff, *An American Heroine in the French Resistance:
The Diary and Memoir of Virginia d'Albert-Lake*

Thomas R. Christofferson and Michael S. Christofferson,
France during World War II: From Defeat to Liberation

Don Whitehead, *Combat Reporter: Don Whitehead's World War II Diary and Memoirs,*
edited by John B. Romeiser

James M. Gavin, *The General and His Daughter: The Wartime Letters of General James M. Gavin
to His Daughter Barbara*, edited by Barbara Gavin Fauntleroy et al.

Carol Adele Kelly, ed., *Voices of My Comrades: America's Reserve Officers Remember World War II,*
Foreword by Senators Ted Stevens and Daniel K. Inouye

John J. Toffey IV, *Jack Toffey's War: A Son's Memoir*

Lt. General James V. Edmundson, *Letters to Lee: From Pearl Harbor to the War's Final Mission,*
edited by Dr. Celia Edmundson

John K. Stutterheim, *The Diary of Prisoner 17326: A Boy's Life in a Japanese Labor Camp,*
Foreword by Mark Parillo

G. Kurt Piehler and Sidney Pash, eds., *The United States and the Second World War:
New Perspectives on Diplomacy, War, and the Home Front*

Susan E. Wiant, *Between the Bylines: A Father's Legacy*, Foreword by Walter Cronkite

Deborah S. Cornelius, *Hungary in World War II: Caught in the Cauldron*

Gilya Gerda Schmidt, *Süssen Is Now Free of Jews: World War II, the Holocaust, and Rural Judaism*

Emanuel Rota, *A Pact with Vichy: Angelo Tasca from Italian Socialism to French Collaboration*

Panteleymon Anastasakis, *The Church of Greece under Axis Occupation*

Louise DeSalvo, *Chasing Ghosts: A Memoir of a Father, Gone to War*